Developing Evidence-Based Practice Skills

Developing Evidence-Based Generalist Practice Skills

Edited by

Bruce A. Thyer
Catherine N. Dulmus
Karen M. Sowers

JOHN WILEY & SONS, INC.

Published by John Wiley & Sons, Inc., Hoboken, New Jersey.
Published simultaneously in Canada.

For general information on our other products and services please contact our Customer Care Department within the United States at (800) 762-2974, outside the United States at (317) 572-3993, or fax (317) 572-4002.

Wiley publishes in a variety of print and electronic formats and by print-on-demand. Some material included with standard print versions of this book may not be included in e-books or in print-on-demand. If this book refers to media such as a CD or DVD that is not included in the version you purchased, you may download this material at http://booksupport.wiley.com. For more information about Wiley products, visit www.wiley.com.

Library of Congress Cataloging-in-Publication Data:
Developing Evidence-Based Generalist Practice Skills / Bruce A. Thyer, Catherine N. Dulmus, Karen M. Sowers.
    pages cm
  Includes bibliographical references and index.
  ISBN 978-1-118-17696-2 (pbk.)
  ISBN 978-1-118-43377-5 (e-bk.)
  ISBN 978-1-118-42117-8 (e-bk.)
  ISBN 978-1-118-41932-8 (e-bk.)
  1. Evidence-based medicine. 2. Physicians (General practice) I. Thyer, Bruce A., editor of compilation. II. Dulmus, Catherine N., editor of compilation. III. Sowers, Karen M. (Karen Marlaine), editor of compilation.
  R723.7.D484 2013
  610.69′5—dc23

                                                                                    2012026666

Printed in the United States of America
10 9 8 7 6 5 4 3 2 1

Developing Evidence-Based Generalist Practice Skills

Edited by

Bruce A. Thyer
Catherine N. Dulmus
Karen M. Sowers

WILEY

JOHN WILEY & SONS, INC.

Library of Congress Cataloging-in-Publication Data:
Developing Evidence-Based Generalist Practice Skills / Bruce A. Thyer, Catherine N. Dulmus, Karen M. Sowers.
    pages cm
  Includes bibliographical references and index.
  ISBN 978-1-118-17696-2 (pbk.)
  ISBN 978-1-118-43377-5 (e-bk.)
  ISBN 978-1-118-42117-8 (e-bk.)
  ISBN 978-1-118-41932-8 (e-bk.)
  1. Evidence-based medicine. 2. Physicians (General practice) I. Thyer, Bruce A., editor of compilation. II. Dulmus, Catherine N., editor of compilation. III. Sowers, Karen M. (Karen Marlaine), editor of compilation.
  R723.7.D484 2013
  610.69′5—dc23

2012026666

Printed in the United States of America
10 9 8 7 6 5 4 3 2 1

We dedicate this book with love and respect to our children, who have so enriched our lives.

Contents

Chapter 6   **Advocacy 123**

*Malabika Misty Das, Cheryl Hiu-Kwan Chui,
and Cecilia Lai-Wan Chan*

Chapter 7   **Crisis Intervention 149**

*Kenneth R. Yeager, Albert R. Roberts, and Wendy
Grainger*

Preface

The editors are pleased to have prepared this volume describing essential skills required for the effective practice of social work. The chapters we have included are revised and updated selections from *The Comprehensive Handbook of Social Work and Social Welfare, Volume 3: Social Work Practice*, originally published in 2008. The publisher requested this revision and asked that we break the earlier volume on practice skills into two separate textbooks suitable for adoption in foundation-level social work education. The present volume thus includes chapters that provide general overviews of the topics of social work and intervention, and the second separate volume addresses specific populations. The issues presented in this work can be considered core skills needed by all social work practitioners. It begins with a review of the increasingly influential perspective known as evidence-informed practice and provides the reader with an orientation to the steps involved in this structured process to help practitioners and clients make joint decisions about assessment and treatment options, decisions made by a careful consideration of the best available research evidence, the client's preferences and values, professional ethical standards, and other key issues.

A chapter on trauma-informed care is newly commissioned for this volume; it was requested due to the growth in this area of practice in the past decade and the rapid developments in both services and research relating to persons whose lives have been touched by serious trauma. Next we have chapters that address interviewing skills and the equally important topics of problem identification, contracting, and case planning. The chapter on case management provides an excellent introduction into this widely used practice skill, and the chapter on advocacy describes how advocacy at multiple levels can be an important part of the practice repertoire of virtually all social workers. The chapter on crisis intervention was included in response to how frequently clients initially seek help when prompted by a crisis in their lives. And skills in helping clients cope with not only the central issue or problem that led them to seek counsel, but also to manage the more immediately urgent problems facing them, are elements of practice all social workers need.

Our profession's primary code of ethics, which was developed by the National Association of Social Workers, contains Standard 5.02, which says that "Social workers should monitor and evaluate policies, the implementation of programs, and practice interventions." Standard 4.01(c) states "Social workers should base practice on recognized knowledge, including empirically based knowledge, relevant to social work and social work ethics." (NASW, 2008).

Other fields have developed even more stringent and explicit standards pertaining to the requirement that practice be thoroughly (although not exclusively) grounded in the latest scientific research, and that practitioners gather data for the purposes of evaluating intervention outcomes. For example, the discipline of Behavior Analysis has its own guidelines for responsible practice, guidelines that include, among others:

"2.10 Treatment Efficacy.

    a. The behavior analyst always has the responsibility to recommend scientifically supported most effective treatment procedures. Effective treatment procedures have been validated as having both long-term and short-term benefits to clients and society.

    b. Clients have a right to effective treatment (i.e., based on the research literature and adapted to the individual client).

    c. In those instances where more than one scientifically supported treatment has been established, additional factors may be considered in selecting interventions, including, but not limited to, efficiency and cost-effectiveness, risks and side-effects of the interventions, client preference, and practitioner experience and training.

3.02 Functional Assessment.

    a. The behavior analyst conducts a functional assessment, as defined below, to provide the necessary data to develop an effective behavior change program.

    b. Functional assessment includes a variety of systematic information-gathering activities regarding factors influencing the occurrence of a behavior (e.g., antecedents, consequences, setting events, or motivating operations) including interview, direct observation, and experimental analysis.

4.07 On-Going Data Collection.

The behavior analyst collects data, or asks the client, client-surrogate, or designated others to collect data needed to assess progress within the program.

4.08 Program Modifications.

The behavior analyst modifies the program on the basis of data."

(All quotes are from the Behavior Analyst Certification Board's *Guidelines for Responsible Practice*, available at http://www.bacb.com/index.php?page = 57)

The behavior analysts clearly have a more stringent standard pertaining to the evaluation of practice, and while contemporary social workers may not be held to a similarly high benchmark, it is nevertheless clear that agency funders, supervisors, and third-party payers are all requiring greater documentation that social work services have been followed by enhanced client functioning. Hence the present volume contains a chapter on the topic of evaluating practice, which is focused on the use of single-system research design methodology. Our last chapter, fittingly enough, addresses the topics of termination, stabilization, and continuity of care, crucial issues associated with every case or client.

We believe that each of these chapters contains essential information needed in order for social workers to practice effectively and ethically. These are foundation skills expected of all practitioners and are thus linked to the accreditation standards established by the Council on Social Work Education (2008), which address these skills. Specifically, this book is designed as a beginning social work practice skills text for undergraduate and graduate students in social work programs and the text conveys the foundation of skills required for beginning social work practice. We designed this book to cover certain Council on Social Work Education (CSWE)–required competencies for accreditation. Specifically, the book addresses the following required accreditation competencies:

- Educational Policy 2.1.2: Apply social work ethical principles to guide professional practice
- Educational Policy 2.1.3: Apply critical thinking to inform and communicate professional judgments
- Educational Policy 2.1.6: Engage in research-informed practice and practice-informed research
- Educational Policy 2.1.9: Respond to contexts that shape practice
- Educational Policy 2.1.10: Engage, assess, intervene, and evaluate with individuals, families, groups, organizations, and communities

Each chapter begins with an overarching theme or question which is the focus of that chapter's topic, and concludes with a brief list of key words, questions for critical thinking, and a list of websites providing additional information on that chapter's subject. We crafted this book so that it could easily be used as a stand-alone required text or an ancillary practice textbook for BSW programs and for practice classes in the foundation year of MSW programs. Undergraduate students typically take this content in the junior year. Graduate students will typically obtain this foundation practice skills content in their first year of study. We hope our new edition is well-received by the academic and practice communities, and we would like to express our enormous debt to the busy experts who agreed to prepare new or revised chapters for inclusion in this volume.

Bruce A. Thyer
Catherine N. Dulmus
Karen M. Sowers

About the Editors

Bruce A. Thyer, PhD, LCSW, is Professor and former Dean, College of Social Work, at Florida State University. He received his MSW from the University of Georgia in 1978 and his PhD in social work and psychology from the University of Michigan in 1982. He is a member of the National Academies of Practice–Social Work, and a Fellow of the American Psychological Association (Divisions 12–Clinical and 25–Behavior Analysis). He is the founding and current editor of the bimonthly journal *Research on Social Work Practice*, which was established in 1991, and is one of social work's most widely subscribed-to journals. He has published extensively in the areas of social work theory, evaluation research, behavior analysis, and evidence-based practice.

    Catherine N. Dulmus, PhD, LCSW, is Professor, Associate Dean for Research, and Director of the Buffalo Center for Social Research at the University at Buffalo and Research Director at Hillside Family of Agencies in Rochester, NY. She received her baccalaureate degree in Social Work from Buffalo State College in 1989, the master's degree in Social Work from the University at Buffalo in 1991 and a doctoral degree in Social Welfare from the University at Buffalo in 1999. As a researcher with interests that include community-based research, child and adolescent mental health, evidence-based practice, and university–community partnerships, Dr. Dulmus' recent contributions have focused on fostering interdependent collaborations among practitioners, researchers, schools, and agencies critical in the advancement and dissemination of new and meaningful knowledge. She has authored or coauthored several journal articles and books and has presented her research nationally and internationally. Prior to obtaining the PhD, her social work practice background encompassed almost a decade of experience in the fields of mental health and school social work.

    Karen M. Sowers, PhD, is Professor and Dean of the College of Social Work at the University of Tennessee, Knoxville. She is the University of Tennessee Beaman Professor for Outstanding Research and Service. Dr. Sowers received her baccalaureate degree in Sociology from the University of Central Florida, and her master's degree and PhD in social work from Florida State University. Dr. Sowers serves on several local, national, and international boards. Dr. Sowers is nationally known for her research and scholarship in the areas of international practice, juvenile justice, child welfare, cultural diversity, and culturally effective intervention strategies for social work practice, evidence-based social work practice, and social work education.

Contributors

Cecilia Lai-Wan Chan, PhD
Department of Social Work and Social
  Administration
University of Hong Kong
Hong Kong

Cheryl Hiu-Kwan Chui, MSW
Department of Social Work and Social
  Administration
University of Hong Kong
Hong Kong

Malabika Misty Das, MSW
Department of Social Work and Social
  Administration
University of Hong Kong
Hong Kong

Sophia F. Dziegielewski, PhD
School of Social Work
University of Central Florida
Orlando, FL

Eileen Gambrill, PhD
School of Social Welfare
University of California at Berkeley
Berkeley, CA

Wendy Grainger, MHSA
Ohio State University Medical Center
Ohio State University
Columbus, OH

Laura Greyber, MSW
School of Social Work
University at Buffalo
Buffalo, NY

Valerie Holton, MSW
School of Social Work
Virginia Commonwealth University
Richmond, VA

Samuel A. MacMaster, PhD
College of Social Work
University of Tennessee
Nashville, TN

Albert R. Roberts, PhD (deceased)
Criminal Justice Department
Rutgers – The State University
  of New Jersey
Piscataway, NJ

Sara Sanders, MSW
College of Social Work
University of Tennessee
Nashville, TN

Nancy J. Smyth, PhD
School of Social Work
University at Buffalo
Buffalo, NY

Bruce A. Thyer, PhD
College of Social Work
Florida State University
Tallahassee, FL

Francis J. Turner, DSW
Faculty of Social Work
Wilfrid Laurier University
Waterloo, Ontario

Joseph Walsh, PhD
School of Social Work
Virginia Commonwealth University
Richmond, VA

Kenneth R. Yeager, PhD
Department of Psychiatry
Ohio State University
Columbus, OH

Developing Evidence-Based Generalist Practice Skills

Chapter 1
Evidence-Informed Practice

Eileen Gambrill

> Should we take our ethical obligations to clients seriously (e.g., to offer them services most likely to help them achieve outcomes they value)?

Social workers make life-affecting decisions under conditions of time pressures, scarce resources, and uncertainty about the effects of their choices. Evidence-based practice (EBP), also referred to as evidence-informed practice, was developed to help professionals make informed decisions in these difficult circumstances. EBP and health care originated in medicine in part because of variations in services offered and their outcomes (Wennberg, 2002). Variations in services naturally raise questions such as "Are they of equal effectiveness?" or "Do some cause harm?" The history of the helping professions shows that common practices thought to help people were found to harm them (e.g., see Blenkner, Bloom, & Neilson, 2001; McCord, 2003). EBP was developed to help professionals to draw on research findings regarding important decisions in a timely manner, using their clinical expertise to integrate data from varied sources. There were (and are) troubling gaps between available knowledge and what is used by professionals. Literature suggests that professionals do not draw on practice-related research findings to inform practice decisions (e.g., Mullen & Bacon, 2004). Not keeping up with new research findings related to important decisions renders knowledge increasingly out of date. As a result, decisions may be made that harm rather than help clients (e.g., Jacobson, Foxx, & Mulick, 2005; Lilienfeld, Lynn, & Lohr, 2003; Thyer & Pignotti, 2010; Thyer & Pignotti, in press). Lipsey (2009) argues that "interjection of unproven social programs into people's lives under the guise of helping is little more than quackery" (p. 19). Many clinicians do not honor obligations described in professional codes of ethics regarding informed consent (e.g., see Braddock, Edwards, Hasenberg, Laidley, & Levinson, 1999).

EBP suggests and explores ways to decrease gaps at the levels of both clinical practice and decision making about groups and populations, for example, purchasing services. It is as much about the ethics of educators and researchers as it is about the ethics of practitioners and agency administrators. Gray (2001a) suggests that the helping process can be undermined by the following problems:

1. Overenthusiastic adoption of interventions of unproven efficacy or even proven ineffectiveness;

2. Failure to adopt interventions that do more good than harm at a reasonable cost;

3. Continuing to offer intervention services that have been demonstrated to be ineffective;

4. Adoption of interventions without adequate preparation such that the benefits demonstrated in a research setting cannot be reproduced in the ordinary service setting;

5. Wide variation in the rates at which interventions are adopted or discarded. (p. 366)

Although interlinked in professional codes of ethics and accreditation standards, ethical and evidentiary issues are often worlds apart in practice. If professionals are not familiar with the evidentiary status of alternative practices and policies, they cannot pass this information on to their clients; they cannot honor informed consent obligations (NASW, 2008). If some alternatives are more effective than others in helping clients, and practice proceeds in ignorance of this information, clients are deprived of opportunities to achieve hoped-for outcomes. Currently, gaps between what research suggests is effective and what services are provided are hidden. For example, rarely do child protection staffs compare the services offered by agencies to which they refer clients for parent training with what research suggests is effective training and share this information with clients. Clients are typically not informed that recommended services have not been critically tested or have been found to be ineffective or harmful.

Descriptions of EBP differ in how accurately (or if) they describe the original view of EBP, including obstacles, to assist readers to make up their own minds regarding its value to social workers and clients. The most popular use of the term *EBP* refers to interventions deemed effective by a researcher or organization—for example, the "EBPs" approach (Norcross, Beutler, & Levant, 2006). Another popular use of the term is to simply attach it to a practice to make the practice or policy look good or to be "in tune with the times"; this could be the use of the name without the substance. Still others promote total distortions of EBP as described in original sources (see Gambrill, 2011). Many descriptions of EBP ignore hallmarks of this process, such as involving clients as informed participants. Given these different views, it is important to review the vision of EBP and health care as described by their creators. Otherwise, potential benefits to clients and professionals may be lost.

What Is Evidence-Informed Practice?

EBP (AKA evidence-informed practice) describes a process for a new professional educational format (problem-based learning) designed to help practitioners to link evidentiary, ethical, and application issues. It is assumed that professionals often need information to make decisions, for example, concerning risk assessment or what services are most likely to help clients attain outcomes they value. As Gray (2001a, p. 354) suggests, when evidence is not used, important failures in decision making occur, such as:

- Ineffective interventions are introduced.
- Interventions that do more harm than good are introduced.
- Interventions that do more good than harm are not introduced.
- Interventions that are ineffective or do more harm than good are not discontinued.

Although its philosophical roots are old, the blooming of EBP as a process attending to evidentiary, ethical, and application issues in all professional venues (education, practice/policy, and research) is fairly recent, facilitated by the Internet revolution.

EBP describes a philosophy and process designed to promote effective use of professional judgment in integrating information regarding each client's unique circumstances and characteristics, including their preferences and actions, and external research findings. It involves the "integration of best research evidence with clinical expertise and [client] values" (Sackett, Straus, Richardson, Rosenberg, & Haynes, 2000, p. 1):

> Without clinical expertise, practice risks becoming tyrannized by external evidence, for even excellent external evidence may be inapplicable to or inappropriate for an individual patient. Without current best external evidence, practice risks becoming rapidly out of date, to the detriment of patients.
>
> (Sackett, Richardson, Rosenberg, & Haynes, 1997, p. 2)

Evidence-informed practice is a guide for thinking about how decisions should be made (Haynes, Devereaux, & Guyatt, 2002). It requires the "conscientious, explicit, and judicious use of current best evidence in making decisions about the care of individual [clients]" (Sackett et al., 1997, p. 2). It is a process for handling the uncertainty surrounding decisions that must be made in real life, in real time. Sources of uncertainty include limitations in current knowledge, lack of familiarity with what knowledge is available, and difficulties in distinguishing between personal ignorance and lack of competence and actual limitations of knowledge (Fox & Swazy, 1974). Uncertainties may be related to lack of information about problem-related causes, clients' ambivalence about pursuit of certain goals, and whether resources are available to help clients.

A willingness to acknowledge ignorance and uncertainty, combined with taking steps to see if needed information is available, increases the likelihood that important uncertainties can be decreased or identified (Chalmers, 2004). This helps us to honor ethical obligations to involve clients as informed participants. Intuition and unsystematic clinical expertise are considered insufficient grounds on which to make decisions.

On the other hand, the "value-laden nature of clinical decisions" (Guyatt & Rennie, 2002, p. 4) implies that we cannot rely on evidence alone:

> *Thus, knowing the tools of evidence-based practice is necessary but not sufficient for delivering the highest quality of [client] care. In addition to clinical expertise, the clinician requires compassion, sensitive listening skills, and broad perspectives from the humanities and social sciences. These attributes allow understanding of [clients' concerns] in the context of their experience, personalities, and cultures. (p. 9)*

> *[A]ny external guideline must be integrated with individual clinical expertise in deciding whether and how it matches the [client's] clinical state, predicament, and preferences and thus whether it should be applied.*

> *(Sackett et al., 1997, p. 4)*

Critical thinking is integral to EBP (Gambrill, 2012a). In both critical thinking as well as EBP, attention is given to ethical issues. The intellectual traits inherent in critical thinking suggested by Paul (1993) such as courage, integrity, and perseverance, reflect the philosophies of EBP described by the originators of EBP (see also Paul & Elder, 2004). Honesty and transparency (clear description of what is done to what effect) are emphasized in both. This applies to all venues of interest in the helping professions: professional education, practice, and policy (what is done to what effect), and related research (its design, conduct, and reporting).

The philosophy of evidence-based practice encourages practitioners to be effective advocates for their clients: "physicians concerned about the health of their patients as a group, or about the health of the community, should consider how they might contribute to reducing poverty" (Guyatt & Rennie, 2002, p. 9). The National Association of Social Workers (NASW) encourages social workers to stand up for others. Service is the first value described in NASW's Code of Ethics (2008). A key characteristic of EBP is breaking down the division between research and practice, for example, highlighting the importance of clinicians critically appraising research reviews and developing a technology to help them do so: "[T]he leading figures in EBM . . . emphasized that clinicians had to use their scientific training and their judgment to interpret [guidelines] and individualize care accordingly" (Gray, 2001b, p. 26).

Clinical expertise includes use of effective relationship skills and the experience of individual helpers to rapidly identify each client's unique circumstances, characteristics, and "their individual risks and benefits of potential interventions and their personal values and expectations" (Sackett et al., 2000, p. 1). Using clinical expertise, practitioners integrate information about a client's characteristics and circumstances with external research findings, client expectations and values, and their preferences and actions (Straus et al., 2005; Sackett et al., 1997). Sackett and his colleagues (1997) suggest that "Increased expertise is reflected in many ways, but especially in more effective and efficient [assessment] and in the more thoughtful identification and compassionate use of individual [clients'] predicaments, rights and preferences in making clinical decisions about their care" (p. 2). Client values refer to "the unique preferences, concerns and expectations each [client] brings to a clinical encounter and which must be integrated into clinical decisions if they are to serve the [client]" (Sackett et al., 2000, p. 1). Evidence-based health care refers to use of best current knowledge as evidence in decision making about groups and populations (Gray, 2001a). Professional codes of ethics call for key characteristics of EBP such as drawing on practice- and policy-related research and involving clients as informed participants.

Evidence-based decision making arose as an alternative to authority-based decision making, in which consensus, anecdotal experience, or tradition are relied on to make decisions (see Table 1.1). The following examples illustrate reliance on authority-based criteria for selection of service methods.

Ms. Riverton has just been to a workshop on eye movement desensitization therapy. The workshop leader told the participants that this method "works and can be used for a broad range of problems." Ms. Riverton suggests to her supervisor at the mental health clinic where she works that agency staff should use this method. When asked why, she said because the workshop leader is a respected authority in the field.

Mr. Davis read an editorial that describes the DARE programs as very effective in decreasing drug use. No related empirical literature was referred to. He suggests to his agency that they use this method.

In the first example, the authority of a workshop leader is appealed to; in the second, the authority of an author of an editorial. Evidence-based

Table 1.1 Differences Between Authority-Based and Evidence-Based Practitioners

Authority-Based Decision Making	Evidence-Based Decision Making
• Does not inform clients, or misinforms them.	• Involves clients as informed participants.
• Ignores client preferences (e.g., "We know best").	• Seeks and considers client values and preferences.
• Does not pose specific questions about information needs, nor search for and critically appraise related literature and share results with clients.	• Poses clear questions related to information needs, seeks for and critically appraises related research findings, and shares what is found with clients.
• Motivated to appear well informed, to preserve status and save time.	• Motivated to be an honest and competent broker of knowledge and ignorance.
• Ignores errors and mistakes.	• Seeks out errors and mistakes; values criticism as vital for learning.
• Accepts practice- and policy-related claims based on misleading criteria such as tradition and consensus.	• Relies on rigorous criteria to appraise claims and select practices and policies (e.g., those that control for biases).
• Relies solely on self-report of clients or anecdotal observations to evaluate progress.	• Uses objective as well as subjective measures to evaluate progress with a focus on outcomes of value to the client.

decision making involves the use of quite different criteria. A key one is information about the accuracy of knowledge claims. Although misleading in the incorrect assumption that EBP means only that decisions made are based on evidence of their effectiveness, use of the term does call attention to the fact that available evidence may not be used or the current state of ignorance shared with clients. It is hoped that professionals who consider related research findings regarding decisions and inform clients about them will provide more effective and ethical care than those relying on criteria such as anecdotal experience or popularity.

In discussing the origins of EBP, Gray (2001b) emphasizes the increasing lack of confidence in data of potential use to clinicians, including peer review, which he referred to as "feet of clay." He highlights the role of gaps between obligations of researchers to report limitations of research, prepare systematic reviews, and accurately describe well-argued alternative views and what we find in published literature. We find:

- Inflated claims.
- Biased estimates of the prevalence of a concern: Propagandistic advocacy in place of careful weighting of evidence.
- Lack of information on the limitations of research.
- Fragmented, incomplete literature reviews.
- Lack of counterevidence to preferred views.
- Lack of well-argued alternative perspectives and related evidence.
- Pseudoinquiry: Poor match between questions addressed and methods used to address them (e.g., see Rubin & Parrish, 2007).
- Ad hominem rather than ad rem argument.
- Disregard of unique knowledge of clients and service providers in making decisions about the appropriateness of a practice guideline.

We find incomplete, uncritical research reviews. Most reviews do not tell us how the authors researched, where they searched, what criteria they used to review studies, and whether they searched for unpublished as well as published reports. Conclusions drawn based on haphazard reviews are often misleading. Recognition of limitations in such reviews related to practice and policy questions encouraged development of the systematic review for synthesizing research findings.

> The purpose of a systematic review is to sum up the best available research on a specific question. This is done by synthesizing the results of several studies.
>
> A systematic review uses transparent procedures to find, evaluate and synthesize the results of relevant research. Procedures are explicitly defined in advance, in order to ensure that the exercise is transparent and can be replicated. This practice is also designed to minimize bias.
>
> Studies included in a review are screened for quality, so that the findings of a large number of studies can be combined. Peer review is a key part of the process, qualified independent researchers control the author's methods and results.

A systematic review must have:

- *Clear inclusion/exclusion criteria*
- *An explicit search strategy*
- *Systematic coding and analysis of included studies*
- *Meta-analysis (where possible). (www.campbellcollaboration.org)*

The Internet offers rapid access to relevant databases, including the Campbell and Cochrane databases of reviews. Economic considerations were also a factor. No matter what system of care exists, resources are limited with pressures to use them justly and wisely including considering both individuals and populations (e.g., "Do all residents with a particular need have access to similar quality care?").

Three Philosophies of Evidence-Based Practice

Evidence-based practice and social care involve a philosophy of ethics of professional practice and related enterprises such as research and scholarly writing, a philosophy of science (epistemology—views about what knowledge is and how it can be gained), and a philosophy of technology. Ethics involves decisions regarding how and when to act; it involves standards of conduct. Epistemology involves views about knowledge and how to get it, or if we can. The philosophy of technology involves questions such as: Should we develop technology? What values should we draw on to decide what to develop? Should we examine the consequences of a given technology? Evidence-informed practice encourages the integration of research and practice, for example, by highlighting the importance of clinicians critically appraising research reviews and developing a technology to help them to do so; "the leading figures in EBM . . . emphasized that clinicians had to use their scientific training and their judgment to interpret [guidelines] and individualize care accordingly" (Gray, 2001b, p. 26). It encourages clinicians to think for themselves—to develop critical appraisal skills. It offers practitioners and administrators a philosophy that is compatible with obligations described in professional codes of ethics as well as an evolving technology for integrating evidentiary, ethical, and practical issues. The uncertainty associated with decisions is acknowledged, not hidden. EBP requires considering research findings related to important practice/policy decisions and sharing what is found (including nothing) with clients. Transparency and honesty regarding the evidentiary status of services is a hallmark of this philosophy.

Steps in Evidence-Based Practice

Steps in EBP include the following:

1. Converting information needs related to decisions into clear questions.
2. Tracking down, with maximum efficiency, the best evidence with which to answer them.

3. Critically appraising that evidence for its validity, impact (size of effect), and applicability (usefulness in practice).

4. Integrating the critical appraisal with our clinical expertise and with our client's unique characteristics and circumstances, including their preferences and values. This involves deciding whether evidence found (if any) applies to the decision at hand (e.g., is a client similar to those studied, is there access to services described) and considering client values and preferences in making decisions.

5. Evaluating our effectiveness and efficiency in carrying out steps 1 to 4 and seeking ways to improve them in the future. (Straus, Richardson, Glasziou, & Haynes, 2005, pp. 3–4)

Questions that arise in the fourth step include: Do research findings apply to my client? That is, is a client similar to clients included in related research findings? Can I use this practice method in my setting (e.g., Are needed resources available?)? If not, is there some other access to programs found to be most effective in seeking hoped-for outcomes? What alternatives are available? Will the benefits of service outweigh harms of service for this client? What does my client think about this method? Is it acceptable to clients? What if I don't find anything (Glasziou, Del Mar, & Salisbury, 2003)? What is the number needed to treat, that is, how many people must receive a service for one person to be helped? What is the number needed to harm? Evidence-informed practitioners take advantage of efficient technology for conducting electronic searches to locate the current best evidence regarding a specific question; information literacy and retrievability are emphasized.

Different Kinds of Questions

Different questions require different kinds of research methods to critically appraise proposed assumptions (e.g., Greenhalgh, 2010; Guyatt, Rennie, Mead, & Cook, 2008; Straus et al., 2005). These differences are reflected in the use of different "quality filters" to search for research findings that reflect the particular terms associated with research likely to offer critical tests of questions. Kinds of questions include the following:

- *Effectiveness*: Do job-training programs help clients get and maintain jobs?
- *Prevention*: Do Head Start programs prevent school drop-out?
- *Screening (risk/prognosis)*: Does this measure accurately predict suicide attempts?
- *Description/assessment*: Do self-report data provide accurate descriptions of parenting practices?
- *Harm*: Does (or will) this intervention harm clients?
- *Cost*: How much does this program cost compared to others?

- *Practice guidelines*: Are these practice guidelines valid and are they applicable to my client/agency/community?
- *Self-development*: Am I keeping up-to-date? How can I keep up-to-date?

Sackett et al. (1997, 2000) suggest posing four-part questions (called PICO questions) that describe the *p*opulation of clients, the *i*ntervention of interest, what it may be *c*ompared to (including doing nothing), and hoped-for *o*utcomes. Gibbs (2003) refers to these as COPES questions. First, they are *c*lient-*o*riented. They are questions clinicians pose in their daily practice that affect clients' welfare. Second, they have *p*ractical importance. They concern problems that arise frequently in everyday practice and that are of concern to an agency. For example, child protective service workers must assess risk. Asking the question about what types of clients present the greatest immediate risk for child abuse is a critical one. Third, COPES (PICO) questions guide an *e*lectronic search for related research findings. The process of forming a specific question often begins with a vague general question and then proceeds to a well-built question. Fourth, hoped-for outcomes are identified.

A careful search requires actively seeking information that challenges or disconfirms our assumptions as well as information that supports them. The availability of the Internet has revolutionized the search for information, making it more speedy and more effective. The Cochrane and Campbell Collaborations prepare, maintain, and disseminate high-quality reviews of research related to specific questions (see earlier discussion). Abstracts of reviews are available without charge and can be searched. Reviews are prepared and maintained, based on standards in *The Reviewers' Handbook* (Higgins & Green, 2008), which is revised often to ensure that it remains up to date. The Cochrane Collaboration focuses on health concerns, however, many reviews are relevant to a wide variety of professionals. Examples are "Psychoeducation for Schizophrenia" (Pekkala & Merinder, 2004) and "Psychological Debriefing for Preventing Posttraumatic Stress Disorder" (Rose, Bisson, Churchill, & Wessely, 2002). The Campbell Collaboration, patterned after the Cochrane Collaboration, prepares reviews related to education, social intervention, and criminal justice. Coordinating groups include communication and dissemination, crime and justice, education, social welfare, and a methods group.

Different Styles of Evidence-Based Practice

Sackett and his colleagues (2000) distinguish among three different styles of EBP, all of which require integrating evidence with a client's unique characteristics and environmental circumstances. They suggest that for problems encountered on an everyday basis, we should search and critically appraise reports found. For level 2 (problems encountered less often), they suggest that we seek out critical appraisals already prepared by others who describe and use explicit criteria for deciding what evidence they select and whether it is valid. Here, step 3 can be omitted and step 2 restricted to sources that have already undergone critical appraisal. A third style applies to problems encountered very infrequently in which we "blindly seek, accept, and apply the recommendations we receive from authorities" (Sackett et al., 2000, p. 5). As they note, the trouble with this mode is that it is "blind" to whether the advice received from the experts "is authoritative (evidence-based, resulting from their operating in the appraising mode) or merely authoritarian (opinion-based, resulting from pride and prejudice)" (p. 5). Lack of time may result in using style 2 with most problems. Guyatt and Rennie (2002) recommend the highest possible skill levels: "Only if you develop advanced skills in interpreting the [practice- and policy-related] literature will you be able to determine the extent to which these attempts are consistent with the best evidence. Second, a high level of EBP skills will allow you to use the original literature effectively, regardless of whether preappraised synopses and evidence-based recommendations are available" (p. 208).

Examples of Evidence-Based Decision Making

Dr. Price works in a mental health crisis center. The administrator of this agency sent a memo to staff that he had heard that brief psychological debriefing was effective in decreasing posttraumatic stress disorder following a crisis and suggested that his staff use this method. Dr. Price decided to see if this was accurate. He formed the following question: In clients experiencing a potentially traumatic event, is brief (1-hour) psychological debriefing, compared to no service, more effective in preventing posttraumatic stress disorder? This is an effectiveness question. He looked in the Cochrane Database and found the systematic review prepared by Rose, Bisson, Churchill and Wessely (2002). To his surprise, this review concluded that not only was this method not effective, there was some indication that it had harmful effects; one study reported that those receiving such counseling were *more* likely to experience stressful reactions a year later. Based on this review, he sent an e-mail to his colleagues questioning the use of this method for clients.

Richard works in a child protection agency that requires him to use a risk assessment measure to estimate the likely recurrence of child abuse among parents alleged to have abused their children. The method used by his agency is a consensus-based instrument; that is, it is based on the opinions of a group of experts on what they consider risk factors. His question is as follows: Among parents alleged to have abused their children, are actuarial measures, compared to consensus-based measures, more accurate in predicting the likelihood of future abuse? Notice again that this is a four-part question: (1) a client group, (2) a particular predictive measure, (3) another kind of risk measure, and (4) the hoped-for outcome. He located relevant articles by Barber (2008) and Johnson (2011). These articles concluded that an actuarial method was the most accurate. Actuarial measures are based on empirical relationships between certain factors and the likelihood of an outcome such as abuse.

These examples illustrate distinctive features of evidence-informed decision making. Well-structured questions related to information needs were posed that guided an effective, efficient electronic search. Searches can be done in the office using appropriate search methods including Boolean logic (and/or), relevant databases, and quality filters designed to locate the best evidence for a particular kind of question. Critical appraisal skills are used to review what is found. Many sources are available to guide this appraisal that include user-friendly checklists for different kinds of questions (e.g., Greenhalgh, 2010). A search for research findings may reveal that a practice method is harmful. We may discover that there is no research that critically appraises the effectiveness of a practice or policy or that the research is too weak to draw an inference. (Ioannidis [2005] argues that most research findings are false.) All these are findings related to important decisions that must be made. If no research findings are available that provide guidance, decisions must be based on other criteria, such as an empirically grounded practice theory. This is a finding and is shared with clients.

Hallmarks and Implications of the Philosophy of Evidence-Based Practice and Care

The philosophy and related technology of EBP have implications for all individuals and institutions involved with helping clients, including educators, researchers, practitioners/policy makers, and those who provide funding. Research, practice, and educational issues are closely intertwined. For example, poor quality reviews of research related to practice and policy questions may result in bogus practice guidelines that result in poor quality services for clients. Clinicians may be misinformed about the evidentiary status of practice and policy claims and so harm rather than help clients. Hallmarks and implications are interrelated; for example, promotion of transparency contributes to both knowledge flow and honoring ethical obligations.

Move Away From Authoritarian Practices and Policies

The key contribution of EBP is moving from authority-based professions to those in which ethical obligations to clients and students are honored and critical appraisal and honest brokering of knowledge and ignorance thrive. A preference for authoritarian beliefs and actions is by no means limited to clinicians. It flourishes among researchers and academics as well. Examples include misrepresenting views, hiding limitations of research studies, ignoring counterevidence to preferred views, and not involving clients and clinicians as informed participants in decisions made (e.g., about whether to use a certain practice guideline). Indicators of the authority-based nature of practice include large gaps between what is said and what is done (e.g., professional codes of ethics and current practices and policies) — basing decisions on criteria such as consensus and tradition, lack of informed consent, and censorship of certain kinds of knowledge such as variations in services and their outcomes.

Honor Ethical Obligations

Evidence-informed practice has ethical implications for practitioners and policy makers as well as for researchers and educators. Implications of evidence-informed practice for assessment include: (a) selecting empirically grounded assessment frameworks that reflect research findings regarding outcomes of interest; (b) using reliable, valid assessment measures; (c) involving clients as informed participants and considering their values and preferences. Implications for intervention include using practices and policies found to do more good than harm and accurately informing clients concerning the evidentiary status of methods recommended and alternatives. Implications for evaluation include using methods that accurately reflect degree of change and keeping track of progress on an ongoing basis. A striking characteristic of EBP and related developments is the extent to which clients are involved in many different ways. One is in the attention given to individual differences in client characteristics, circumstances, actions, values, and preferences in making decisions (e.g., see earlier description of EBP). The client-focused nature of evidence-informed decision making requires helpers to attend to client interests: What are *their* desired outcomes? What information would *they* like? What are *their* preferences regarding practices and policies? Considerable attention has been devoted to the creation of decision aids (O'Conner et al., 2009). A second way clients are involved is helping them to develop critical appraisal skills. A third is involving clients in the design and critique of practice- and policy-related research (e.g., Hanley, Truesdale, King, Elbourne, & Chalmers, 2001). A fourth is attending to outcomes that clients value and a fifth is involving them as informed participants. A sixth is recognizing their unique knowledge in relation to application concerns. Decisions concerning the distribution of scarce resources is also a key ethical concern in the helping professions; this requires consideration of populations as well as individuals (Gray, 2001a). Decisions concerning populations may pose hardships for individual clients.

Making Practices, Policies, and Their Outcomes Transparent

Evidence-informed practice encourages transparency of what is done to what effect in all venues of interest, including practice and policy, research, and professional education. It is a democratic endeavor in which clients are apprised of the evidentiary status of services (e.g., the likelihood that they will do more good than harm). There is candidness and clarity in place of secrecy and obscurity (Chalmers, 2003). These characteristics are at odds with authority-based practice. For example, is there evidence for the following claims:

- Psychological debriefing prevents posttraumatic stress syndrome.
- Eyewitness testimony can be trusted.
- Genograms contribute to accurate assessment.
- Screening programs for depression do more good than harm.

Transparency calls for blowing the whistle on pseudoscience, fraud, quackery, and professional propaganda. It will highlight gaps between resources needed to attain hoped-for outcomes as suggested by related research and what is used and thus may (and should) encourage advocacy on the part of clients and professionals for more effective services. It will reveal services that are ineffective, allowing a more judicious distribution of scarce resources (see Eddy, 1994a, 1994b). It will highlight gaps between contributions to client problems (e.g., lack of health care and high-quality educational opportunities) and interventions used and promoted. Identification of gaps will suggest ways to rearrange resources. Transparency will reveal the extent to which different kinds of ethical obligations are met, such as involving clients as informed participants. It will reveal impossible tasks; consider the unrealistic expectation to "ensure" that no child in protective care be harmed. This cannot be done. Transparency encourages clear language that should discourage propagandistic ploys that hide what is done to what effect. There is no longer a need to veil the lack of evidentiary status for practices and policies, or the lack of focus on client outcomes and failure to consider client preferences.

Increased transparency also has implications for the conduct, reporting, and dissemination of research findings. It requires accurate description of well-argued alternative views and related evidence and encourages rigorous testing of claims. Biases intrude both on the part of researchers when conducting and reporting research and when preparing research reviews (e.g., see Jadad & Enkin, 2008; MacCoun, 1998) as well as on the part of practitioners when making decisions. EBP calls for candid descriptions of limitations of research studies and use of methods that critically test questions addressed; it calls for systematic reviews (see Cochrane and Campbell Collaborations protocols). A key contribution of EBP is discouraging inflated claims of knowledge that mislead involved parties and hinder the development of knowledge. Consider terms such as *well established* and *validated*, which convey a certainty that is not possible. Bogus claims based on uncritical appraisals of related research hinder exploration and may result in harmful practices and policies.

Encourage a Systemic Approach for Integrating Practical, Ethical, and Evidentiary Issues

Evidence-informed practice describes a process designed to encourage integration of ethical, evidentiary, and application concerns. It advocates a systemic approach to improving the quality of services: (a) educating professionals who are lifelong learners, (b) involving clients as informed participants, (c) attending to management practices and policies that influence practice (i.e., evidence-based purchase of services), (d) considering the implications of scarce resources, and (e) attending to application challenges. Quality of services is unlikely to improve without attending to *all* links in the system of service provision. Gray (2001a, p. 354) suggests that performance (P) is directly related to an individual's motivation (M) and competence and inversely related to the barriers (B) that individual has to overcome: $P = (M \times C)/B$. Related literature describes a wide variety of efforts to address application concerns including the creation of tools and training programs designed to develop and encourage use of critical appraisal skills.

Maximize Knowledge Flow

EBP and social care are designed to maximize knowledge flow. Exploring ways to diffuse and disseminate knowledge encourages knowledge flow and related literature is rich in the variety of efforts described. In a culture in which knowledge flow is free, critical appraisal flourishes and questions are welcomed. Evidence-informed decision making emphasizes the importance of involving all interested parties, including clients, and its advocates have actively pursued the development of a technology and political base to encourage this. (See http//:www.cochraneconsumers.org). Gray (2001a) notes that evidence-based organizations should include systems that are capable of providing evidence and promoting the use of evidence, including both explicit (created by researchers) and tacit (created by clinicians, clients, and managers). Clinicians and clients are involved as informed participants—there is no privileged knowledge in the sense of not sharing information about the evidentiary status of practices and policies. Such sharing poses a threat to those who forward bogus claims and carry out pseudo inquiry, perhaps to retain funding and maintain status. Benefits of a free, efficient, knowledge market include:

- Critical appraisal of knowledge claims.
- Honoring informed consent obligations.
- Increased staff morale because decisions will be more informed and staff are rewarded for sharing knowledge and are free to discuss problems, including errors, and learn from colleagues and others throughout the world.
- Increase in the ratio of informed to uninformed or misinformed decisions.
- Recognizing uncertainty. This is often swept under the rug, resulting in blaming staff for not acting on knowledge that does not (or did not) exist.

- Reducing bogus claims of knowledge that may result in harm to clients among all parties including researchers. We often find little match between questions addressed and use of methods that can critically test them together with hiding limitations and inflated claims of effectiveness regarding what has been found.

- Lack of censorship of well-argued alternative views and counterevidence regarding popular views.

Identifying errors, mistakes, and related factors and using this information to minimize avoidable mistakes contributes to knowledge flow. Thus, we have an obligation to recognize and learn from our mistakes (Popper, 1992; 1994). We learn from our mistakes, and we lose valuable learning opportunities by overlooking opportunities to "educate our intuition" (Hogarth, 2001). Research regarding errors shows that systemic causes, including quality of staff training and agency policies, contribute to mistakes and errors (Munro, 2010; Reason, 1997). Accountable complaint systems are another way to maximize knowledge flow. Evidence-informed agencies encourage knowledge flow by using services likely to maximize the likelihood of attaining outcomes that clients value and not using services of unknown effectiveness or those found to do more harm than good.

Educational Implications

The importance of developing professionals who are lifelong learners is highlighted by research that shows that the typical professional education program produces graduates who do not keep up with the literature, which results in knowledge rapidly becoming out of date, with all the implications of this for clients (Sackett et al., 2000). Traditional forms of continuing education are not effective (Forsetlund et al., 2009). A unique form of problem-based learning (PBL) was developed at the McMaster University Faculty of Health Sciences in Canada. This involves a totally different form of professional education in which students are placed in small groups of five or seven, together with a tutor who is trained in group process as well as in skills involved in evidence-informed practice, such as posing well-structured questions and searching effectively and efficiently for related literature. This kind of problem-based learning in medicine has spread throughout the world. It provides repeated opportunities for corrective feedback that is so vital for learning.

A problem focus grounds content squarely on practice concerns, highlights key decisions and related questions and options, and links curriculum areas in a manner required when making decisions "on the job," including research and practice, policy and practice, and knowledge about human behavior and the environment. It emphasizes the unstructured and uncertain nature of problem solving and provides repeated opportunities to help students learn how to handle this. Focusing on problems of concern to clients and/or significant others in no way implies that client strengths are overlooked. It would be a poor problem solver indeed who did not take advantage of available resources. Another implication is describing methodological and conceptual controversies, including problem framing, so that social workers are informed and thus can accurately inform clients as required by our code of ethics. Consider for example the continuing medicalization of problems-in-living (Conrad, 2007; Kirk, 2005; Rapley, Moncrieff, & Dillon, 2011). Such medicalized problem framing may not be emphasized in professional education, as suggested by a review of course outlines in social work courses on psychopathology (Lacasse & Gomory, 2003).

Controversies

Both the origins of EPB and objections to it reflect different views of "evidence." There are many kinds of evidence. Differences of opinion regarding what evidence is can be seen in the professional literature as well as in the media. When do we have enough to recommend a practice or policy? Do criteria for "having enough" differ in relation to different kinds of decisions. Davies (2004) suggests that a broad view of evidence is needed to review policies including (a) experience and expertise, (b) judgment, (c) resources, (d) values, (e) habits and traditions, (f) lobbyists and pressure groups, and (g) pragmatics and contingencies. He argues that we should consider all of these factors in making decisions about whether or not to implement a policy. Davies identifies six kinds of research related to evidence of policy impact: (1) implementation, (2) descriptive analytical, (3) attitudinal, (4) statistical modeling, (5) economic/econometric, and (6) ethical. Key controversies include the degree of rigor that should be used to evaluate knowledge claims and the extent to which clients should be involved as informed participants. For example, multisystemic family therapy (MST) is widely described as effective and as an "evidence-based practice." Based on a critical appraisal of reviews of MST using Cochrane Collaboration guidelines, Littell and her colleagues (2005) concluded that such programs are neither more nor less effective than are other programs. This review, as well as many others, show that haphazard reviews came to different conclusions than do systematic reviews. Concerns about inflated claims was a key reason for the origin of EBP and health care. Inflated claims obscure uncertainties that, if shared, may influence client decisions.

Different opinions about how much "we know" reflects use of different criteria. The Taskforce on Psychological Intervention Guidelines (1995) of the American Psychological Association suggested that two well-designed RCTs showing positive outcomes represent an "empirically validated treatment." A more measured statement would be to say that a claim has been critically tested in two high-quality randomized controlled trials and has passed both tests; this keeps uncertainty in view. Professionals rely on weaker criteria when evaluating the evidentiary status of claims that affect their clients than they rely on when evaluating claims that affect their personal well-being (see Gambrill & Gibbs, 2002).

Obstacles

Many challenges confront helpers who want to make evidence-informed decisions such as gaining access to research findings related to important questions and critically appraising this knowledge in a timely manner (e.g., see Bogenschneider & Corbett, 2010). Straus and McAlister (2000) note that some limitations of EBP are universal in helping efforts such as challenges in applying evidence to the care of individuals. Barriers they suggest include the need to develop new skills and limited funds and resources (see also Gibbs & Gambrill, 2002). Obstacles lie at many levels, including the very culture in which we live — in which it is common to find exaggerated reports of risks and remedies — making it a challenge to separate the wheat from the chaff regarding claims of what "we know" and what "we do not know." Poor-quality research continues to appear in professional journals. There are many reasons for this, including the special interests of players in the biomedical industrial complex, such as pharmaceutical companies (Gambrill, 2012b). Dysfunctional organizational cultures and climates in which errors are hidden and staff are punished for blowing the whistle on inadequate or harmful practices and policies is an obstacle.

Personal characteristics such as arrogance and flawed self-assessments may compromise decisions (Dunning, Heath, & Suls, 2004). Biases such as wishful thinking and searching only for data that support a favored position (confirmation bias) compromise the quality of decisions (Gambrill, 2012b; Nickerson, 1998). A reluctance to acknowledge uncertainty and controversy compromises fulfillment of ethical obligations to accurately inform clients. Consider critiques of practice guidelines and controversies regarding the role of common factors (see Norcross, Beutler, & Levant, 2006; Wampold, 2006; 2010). Challenges include gaining timely access to research findings related to important practice and policy questions and critically appraising this knowledge (Greenhalgh, Robert, Macfarlane, Bate, & Kyriakidou, 2004). Lack of transparency regarding limitations of research remains widespread, as does the publication of incomplete, uncritical reviews that provide an overly rosy picture of alleged effectiveness of practice methods. Inflated claims are more the rule than the exception in the helping professions, misleading clients and others. Money may not be available for computers allowing rapid access to needed databases or for knowledge resource personnel who can help staff locate valuable research related to information needs in a timely manner. Skills are needed in evidence management, searching, appraisal, and storage (Gray, 2001a).

Special training, repeated guided practice, and related tools and resources are needed to carry out the steps of EBP in real time. Even then, many obstacles remain, such as authoritarian agency cultures. Although the steps involved in EBP may sound simple and straightforward, they are often difficult and sometimes impossible to carry out successfully in the real world. A lack of assessment knowledge and skills may contribute to posing misleading questions and overlooking important individual differences in a client's circumstances or characteristics. For example, posing an effectiveness question before discovering factors that contribute to depression (such as "In adults who are depressed, is cognitive-behavioral therapy, compared to medication, more effective in decreasing depression?") may overlook the fact that, for this client, recent losses in social support are uppermost, which suggests a different question, such as "In adults who are depressed because of a recent loss in social support, is a support group or individual counseling more effective in decreasing depression?" Developing technologies to address application problems has been a key contribution of evidence-informed practice; it is an ongoing challenge. Still today, as years ago, there are "no magic bullets" (Oxman, Thomson, Davis, & Haynes, 1995).

Conclusion

Views of EBP differ in their breadth and attention to application and ethical issues ranging from the broad, systemic philosophy and related evolving technology envisioned by its originators to narrow views (use of practice guidelines) and total distortions. It is important to distinguish between objections based on inaccurate views of EBP and those based on an accurate understanding. Otherwise, we may prematurely discard promising approaches and lose opportunities to address real challenges. So far, distortions of EBP, propagandistic use of the term (the label without the substance), and the "EBPs approach" have won the day. Clearinghouses and texts using the term *evidence-based* abound. But are these "evidence-based"? Are practices and polices described in such sources "best"? Critical appraisal of content promoted in such sources often show that what is proclaimed as best may not be (e.g., Gorman & Huber, 2009; Littell, 2008).

Readers may not be informed about successful practices and policies and related theoretical approaches (e.g., see Angell, 2004). Consider misrepresentation and ignoring of applied behavior analysis and its application to areas of direct concern to social workers including mental health, (mis)use of alcohol and drugs, and child welfare (Thyer, 2005). Consider also ignoring of successful policies. For example, in A. Abbott's *Alcohol, Tobacco and Other Drugs: Challenging Myths, Assessing Theories, Individualizing Interventions* (second edition), a recent book published by the National Association of Social Workers (2010), there is no mention of the successful policy of decriminalization of all drugs in Portugal in 2001 (Greenwald, 2009; Hughes & Stevens, 2010). Nor is there any mention of this policy in the fourth edition of *Chemical Dependency: A Systematic Approach* by McNeece and DiNitto (2012). Why is this? Ignoring successful policies contributes to the continuation of the unsuccessful and harmful "war on drugs" promoted by the federal government in the United States—one that has been, and continues to be, especially harmful to minorities (e.g., Alexander, 2010; Wacquant, 2009). By ignoring successful policies in social work, academics become complicit in maintaining harmful policies.

The practice and philosophy of EPB as described by its originators offers practitioners and administrators a philosophy that is compatible with obligations described in professional codes of ethics and educational accreditation policies and standards (e.g., aligned with informed consent and drawing on practice- and policy-related research findings) as well as an evolving technology for integrating evidentiary, ethical, and practical issues. Key steps in EBP increase the likelihood that involved parties will be accurately informed about the uncertainties associated with decisions. Perhaps the greatest challenge is a willingness to acknowledge gaps in our current knowledge regarding decisions and what may be "out there." A willingness to say "I don't know" and a commitment to clients to discover what is out there (including nothing) are vital. So, too, is a willingness and the courage to advocate for effective services—a willingness to "stand up for others." In the everyday world, "best practice" may have to be based on shaky evidentiary grounds. Evidence-informed practice and policy encourages professionals to be honest about these grounds so that clients are involved as informed participants in decisions made. Will social workers be "conscientious, explicit and judicious" in their "use of current best evidence in making decisions about the care of individual [clients]" (Sackett et al., 1997, p. 2)? To what extent will content in the chapters in this volume facilitate such characteristics?

Key Terms

Evidence

Knowledge

Evidence-based practice

Evidence-based health care

Haphazard research review

Methodological filters

Quackery

Science

Systematic research review

Review Questions for Critical Thinking

1. Should we offer clients services we ourselves would like to receive?
2. Can we trust the "experts" to accurately inform us regarding the evidentiary status of claims of "what works"?
3. Are clients being harmed in the name of helping?
4. Do good intentions protect clients from harm?

Online Resources

DUETS: http://www.library.nhs.uk/duets

Database of uncertainties about the effects of intervention.

Campbell Database of reviews: http://www.campbellcollaboration.org

Coalition for Evidence-Based Policy: http://www.coalition4evidence.org

Cochrane Database of reviews: http://www.cochrane.org

Evidence-based behavioral practice (EBBP): http://www.ebbp.org

Patient decision aids: http://decisionaid.ohri.ca

Social Care Institute for Excellence (SCIE): http://scie.org.uk

Provides reports regarding best practices in social care.

TRIP Database: http://www.tripdatabase.com

Searches more than 75 sites of high quality medical information.

References

Abbott, A. (2010). *Alcohol, tobacco, and other drugs: Challenging myths, assessing theories, individualizing intervention*. Washington, DC: NASW Press.

Alexander, M. (2010). *The new Jim Crow laws: Mass incarceration in the age of color blindness*. New York, NY: New Press.

Angell, M. (2004). *The truth about drug companies: How they deceive us and what to do about it*. New York, NY: Random House.

Barber, J. G. (2008). Putting evidence-based practice into practice. In B. W. White (Ed.). *Comprehensive handbook of social work and social welfare volume 1: The profession of social work* (pp. 441–449). Hoboken, NJ: Wiley.

Blenkner, M., Bloom, M., & Nielson, M. (2001). A research and demonstration project of protective services. *Social Casework, 52*, 483–499.

Bogenschneider, K., & Corbett, T. (2010). *Evidence-based policy making: Insights from policy minded researchers and research-minded policy-makers*. New York, NY: Taylor & Francis.

Braddock, C. H., Edwards, K. A., Hasenberg, N. M., Laidley, T. L., Levinson, W. (1999). Informed decision making in outpatient practice: Time to get back to the basics. *JAMA, 282*, 2313–2320.

Chalmers, I. (2003). Trying to do more good than harm in policy and practice: The role of rigorous, transparent, up-to-date evaluation. *Annals of the American Academy of Political and Social Science, 589*, 22–40.

Chalmers, I. (2004). Well-informed uncertainties about the effects of treatment. *British Medical Journal, 328*, 425–426.

Conrad, J. (2007). *The medicalization of society: On the transformation of human conditions into treatable disorders*. Baltimore, MD: John Hopkins University Press.

Davies, P. (2004, February). *Is evidence-based government possible?* Jerry Lee lecture, 4th annual Campbell Collaboration Colloquium, Washington, DC.

Dunning, D., Heath, C., & Suls, J. M. (2004). Flawed self-assessment: Implications for health, education, and the workplace. *Psychological Science in the Public Interest, 5*, 69–106.

Eddy, D. M. (1994a). Principles for making difficult decisions in difficult times. *Journal of the American Medical Association*, *271*, 1792–1798.

Eddy, D. M. (1994b). Rationing resources while improving quality. *Journal of the American Medical Association*, *373*, 817–824.

Forsetlund, L, Bjørndal, A., Rashidian, A., Jamtvedt, G., O'Brien, M. A., Wolf, F.,...Oxman, A. D. (2009). Continuing education meetings and workshops: Effects on professional practice and health care outcomes. *Cochrane Database of Systematic Reviews, 2*, Article CD003030.

Fox, R. C., & Swazey, J. P. (1974). *The courage to fail: A social view of organ transplants and dialysis*. Chicago, IL: University of Chicago Press.

Gambrill, E. (2011). Evidence-based practice and the ethics of discretion. *Journal of Social Work*, *11*, 26–48.

Gambrill, E. (2012a). *Critical thinking in clinical practice* (3rd ed.). Hoboken, NJ: Wiley.

Gambrill, E. (2012b). *Propaganda in the helping professions*. New York, NY: Oxford University Press.

Gambrill, E., & Gibbs, L. (2002). Making practice decisions: Is what's good for the goose good for the gander? *Ethical Human Services and Services, 4*, 31–46.

Gibbs, L. (2003). *Evidence-based practice for the helping professions*. Pacific Grove, CA: Brooks/Cole.

Gibbs, L., & Gambrill, E. (2002). Arguments against evidence based practice. *Research on Social Work Practice, 14*, 452–476.

Glasziou, P., Del Mar, C., & Salisbury, J. (2003). *Evidence-based medicine workbook*. London, U.K.: BMJ Publishing Group.

Gorman, D. M., & Huber, J. C. (2009). The social construction of "evidence-based" drug prevention programs: A reanalysis of data from the Drug Abuse Resistance Education (DARE) Program. *Evaluation Review, 33*, 396–414.

Gray, J. A. M. (2001a). *Evidence-based health care: How to make health policy and management decisions* (2nd ed.). New York, NY: Churchill Livingstone.

Gray, J. A. M. (2001b). Evidence-based medicine for professionals. In A. Edwards & G. Elwyn (Eds.), *Evidence-based patient choice: Inevitable or impossible?* (pp. 19–33). New York, NY: Oxford University Press.

Greenhalgh, T. (2010). *How to read a paper: The basics of evidence-based medicine* (4th ed.). London, U.K.: BMJ Publishing Group.

Greenhalgh, T., Robert, G., Macfarlane, F., Bate, P., & Kyriakidou, O. (2004). Diffusion of innovations in service organizations: Systematic review and recommendations. *Milbank Quarterly, 82*, 581–629.

Greenwald, G. (2009), *Drug decriminalization in Portugal: Lessons for creating fair and successful drug policies*. Washington, DC: CATO Institute.

Guyatt, G., & Rennie, D. (2002). *Users' guides to the medical literature: A manual for evidence-based clinical practice*. Chicago, IL: American Medical Association.

Guyatt, G., Rennie, D., Meade, M. O., & Cook, D. J. (2008). *Users' guides to the medical literature: A manual for evidence-based clinical practice* (2nd ed.). Chicago, IL: American Medical Association.

Hanley, B., Truesdale, A., King, A., Elbourne, D., & Chalmers, I. (2001). Involving consumers in designing, conducting, and interpreting randomised controlled trials: Questionnaire survey. *British Medical Journal, 322*, 519–523.

Haynes, R. B., Devereaux, P. J., & Guyatt, G. H. (2002, March/April). Clinical expertise in the era of evidence-based medicine and patient choice [Editorial]. *ACP Journal Club, 136* (A11), 1–7.

Higgins, J. P. T., & Green, S. (Eds.). (2008, March). Cochrane handbook for systematic reviews of interventions 4.2.4. In *Cochrane Library* (Vol. 2). Chichester, U.K.: Wiley.

Hogarth, R. M. (2001). *Educating intuition*. Chicago, IL: University of Chicago Press.

Hughes, C. E., & Stevens, A. (2010). What can we learn from the Portuguese decriminalization of illicit drugs? *British Journal of Criminology, 50*, 999–1022.

Ioannidis, J. P. A. (2005). Why most published research findings are false. *PLoS Medicine, 2*, e124.

Jacobson, J. W., Foxx, R. M., & Mulick, J. A. (Eds.). (2005). *Controversial therapies for developmental disabilities: Fads, fashion, and science in professional practice*. Mahwah, NJ: Erlbaum.

Jadad, A. R., & Enkin, M. W. (2007). *Randomized controlled trials: Questions, answers, and musings* (2nd ed.). Malden, MA: Blackwell.

Johnson, W. L. (2011). The validity and utility of the California Family Risk Assessment under practice conditions in the field: A prospective study. *Child Abuse and Neglect, 35*, 18–28.

Kirk, S. A. (Ed.). (2005). *Mental disorders in the social environment: Critical perspectives*. New York, NY: Columbia University Press.

Lacasse, J. R., & Gomory, T. (2003). Is graduate social work education promoting a critical approach to mental health practice? *Journal of Social Work Education, 39*, 383–408.

Lilienfeld, S. O., Lynn, S. J., & Lohr, J. M. (Eds.). (2003). *Science and pseudoscience in clinical psychology*. New York, NY: Guilford Press.

Lipsey, M. W. (2009). Better evidence for a better world. In M. W. Lipsey & E. Noonan (Eds.), *International initiative for impact evaluation* (pp. 19–21). Working Paper 2. The Campbell Collaboration.

Littell, J. H. (2008). Evidence based or evidence biased? The quality of published reviews. *Children and Youth Services Review, 30*, 1299–1317.

Littell, J. H., Popa, M., & Forsythe, B. (2005). Multisystemic therapy for social, emotional, and behavioral problems in youth aged 10–17. In *Cochrane Database of Systematic Reviews* (Vol. 3). Chichester, U.K.: Wiley.

MacCoun, R. (1998). Biases in the interpretation and use of research results. *Annual Review of Psychology, 49*, 259–287.

McCord, J. (2003). Cures that harm: Unanticipated outcomes of crime prevention programs. *The Annals of the American Academy of Political and Social Science, 587*, 16–30.

McNeece, C. A., & DiNitto, D. M. (2012). *Chemical dependency: A systems approach* (4th ed.). Boston, MA: Pearson.

Mullen, E. J., & Bacon, W. (2004). A survey of practitioner adoption and implementation of practice guidelines and evidence-based treatments. In A. R. Roberts & K. Yeager (Eds.), *Evidence-based practice manual: Research and outcome measures in health and human services* (pp. 210–218). New York, NY: Oxford University Press.

Munro, E. (2010). Learning to reduce risk in child protection. *British Journal of Social Work, 40*, 1135–1151.

National Association of Social Workers (NASW). (2008). *Code of ethics*. Washington, DC: Author.

Nickerson, R. S. (1998). Confirmation bias: A ubiquitous phenomena in many guises. *Review of General Psychology, 2*, 175–220.

Norcross, J. C., Beutler, L. E., & Levant, R. F. (Eds.). (2006). *Evidence-based practices in mental health: Debate and dialogue on the fundamental questions*. Washington, DC: American Psychological Association.

O'Conner, A. M., Bennett, C. L., Stacey, D., Barry, M., Col, N. F., Eden, K. B., et al. (2009). Decision aids for people facing health treatment or screening decisions. *Cochrane Database of Systematic Reviews, 3*, Article CDOO 1431.

Oxman, A. D., Thomson, M. A., Davis, D., & Haynes, R. B. (1995). No magic bullets: A systematic review of 102 trials of interventions to improve professional practice. *Canadian Medical Association Journal, 153*, 1423–1431.

Paul, R. (1993). *Critical thinking: What every person needs to survive in a rapidly changing world* (3rd ed.). Sonoma, CA: Foundation for Critical Thinking. Available from www.criticalthinking.org

Paul, R. W., & Elder, I. (2004). *Critical thinking: Tools for taking charge of your professional and personal life*. Upper Saddle River, NJ: Prentice Hall.

Popper, K. (1992). *In search of a better world: Lectures and essays from thirty years*. London, U.K.: Routledge & Kegan Paul.

Popper, K. (1994). *The myth of the framework: In defense of science and rationality* (M. A. Notturno, Ed.). New York, NY: Routledge.

Rapley, M., Moncrieff, J., & Dillon, J. (Eds.). (2011). *De-medicalizing misery: Psychiatry, psychology and the human condition*. Houndsmills, Basingstoke Hampshire, England: Palgrave Macmillan.

Reason, J. (1997). *Managing the risks of organizational accidents*. Brookfield, VT: Ashgate.

Rose, S., Bisson, J., Churchill, R., & Wessely, S. (2002). Psychological debriefing for preventing posttraumatic stress disorder (PTSD). In *Cochrane Database in Systematic Reviews, 1*. Chichester, U.K.: Wiley.

Rubin, A., & Parrish, D. (2007). Problematic phrases in the conclusions of published outcome studies: Implications for evidence-based practice. *Research on Social Work Practice, 17*, 334–347.

Sackett, D. L., Richardson, W. S., Rosenberg, W., & Haynes, R. B. (1997). *Evidence-based medicine: How to practice and teach EBM*. New York, NY: Churchill Livingstone.

Sackett, D. L., Rosenberg, W. M. C., Gray, J. A. M., Haynes, R. B., & Richardson, W. S. (1996). Evidence-based medicine: What it is and what it isn't [Editorial]. *British Medical Journal, 312*, 71–72.

Sackett, D. L., Straus, S. E., Richardson, W. C., Rosenberg, W., & Haynes, R. M. (2000). *Evidence-based medicine: How to practice and teach EBM* (2nd ed.). New York, NY: Churchill Livingstone.

Straus, S. E., & McAlister, D. C. (2000). Evidence-based medicine: A commentary on common criticisms. *Canadian Medical Journal, 163*, 837–841.

Straus, S. E., Richardson, W. S., Glasziou, P., & Haynes, R. D. (2005). *Evidence-based medicine: How to practice and teach EBP* (3rd ed.). New York, NY: Churchill Livingston.

Task Force on Psychological Intervention Guidelines. (1995). *Template for developing guidelines: Interventions for mental disorders and psychosocial aspects of physical disorders*. Washington, DC: American Psychological Association.

Thyer, B. A. (2005). The misfortunes of behavioral social work: Misprized, misread, and misconstrued. In S. A. Kirk (Ed.), *Mental disorders in the social environment: Critical perspective* (pp. 330–343). New York, NY: Columbia University Press.

Thyer, B. A., & Pignotti, M. (2010). Science and pseudoscience in developmental disabilities: Guidelines for social workers. *Journal of Social Work in Disability & Rehabilitation, 9*, 110–129.

Thyer, B. A., & Pignotti, M. (in press). *Science and pseudoscience in social work*. New York, NY: Oxford University Press.

Wacquant, L. (2009). *Punishing the poor: The neoliberal government in social insecurity*. Durham, NC: Duke University Press.

Wampold, B. E. (2006). The psychotherapist. In J. C. Norcross, L. E. Beutler, & R. F. Levant (Eds.), *Evidence-based practices in mental health: Debate and dialogue on the fundamental questions* (pp. 202–207). Washington, DC: American Psychological Association.

Wampold, B. E. (2010). The research evidence for the common factors models: A historically situated perspective. In B. M. Duncan, S. D. Miller, M. A. Hubble, & B. E. Wampold (Eds.), *The heart and soul of therapy* (2nd ed., pp. 49–82). Washington, DC: American Psychological Association.

Wennberg, J. E. (2002). Unwarranted variations in healthcare delivery: Implications for academic medical centers. *British Medical Journal, 325*, 961–964.

Chapter 2
Trauma-Informed Practice

Nancy J. Smyth and Laura Greyber

> What changes do we need to make to improve social work practice to better address the needs of people who have experienced significant trauma over the course of their lives?

Overview

Researchers estimate that approximately 60% of youth have experienced a traumatic event, 15.5 million witness and/or experience domestic violence, and that 7 million were subjected to severe and chronic familial violence (Berkowitz, Stover, & Marans, 2011). In the adult population, the 1995 National Comorbidity Study found rates of trauma exposure of 51% (women) and 61% (men) using a narrower definition of trauma than is used in the current diagnostic manual (Kessler, 2000). More recent community-based studies suggest that the rates of exposure may go as high as 90% in some communities, although a national study has not been conducted in the United States using the expanded definition of trauma that includes diagnosis of a life-threatening illness and the sudden death of a close friend/loved one (Kessler, 2000). Generally, it's estimated that clinical populations demonstrate consistently much higher rates of lifetime exposure to trauma, especially recipients of public mental health services (Cusack, Frueh, & Brady, 2004).

Not only do traumatic experiences affect all levels of well-being, including mental, physical, emotional, social, and behavioral health, but they also are associated with a heavy burden on society. For instance, it is estimated that $8.3 billion is spent on an annual basis for the medical care, mental health services, and lost productivity for survivors of intimate partner violence. Additionally, the current conflicts in the Middle East, both Afghanistan and Iraq, have created a groundswell of service members returning with posttraumatic stress disorder (PTSD) and/or depression (18.5%) (Substance Abuse and Mental Health Services Administration [SAMHSA], 2011).

Given the startling statistics and prevalence rates of trauma and violence, and the impact of such events on youth and adult populations, it becomes evident that appropriate and effective techniques for assessment and treatment of trauma-related symptoms is imperative. In addition, there is recognition that existing service systems need to be examined to ensure that they are supportive environments in light of what is currently known about how trauma affects people. SAMHSA's National Center for Trauma-Informed Care describes this best practice as follows:

> Trauma-informed care *is an approach to engaging people with histories of trauma that recognizes the presence of trauma symptoms and acknowledges the role that trauma has played in their lives. NCTIC facilitates the adoption of trauma-informed environments in the delivery of a broad range of services including mental health, substance use, housing, vocational or employment support, domestic violence and victim assistance, and peer support. In all of these environments, NCTIC seeks to change the paradigm from one that asks, "What's wrong with you?" to one that asks, "What has happened to you?"*
>
> (SAMHSA, National Center for Trauma Informed Care, n.d., p. 1)

As part of this effort to transform the paradigms around which service systems are organized, SAMHSA has developed a strategic initiative focused on Trauma and Justice. Goals for Trauma and Justice include: (a) develop a comprehensive public health approach to trauma; (b) make screening for trauma and early intervention and treatment common practice; (c) reduce the impact of trauma and violence on children, youth, and families; (d) address the needs of people with mental disorders, substance use disorders, co-occurring disorders, or a history of trauma in the criminal and juvenile justice systems; (e) reduce the impact of disasters on the behavioral health of individuals, families, and communities (SAMHSA, Strategic Initiative #2: Trauma and Justice, n.d.).

Defining Trauma

There are multiple definitions of trauma, many of which have evolved over time as our understanding of this phenomenon has developed and progressed. Resick (2001) defines trauma as "events that are life threatening (and/or threatening to 'self'...) and that are accompanied by intense fear, helplessness, or horror" (p. 2). The International Society for the Study of Traumatic Stress (ISTSS) describes traumatic events as "emotionally shocking events that overwhelm a person in a variety of ways" (ISTSS, n.d.). There can be wide variation in peoples' responses to a traumatic event. While some people may have only a mild reaction, others can experience debilitating symptoms. Common reactions can include shock, fear, anxiety, emotional numbing, feelings of disconnection from self and others, intrusive thoughts and images of the event, amnesia for parts of the experience, and dissociation (ISTSS).

Although definitions may vary depending on the source, it is important to note that woven into each definition is the concept of an event combined with an individual's perception of and reaction to an event. While one individual may perceive an experience as traumatic, another individual may not, and thus, the sequelae of symptoms vary widely depending on the event and the person.

In the United States, the *Diagnostic Statistical Manual-TR IV* (*DSM-IV TR*; American Psychiatric Association [APA], 2000) is the diagnostic framework used most often for practice and research. The *DSM-IV TR* defines trauma as:

> ...*an event that involves actual or threatened death or serious injury, or other threat to one's physical integrity; or witnessing an event that involves death, injury, or a threat to the physical integrity of another person; or learning about unexpected or violent death, serious harm, or threat of death or injury experienced by a family member or other close associate.*

> *(APA, 2000, p. 463)*

Types of Trauma

Trauma is often divided into two large categories: simple and complex trauma. *Simple trauma* is the term often used to refer to acute traumatic events. According to the National Child Traumatic Stress Network (NCTSN), acute events can include school shootings, gang-related violence, terrorist attacks, natural disasters, serious accidents, sudden or violent loss of loved one, and physical or sexual assault (NCTSN, *Types of Traumatic Stress*, n.d.). Conversely, *complex trauma*, often referred to as chronic traumatic situations, includes some forms of physical abuse, long-standing abuse including sexual abuse, domestic violence, and wars or other forms of ongoing violence. According to NCTSN, complex trauma describes:

> ...*exposure to multiple or prolonged traumatic events...involves the simultaneous or sequential occurrence...maltreatment, neglect, physical and sexual abuse, and domestic violence—that is chronic, begins early in childhood, and occurs within the primary caregiving system. Exposure to these initial traumatic experiences—and the resulting emotional dysregulation and the loss of safety, direction, and the ability to detect or respond to danger cues—often sets off a chain of events leading to subsequent or repeated trauma exposure in adolescence or adulthood.*

> *(NCTSN, n.d.a)*

Children who experience chronic, repeated trauma are more likely to have symptoms of intense distress such as problems with sleeping, paying attention, concentration, and they may be more angry, irritable, withdrawn, and have recurrent intrusive thoughts. In the adult population, symptoms related to trauma include poor interpersonal relationships and problems with employment to name a few. Individuals, regardless of age, are more likely to develop a mental illness or a psychiatric condition such as PTSD, depression, anxiety, and behavior disorders if they are exposed to chronic, complex trauma (NCTSN, *Defining Trauma and Child Traumatic Stress*, n.d.c).

Trauma-Related Diagnoses

Although experiencing a traumatic event does not necessarily lead into a diagnosable mental health disorder, a range of disorders can be considered a direct result of or reaction to trauma. The *DSM-IV TR* lists mental health disorders and includes the following related to trauma: adjustment disorders, bereavement disorders, PTSD, acute stress disorder (ASD), and dissociative disorders (APA, 2000). In addition to diagnosable mental illnesses listed in the *DSM-IV TR*, trauma reactions are often associated with impairment in functioning, adjustment problems, stress-related illnesses, and other physical disorders; trauma often impacts a range of domains including attachment, biology, affect regulation, dissociation, behavioral control, cognition, and self-concept (NCTSN, 2003a). Research indicates that approximately 6% to 20% of individuals who experience a traumatic event go on to develop PTSD (Berkowitz et al., 2011).

Although any type of traumatic event can result in pathology, there are certain traumatic experiences that are more likely to cause PTSD. These often include but are not limited to events such as rape, molestation, physical attack, combat, threat with weapon, neglect, and physical abuse (Resick, 2001). Furthermore, individuals who are diagnosed with PTSD are more at-risk for developing comorbid disorders including major depressive disorder (MDD), dysthymia, mania, generalized anxiety disorder (GAD), panic, various phobias, drug and/or alcohol problems, and conduct disorder. In a national study conducted by Kessler, Sonnega, and Bromet (1995), it is estimated that approximately 50% of men and women diagnosed with PTSD are also diagnosed with MDD. Research also indicates that PTSD often marks the onset of comorbid psychiatric disorders (Cusack et al., 2004). Indicated by research, trauma histories are highly correlated with substance and/or alcohol abuse, which is often linked to negative outcomes such as more severe symptomology, high rates of rehospitalization, treatment noncompliance, and housing instability (Gearon, Kaltman, Brown, & Bellack, 2003). While traumatic events can often be a catalyst to drug and/or alcohol abuse problems, the use of drugs and alcohol can also make individuals more vulnerable—essentially increasing the chances of traumatic events (Gearon et al., 2003). Furthermore, individuals who are diagnosed with PTSD are much more likely to attempt suicide—compared to control populations, approximately 6 times more likely (Cusack et al., 2004).

In the child population, it is reported that "exposures to such traumas, in turn, has been associated with a wide variety of negative mental health outcomes, including anxiety and depression" (Briere et al., 2001, p. 1002). Youth who have been exposed to or have directly experienced a traumatic event are also much more likely to develop subclinical disorders and general psychological distress (Graham-Bermann et al., 2008). Exposure at a young age can affect behavior, mental health, academics, sleeping, eating problems, and other physical symptoms, such as aches and pains (NCTSN, 2003a). Youth who have repetitive, chronic, and severe exposure to trauma are much more likely to develop PTSD and related symptoms (NCTSN, 2003b).

Risk Factors

Certain factors or characteristics can place individuals at higher risk for experiencing trauma and subsequent symptoms. One such factor is age, which is the "strongest risk factor for predicting global distress following traumas" (Resick, 2001, p. 95), with younger people being more likely to have distress. In addition, gender is consistently identified as a risk factor across studies, with women being at higher risk for PTSD than men. Resick (2001, pp. 97–100) notes that other commonly investigated factors, like socioeconomic status, income, and education levels, have emerged as risk factors in some studies and not in others.

Besides demographic variables, there are pretrauma factors that affect the likelihood of people experiencing distress from a traumatic event. For example, a prior childhood trauma, other stressors in the family environment, experiencing prior stressful life events, and prior psychological problems all increase the risk of experiencing distress when a traumatic event is experienced (Resick, 2001, pp. 100–102). To illustrate further, Mueser and colleagues found that "trauma is a common experience in persons with severe mental illnesses such as schizophrenia and bipolar disorder and that it is correlated with a variety of poor outcomes, including symptom severity, substance abuse, and homelessness" (2001, p. 110). Lastly, some research suggests that individuals who have experienced trauma are much more likely to reexperience trauma (Lewis et al., 2006).

Social Work and Trauma

Social workers have worked with vulnerable populations—many of whom have lived through traumatic life events—since the beginning of our profession. For this reason, we are likely to encounter clients with trauma histories across all of the service settings in which we work. However, the knowledge base on trauma reactions and trauma intervention has developed rapidly since 1980, when PTSD first became listed as a diagnosis in the *DSM*. As a result, social workers are recognizing the need to stay abreast of the new research on how trauma affects people and what the most effective practices are for treating people who have experienced trauma. Providing trauma-informed practice means first recognizing that based on the prevalence rates from research, most of the clients we see will have a history of exposure to one or more traumatic events. While trauma-informed practice involves the need to incorporate trauma assessment into routine practice and to ensure that clients have access to interventions that address their trauma-related symptoms and problems, it also focuses our attention on how all services are delivered (Bloom & Farragher, 2011). For example, the ways in which psychiatric hospital staff uses restraints on clients could well result in higher levels of distress for the many clients who have a history of physical abuse. Similarly, the process of nightly bed checks in residential or inpatient facilities might trigger traumatic reactions from the large number of clients who have sexual abuse histories. Finally, trauma-informed practice also requires that we examine how working with traumatized clients can affect our own vulnerability to experiencing *secondary traumatic stress* (STS), that is, the stress-related symptoms that develop as a result of close contact with people who have experienced significant trauma.

While much of the content on STS is anecdotal, some research is beginning to emerge that identifies it is a significant problem that deserves attention. For example, one study found that half the social workers surveyed reported significant levels of STS (Bride, 2007). An instrument that assesses STS is the Secondary Traumatic Stress Scale (Bride, Robinson, Yegidis, & Figley, 2004).

Assessment of Trauma

Although trauma is often a major comorbid disorder with other mental illnesses, trauma assessments are rarely employed on a standard basis in mental health settings. For example, research from a community mental health center indicated that 43% of individuals receiving services met the criteria to be diagnosed with PTSD; however, only 2% were documented with PTSD (Cusack et al., 2004). "Given the unfortunate sequelae that can result from traumatic events, comprehensive and effective trauma-related assessment is necessary for all populations" (de Arellano & Danielson, 2008, p. 54). It is extremely important to consider the development of trauma-related symptoms and conduct thorough assessments of trauma histories. For example, research indicates that trauma-related symptoms and consequences can, oftentimes, be delayed, and do not become apparent until adulthood (Lewis et al., 2006).

Trauma Specific Versus Generic Assessments

Recent literature indicates the need for a battery of assessments when assisting children and adolescents who may have or are experiencing traumatic events. A range of assessments, from generic to specific trauma questionnaires, are recommended. By collecting a number of assessments, it is less likely that trauma is either overlooked with generic questionnaires, or focused on too heavily, which "runs the risk of overlooking other outcomes that are potentially integral" (Briere & Scott, 2007, p. 351). It is indicated that the battery of tests should ascertain data related to presenting symptomology, trauma exposure, generic symptoms and trauma-related symptoms, and other tests indicated based on the client's presenting symptoms. Furthermore, a specific test of PTSD may be indicated based on assessment of trauma exposure and related symptoms (Briere & Scott, 2007). Fricker and Smith (2001) examined the sensitivity of generic versus trauma-specific assessments and found that the validity scales for the Trauma Symptom Checklist for Children (TSCC) were not as effective in identifying clinical cases, although this scale was more sensitive to PTSD-related symptoms when compared to the Personality Inventory for Youth (PIY). The results from this study indicate the necessity for both generic and trauma-specific assessments to be included in a battery of tools to gather information from youth.

Administering Trauma Assessments

Researchers de Arellano and Danielson (2008) advise that there are a variety of factors that must be examined when determining an assessment approach related to trauma. First, they recommend a general approach, which utilizes core questions related to trauma experiences, and should be inclusive of the child and family members. Next, if trauma is identified, the person is then asked a specific set of questions that are directly related to the trauma and trauma history. When asking specific questions related to trauma, they should be prefaced with an introductory narrative, a rationale, and a behavioral description. Briere and Scott (2007) also indicate the importance in ordering: symptomatology, trauma exposure, generic symptoms, trauma-related symptoms, if necessary a diagnostic test for PTSD, and other tests as indicated. This order of questioning is intended to reduce the likelihood of distress by creating a sense of normalization of feelings and experiences related to trauma. Additionally, a behavioral approach should be utilized when assessing trauma history, which reduces stigmatization, improves rapport, and helps to clarify terms related to trauma. For example, instead of asking, "Were you physically abused?" it is more effective to inquire, "How were you disciplined?" or "Sometimes people in families get very upset and throw things, threaten each other, or hit each other. Did anything like that happen in your family?" ... [if yes] ... "Tell me more about that ... " or "Would you give me some examples so I can get a clearer picture of what that was like?"

When working with youth, it is important to consider their safety and risk of harm at all times. It is therefore recommended that all family members must be assessed individually when a family unit seeks services. Lastly, the use of multiple assessments, including clinical interviews, family self-report, and child self-report measures allows for a more comprehensive evaluation and will assist in the development phases of treatment planning (de Arellano & Danielson, 2008).

Client Age Considerations

When choosing the most appropriate measure to assess trauma-related symptoms, a clinician must determine which assessments are age-appropriate. For example, the TSCC requires that the client must be 8 years of age or older. Researchers indicate that "This age limit reflects the concern that younger children may have insufficient cognitive development to fully understand what a given psychological symptom or internal state actually represents, or lack the reading comprehension necessary to respond to written test items regarding that state or symptom" (Briere et al., 2001, p. 1003).

Furthermore, there is a lack of standardized instruments to assess the impact of traumatic events related to mental health. In a 10-year review of trauma related scales, Ohan, Myers, and Collett (2002) report that the assessment of trauma in youth populations is relatively new, and that the clinical utility with regard to treatment planning using assessment data is still ambiguous. In an attempt to fill this void, researchers have developed a number of instruments including: the Children's PTSD Inventory, Child Posttraumatic Stress Reaction Index, Child Dissociative Checklist, Clinician Administered PTSD Scale–Child (CAPS-C), Children's Impact of Traumatic Events Scale–Revised, and the Sexual Abuse Fear Evaluation. Although instruments have been developed for the child and adolescent populations, very few have been psychometrically validated with the exception of the TSCC and the Child Sexual Behavior Inventory (CSBI–Caregiver report) to name two (Briere et al., 2001). In addition to the TSCC and the CSBI, research indicates that the UCLA PTSD Index has high internal consistency, test-retest reliability, sensitivity, and specificity (Ellis, Lhewa, Charney, & Cabral, 2006).

de Arellano and Danielson (2008) also recommend that age, developmental issues, and timelines are necessary to take into account, especially when assessing children and adolescents. In the case in which a child may be too young to answer written test items, or does not have the cognitive capacity, caregiver report can be utilized as a substitute. Instruments such as the CSBI can be administered to caregivers. In addition to caregiver report, clinicians can also utilize diagnostic interviews to ascertain data (Briere et al., 2001). While caregiver report measures can be useful in conjunction with clinician diagnostic tools, there are few caregiver-report measures that are specific to trauma-related symptoms and the experiences of their child; rather, most guardian-report measures are generic assessments of behavior. Furthermore, information is typically less valid and reliable if it is gathered from a third party akin to the client, such as a caregiver, teacher, or clinician (Briere et al., 2001).

Cultural Issues in Assessment

While the above endorsements are suitable for majority populations, culture is a vital component to consider when evaluating trauma. Culture specific guidelines for trauma assessments have been developed and include the following suggestions as part of The Culturally Informed Trauma Assessment: investigate the target population; navigate new ways of delivering assessment services based on study of the target population; further assess extended family and other collaterals; organize background assessment to better accommodate target populations; recognize and broaden the range of

traumatic events to be assessed; modify the types of trauma-related sequelae assessed; evaluate the effectiveness of the modified assessment; develop
the assessment based on its evaluation (de Arellano & Danielson, 2008).

Interpreting Trauma Assessment Data

In addition to age and culture, other factors must be taken into consideration when assessing trauma in child and adolescent populations.
For instance, research indicates that some youth may underreport symptoms, experiences, and reactions related to various traumatic events.
Authors Fricker and Smith (2001) provide the example of children who
have experienced sexual abuse, where it is more likely to misrepresent
symptoms, alter presentation during assessment, minimize emotions, deny
reactions to trauma, and exaggerate distress. Such examples indicate that
youth can often inaccurately interpret trauma, and that assessment of
such experiences are more valid when information is corroborated with
caregiver, teacher, or clinician reports. In addition to eliciting data from
multiple sources, the use of assessments that have built-in validity scales
can help to "detect patterns of unusual over- and underresponding to
items" (Fricker & Smith, 2001, p. 53).

Trauma Assessment Instruments

There are a number of trauma-specific assessments, as well as generic
assessments that may indicate the need for further assessment. Some of
the most widely used trauma-specific assessments are the Trauma History
Questionnaire (THQ), the UCLA Posttraumatic Stress Disorder Index
(PTSD-RI), the Trauma Symptom Checklist (TSC), The Trauma Symptom
Checklist for Young Children (TSC-YC), and the TSCC (Briere et al., 2001;
Ohan, Myers, & Collett, 2002; Stover & Berkowitz, 2005). Although there
are limited psychometric evaluations on trauma-focused instruments, it
appears that the TSCC has relatively high internal consistency (0.7–0.9).
Convergent validity for the TSCC is 0.75–0.82 as reported in a review of
trauma assessments and rating scales (Ohan et al., 2002). Furthermore,
assessments such as the Clinician-Administered PTSD Scale (CAPS and
CAPS-Child Version) and the Child Dissociative Checklist are often utilized
in populations with histories of trauma.

In addition to trauma-specific assessments, the Potential Stressful
Events Inventory, the Stressful Life Events Screening Questionnaire, and the
Impact of Events Scale are often used as generic assessments that may indi-
cate trauma. A more detailed listing of current measures utilized to assess
trauma and related symptoms can be found in Stover and Berkowitz's
2005 article, *Assessing Violence Exposure and Trauma Symptoms in Young
Children: A Critical Review of Measures*, as well as Ohan, Myers, and
Collett's 2002 article, *Ten-Year Review of Rating Scales. IV: Scales Assessing
Trauma and Its Effects*.

Interventions for Trauma

There are a number of approaches to helping persons who have experienced trauma, including both psychosocial and pharmacological treatments. There is also a large literature focusing on the treatment of traumatized children and youth. Several of these approaches have been "graded" in terms of their evidentiary foundations, and some are currently not recommended as treatments. These topics are reviewed in the next section.

Psychosocial Treatments for Trauma

There are many approaches to the treatment of trauma, both preventive and clinically focused modalities. For instance, secondary preventive interventions are often designed to address early symptoms that may occur before a full diagnosis of PTSD. These interventions are intended to alleviate early symptoms, in effect quelling any potential mental health diagnosis. An example of a secondary preventive intervention is the modified version of the Critical Incident Stress Debriefing. However, at this time, there is a lack of empirical evidence to support the benefits of this intervention when compared to control groups with PTSD (Berkowitz et al., 2011). Psychological First Aid is a new preventative intervention that is being received positively; however, it has yet to undergo enough research to determine its effectiveness (Foa, Keane, Friedman, & Cohen, 2009). Although empirical support for preventive interventions is generally quite limited, preliminary research suggests that boosting protective factors and coping skills may be beneficial targets in reducing the likelihood of developing PTSD following a traumatic event (Berkowitz et al., 2011). Berkowitz and colleagues (2011) tested the Child and Family Traumatic Stress Intervention (CFTSI), which is an intervention designed to "prevent the development of chronic posttraumatic stress disorder provided within 30 days of exposure to a potentially traumatic event" (p. 676). Results from this study indicate that targeting coping skills and familial support is a promising practice for youth who experience traumatic events.

Moreover, some treatments of trauma are considered trauma-focused or trauma-specific, and are designed to address the needs of populations with histories of trauma. Conversely, non-trauma-specific interventions are often utilized, or are used in addition to trauma-specific interventions. Some posttrauma approaches include psychodynamic therapies, cognitive behavioral therapies that include exposure-based treatments (Cahill, Foa, Hembree, Marshall, & Nacash, 2006), and other information-processing therapies like Eye Movement Desensitization Reprocessing therapy (EMDR) and trauma-focused cognitive behavior therapy (TF-CBT; Resick, 2001). As the understanding of trauma and its effects develops, more sophisticated therapies are being specifically designed to address traumatic responses and symptoms, and trauma-related disorders.

Many behavioral techniques are utilized for individuals who have experienced trauma. Some of the most commonly reported in the literature include: Trauma-Focused CBT for individuals, groups, or schools (TF-CBT), as well as Dialectical Behavior Therapy. In a recent systematic review from the Cochrane Collaboration, Bisson and Andrew (2009) examined 39 studies of interventions to alleviate PTSD symptoms. "With regards to reduction of clinician-assessed PTSD symptoms measured immediately after treatment, TFCBT did significantly better than waitlist/usual care . . . TFCBT did significantly better than other therapies" (p. 2).

Other interventions include EMDR, pharmacotherapy, Trauma Systems Therapy, and Prolonged Exposure Therapy. Stress Inoculation Therapy (SIT), Stress Management/Relaxation Therapy, Person-Centered Therapy (PCT), and exposure therapy are more general types of interventions that can be utilized to treat symptoms or related consequences of trauma (Bisson & Andrew, 2009; NCTSN, 2005; SAMHSA, 2012).

Other more general therapies include experiential therapies (e.g., Accelerated Experiential Dynamic Psychotherapy [AEDP]) and behavioral therapies (e.g., Prolonged Exposure, CBT) (Gleiser, Ford, & Fosha, 2008; Runyon, Deblinger, & Schroeder, 2009; Scheeringa et al., 2007; Smith et al., 2007). Cognitive behavioral therapies are supported by the NCTSN to: (a) teach stress management and relaxation skills; (b) create a narrative or story of what happened; (c) correct untrue/distorted ideas of what happened and why; (d) change unhealthy/wrong views that result from trauma; and (e) involve caregivers in a recovery environment (NCTSN, n.d.b).

Psychosocial Interventions for Trauma in Youth

While many psychosocial approaches can be used effectively within both youth and adult populations, some therapies have been designed to specifically address the unique needs of the child and adolescent populations that have experienced some form of trauma. Many of these therapies fall under the umbrella of CBT, but are specifically developed for children. Some youth-specific interventions include the Skills Training in Affect and Interpersonal Regulation with Narrative Story Telling (STAIR/NST) and the School-Based Group CBT (Silva et al., 2003; Silverman et al., 2008). In a recent systematic review of interventions for children and adolescents, authors Wethington and colleagues (2008) examined the following interventions: individual CBT, group CBT, play therapy, art therapy, psychodynamic therapy, and pharmacological therapy. Results from the systematic review indicated that both individual and group CBT were effective in reducing symptoms related to exposure of trauma. However, the other therapies did not have a sufficient amount of evidence to determine effectiveness related to trauma symptoms. In addition, Child Centered Therapy (CCT) is also described as a technique that can be utilized to alleviate abuse-related PTSD symptoms in children, although when compared to TF-CBT, it fared less favorably in reducing levels of depression or abuse-specific distress, and produced less improvement in support of child and effective parenting practices (Cohen, Deblinger, Mannarino, & Steer, 2004).

Beyond psychosocial interventions for trauma, models and programs have been developed to address effects related to trauma including the Sanctuary Model and the Trauma Recovery and Empowerment Model (TREM) (Fallot & Harris, 2002; Rivard et al., 2003). Butler and Wolf (2009) summarize the recent national trend of best practice movements focused on macro-level or organizational-level interventions. One such practice/policy effort is often termed Trauma-Informed Care (TIC); it focuses on creating organization or systemic changes by addressing environmental issues, cultures, and climates across agencies. TIC systems are environments that promote safety and trust for recipients as well as for staff members. These organizations pay specific attention to actively reducing and eliminating any form of therapy or service provision that could retraumatize consumers (Butler & Wolf, 2009). For instance, the use of restraints, holds, and seclusions can often be retraumatizing for individuals with a history of trauma. In addition to safety, TIC systems emphasize the importance of understanding trauma and the pervasive effects it can have on biopsychosocial areas of well-being. Within a TIC system, engagement, empowerment, and collaboration are underscored as the organization actively partners with individuals who seek services (Butler & Wolf, 2009).

SAMHSA (2011) reported improved service outcomes for youth receiving services in a TIC system; these service system studies are difficult to test through a randomized study (the highest level of evidence). However, their "real world" evaluations of outcomes across multiple programs can provide some empirical support that can prove useful in the absence of other data. Within TIC systems, trauma-focused therapies are often the interventions of choice, as they were designed to specifically treat survivors of trauma, including those with PTSD, although some TIC agencies might just ensure that clients have access to these interventions, rather than providing them.

Trauma Interventions and Evidence-Based Rating Systems

A multitude of organizations have developed guidelines or rating systems to determine the levels of empirical support for various interventions. Some of these organizations include the National Institute for Clinical Excellence (NICE; 2005), the California Evidence-Based Clearinghouse (CEBC, 2009), and the Agency for Health Care Policy and Research (AHCPR). The AHCPR is one of the nation's leading federal agencies on the quality, costs, outcomes, and safety of various health care practices. The International Society for Traumatic Stress Studies (ISTSS) utilized the AHCPR classification system to identify the degree of empirical support for PTSD interventions (Foa et al., 2009). The Cochrane Collaboration is another organization that primarily disseminates systematic reviews of clinical practices, including PTSD. It should be noted that the NICE guidelines recommendations on debriefing run contrary to the more recent reviews by ISTSS (Foa et al., 2009). In addition, SAMHSA has developed a registry to provide information about evidence-based programs and practices. SAMHSA's National Registry for Evidence-Based Programs and Practices (NREPP) lists a multitude of interventions to address trauma and its related consequences. The criterion used by each organization varies, so the levels of support for a given treatment might be different depending on the framework utilized. See Table 2.1 for a more detailed list of evidence-based rating systems and corresponding psychosocial and pharmacological interventions for trauma.

Pharmacological Treatments for Trauma

In addition to psychosocial treatment approaches, pharmacological and medication efforts have been utilized for individuals who have symptoms related to trauma. However, the research generally doesn't support the use of medication as the sole intervention for PTSD, since the remission rates generally are lower than for evidence-based psychosocial treatments (Friedman, Cohen, Foa, & Keane, 2009).

The ISTSS review of effective PTSD treatments (using the AHCPR classification system) reported that the medications that have the strongest support for adults (Level A) are the selective serotonin reuptake inhibitors (SSRIs), specifically ertraline/paroxetine/fluoxetine (all Level A), and one serotonin and norepinephrine reuptake inhibitor (SNRI), venlafaxine (Level A) (Foa et al., 2009). These drugs help reduce PTSD symptoms, improve overall functioning, and can address comorbid depression. Other medications have some effectiveness with some PTSD symptoms, but only the SSRIs/SNRIs address the range of PTSD symptoms (Foa et al., 2009). There has been minimal research on medications for PTSD in children and adolescents, although medications are routinely prescribed. Because of the limited number of studies that have been conducted, the ISTSS review found no medication that rose to the level of A evidence, although, again, the SSRIs were promising (Foa et al., 2009). A complete list of evidence-based rating systems and corresponding psychosocial and pharmacological treatments can be found in Table 2.1.

Treatments to Avoid

It is generally a good principle to employ research-supported treatments with clients whenever possible. It's also good practice to ensure that clients are informed about the research base of any intervention that they receive, as well as the other research-based alternatives that they aren't receiving, but that may be an option for them. Interventions without research support are best avoided until more research is available, or unless all research-based interventions have been utilized and have failed. In this latter situation, it is imperative that the client have full knowledge of the limits of what is known about a treatment. Also in this situation, it becomes especially important to carefully monitor progress with assessment instruments and to cease any treatment (and then seek consultation) in any situation where a client's functioning deteriorates.

Table 2.1 Evidence-Based Rating Systems and Treatments

Treatment (Alphabetically Ordered)	CEBC	AHCPR (ISTSS)	NICE	SAMHSA's NREPP
Abuse-focused CBT	Level Three (for youth)			
Acceptance and Commitment Therapy		Level F: New or innovative therapies not yet empirically tested (with comorbid substance use)		Considered an evidence-based or promising practice
Boston Consortium: Trauma-Informed Substance Abuse Treatment for Women				Considered an evidence-based or promising practice
CBT (including prolonged exposure and cognitive processing therapy)		Level A (for comorbidities)		
CBT + Exposure Therapy for panic disorders		Level D: Longstanding clinical practice not empirically tested or supported		
CBT + Implosive Therapy for panic disorders		Level D: Longstanding clinical practice not empirically tested or supported		
Child–Parent Psychotherapy	Level Two (for family violence)			Considered an evidence-based or promising practice
Cognitive Behavioral Intervention for Trauma in Schools (CBITS)				Considered an evidence-based or promising practice
Collaborative Care		Level B: Moderate empirical support (for comorbid substance abuse)		
Combined Parent–Child CBT (CPC-CBT)				
Creative Art Therapy		Effectiveness with PTSD populations unknown due to insufficient information		Considered an evidence-based or promising practice

Treatment	Level	Evidence	Notes
EMDR	Level Three (for youth)	Level A: Strongest empirical support (for adults) Level B: Moderate empirical support (for youth) Level C: Compelling clinical observation or naturalistic clinical studies (with comorbid bipolar disorder)	Considered an evidence-based or promising practice
Empowering Families Who Are At-Risk for Physical Abuse			
Helping Women Recover and Beyond Trauma			Considered an evidence-based or promising practice
Hypnosis		Effectiveness with PTSD populations unknown due to insufficient information	Considered an evidence-based or promising practice
Marital and Family Therapy		Effectiveness with PTSD populations unknown due to insufficient information	
Multiple-Channel Exposure Therapy		Level B: Moderate empirical support (for comorbid panic disorder)	
Obsessive-Compulsive Inpatient Treatment		Level C: Compelling clinical observation or naturalistic clinical studies (with comorbid OCD)	
Prolonged Exposure–Stress Inoculation therapy		Level C: Compelling clinical observation or naturalistic clinical studies (with comorbid bipolar disorders)	

(continued overleaf)

Table 2.1 *(continued)*

Treatment (Alphabetically Ordered)	CEBC	AHCPR (ISTSS)	NICE	SAMHSA's NREPP
Psychodynamic Imaginative Trauma Therapy		Level C: Compelling clinical observation or naturalistic clinical studies (with comorbid bipolar disorder)		
Psychodynamic Oriented Therapy (e.g., CPP)		Effectiveness with PTSD populations unknown due to insufficient information		
Psychosocial Rehabilitation		Growing support		Considered an evidence-based or promising practice
Real-Life Heroes				Considered an evidence-based or promising practice
Seeking Safety		Level A: Strongest empirical support (for adults w/comorbid substance use disorder (SUD), & one Level A study for youth w/comorbid SUD		
Selective Serotonin Reuptake Inhibitors (SSRIs)		Level A: Strongest empirical support (for adults) & promising for use with youth		
Single session debriefing interventions			Level A: Strongest empirical support (for early intervention)	
SITCAP-ART	Level Three (for youth)			Considered an evidence-based or promising practice

Treatment	CEBC	AHCPR (Foa et al.)	NICE	NREPP
Substance Dependence–PTSD Therapy		Level C: Compelling clinical observation or naturalistic clinical studies (with comorbid substance abuse)		
TF-CBT	Level One: Strongest empirical support (for youth)	Level A: Strongest empirical support (for youth)	Level B: Moderate empirical support (for 1 month posttrauma)	Considered an evidence-based or promising practice
Trauma Affect Regulation: Guide for Education and Therapy (TARGET) Trauma Recovery Groups		Level C: Compelling clinical observation or naturalistic clinical studies (with comorbid psychotic disorders)		Considered an evidence-based or promising practice
TREM		Level C: Compelling clinical observation or naturalistic clinical studies (with comorbid substance abuse)		Considered an evidence-based or promising practice

Source: Data drawn from CEBC (n.d.) from http://www.cebc4cw.org/topic/trauma-treatment-for-children; AHCPR from Foa et al., 2009; NICE (2005) from http://www.nice.org.uk/CG26; SAMSHA's NREPP (2012) from http://nrepp.samhsa.gov.

Critical Incident Stress Debriefing (CISD), or single-session psychological debriefing, is an intervention that has no significant support for its effectiveness, especially when it's implemented in one-on-one sessions (Foa et al., 2009). There are even studies that demonstrate that single-session, one-on-one CISD has made people worse (Bisson, McFarlane, Rose, Ruzek, & Watson, 2009). The developers of CISD intended it to be a group intervention and for it to be implemented as part of a larger Critical Incident Stress Management package; the research investigating effectiveness of group CISD and as part of CISM still need to be done (Bisson et al., 2009). For all of these reasons it's recommended that CISD be avoided.

There is a group of therapies that are sometimes called "Energy Therapies" that include treatments such as Thought Field Therapy (TFT), Emotional Freedom Technique (EFT), Neuro Emotional Technique (NET), and Reiki therapy—they are presumed to work on the body's energy fields. Sometimes the phrase "Power Therapies" is used to refer to these treatments, and then Traumatic Incident Reduction (TIR) and Visual-Kinesthetic Disassociation (VIR) are often included. While there is some very preliminary research on a couple of these therapies (TFT, TIR, & VKD), there hasn't been enough research conducted to allow for any evaluation of effectiveness (Welch & Rothbaum, 2007). And there is no research on many of the therapies included in these categories. As a general rule, it's best to avoid untested treatments until the research evidence is ascertained (see Pignotti & Thyer, 2009).

Future Issues in Trauma-Informed Practice

As the knowledge surrounding the areas of trauma and related diagnoses continues to grow, so too will areas of assessment, diagnosis, and treatment of individuals who have experienced traumatic events. While there appears to be a plethora of treatments available to intervene across youth and adult populations, refinement and further development of such treatments is necessary, especially as they relate to the unique needs of special populations. In addition to treatments with clinical populations, proactive and preventive modalities should be explored further in an effort to enhance protective and resiliency factors. Protective factors have the potential to boost coping abilities while quelling risk factors that could contribute to the development of pathology following traumatic events.

The future likely will bring more research on the concept of complex trauma or complex PTSD, a concept that has high relevance for many clinical practice settings. While there is a literature on best practices, only recently have there been efforts to operationalize and research the treatments more systematically and to discuss treatment from an evidence-based approach (e.g., Courtois & Ford, 2009). Much more research is needed in the area of diagnosis, assessment, and treatment of complex PTSD.

With regard to emerging treatments, there will be many more efforts focused on the application of virtual technologies in assessment and treatment, including virtual reality (Welch & Rothbaum, 2007), Internet-based assessment and treatment of PTSD (Smyth, 2011b; Welch & Rothbaum,

2007) and the use of mobile devices to enhance treatment (Smyth, 2011a). Another area that is likely to develop in the next decade is the use of pharmacological interventions that target memory and stress reactions so as to prevent PTSD, such the use of propranolol to reduce the likelihood of PTSD (Friedman et al., 2009). Most recently, a sensationalized cover story in the March 2012 *Wired* magazine states that "The forgetting pill erases painful memories forever" (Lehrer, 2012) and explores the possibilities of pills that will disrupt or erase traumatic memories in an article that summarizes some of the preliminary research on this topic.

It is hoped that with the increased interest in trauma-informed practice, the assessment of trauma will become a regular, consistent part of all human-service organizations. The ability to address symptoms related to trauma, or other challenges or impairment in functioning, rests on an accurate detection of trauma histories. Delivery of services, treatment planning, and organizational structure should be attuned to the unique needs of individuals who have experienced trauma. From administrative staff to direct-care staff, safety, collaboration, and empowerment should be concretely intertwined into all aspects of service delivery.

From a research standpoint, it would be beneficial to have more psychometrically validated and empirically supported assessments and instruments to both screen and diagnose trauma-related symptoms and disorders, particularly in the child and adolescent populations. Although difficult, it may also prove beneficial to design research studies with the capability of measuring and testing TIC systems compared to non-TIC systems. Operationalization of terms such as collaboration, empowerment, safety, and other key principles inherent to TIC systems would allow for the measurement and assessment of these principles from a behavioral standpoint.

Anticipated Changes in *DSM-5*

Changes have recently been suggested for some diagnoses within the *DSM-IV TR* for the upcoming and revised *DSM-5* (American Psychiatric Association, 2012b). One particular diagnosis is PTSD, as recent research findings suggest that the "current structure of PTSD symptoms does not accurately describe the disorder in trauma-exposed samples" (Ayer et al., 2011, p. 411).

Some of the proposed changes for the *DSM-5* include grouping disorders that were once categorized as anxiety disorders and adjustment disorders as Trauma- and Stressor-Related Disorders. These disorders may include reactive attachment disorder, disinhibited social engagement disorder, PTSD in preschool children, ASD, PTSD, adjustment disorders, other specified Trauma- or Stressor-Related disorders, and unspecified trauma- or stressor-related disorder (APA, 2012b). Additionally, some changes in the *DSM-5* are related to the heterogeneity of disorders as well as the overlapping of disorders, particularly for those characterized by "fear and avoidance, including posttraumatic stress disorder, panic/agoraphobia, social phobia/social anxiety disorder, and specific phobia" (Kupfer & Regier, 2011). For instance, disorders that are often associated with fear and avoidance are highly related to "stress-induced and fear circuitry spectrum" (Kupfer & Regier, 2011). Neuroscience imaging has demonstrated, in animal samples, that stress-induced and fear circuitry are distinctly relevant to PTSD and other trauma-related disorders as opposed to generalized anxiety disorder, obsessive-compulsive disorders, and impulse control disorders. Some researchers argue that current definition of PTSD is problematic, that it "is insufficiently distinct from other mental disorders,... lacks empirical support for construct validity, and... has moved [us] away from a sophisticated understanding of natural emotional responses to traumatic event[s]" (Elhai, Grubaugh, Kashdan, & Frueh, 2008). For instance, some proposed changes for the diagnosis of PTSD in the *DSM-5* include narrowing the criterion for the traumatic stressor, eliminating indirect experience/witness of trauma (must be directly experienced or witnessed), and symptoms must be present within 1 week of the traumatic event. However, if delayed onset is suspected, the symptoms must be "thematically related" to the trauma (Elhai et al., 2008). Additionally, comorbid disorders can often exacerbate PTSD symptoms, and therefore pre-existing disorders must be carefully examined. Lastly, researchers suggest that specifiers of symptoms, such as acute, chronic, and delayed-onset, should be removed (Elhai et al., 2008). Results from a cross-sectional study indicate that after removing similar PTSD symptoms that were overlapping with anxiety and mood disorders, "the prevalence, comorbidity, and structural validity of PTSD do not diverge considerably from those of symptom criteria for PTSD found in the *DSM-IV* " (Elhai et al., 2008, p. e6). Results from this study indicate that recommendations for changes in PTSD criteria for the *DSM-5* may not be entirely accurate or appropriate.

Authors also question whether or not PTSD is a distinct disorder; or does "criterion creep" occur, in which PTSD has been proposed to be an expanded model that may include disorders such as: prolonged duress stress disorder, posttraumatic grief disorder, posttraumatic relationship syndrome, posttraumatic dental care anxiety, posttraumatic abortion syndrome, and posttraumatic embitterment disorder (Rosen, Spitzer, & McHugh, 2008). For instance, recent research conducted on the phenomenon of bereavement indicates that a certain set of criteria was identified in bereaved persons, and therefore suggests that *Prolonged Grief Disorder* was psychometrically validated and proposed for the *DSM-5* and ICD-11 (Prigerson et al., 2009).

Furthermore, the etiology of PTSD has been called into question as authors point out that many nonthreatening life events are likely to contribute to PTSD, including divorce and financial difficulties. As it stands in the *DSM-IV-TR*, individuals must meet criterion A to be diagnosed with PTSD (Rosen, Spitzer, & McHugh, 2008).

It is apparent that debates regarding the diagnostic categories for the upcoming *DSM-5* and criteria for various disorders will, without a doubt, change the way in which trauma disorders will be assessed, treated, and researched. Full details regarding proposed changes to the *DSM-5* PTSD diagnosis information can be found at the American Psychiatric Association's development website (2010; http://www.dsm5.org/ProposedRevisions/Pages/proposedrevision.aspx?rid=165).

Key Terms

Acute Stress
    Disorder

At-Risk Populations

Complex Trauma

Coping

Flashback

Dissociation

Posttraumatic Stress
    Disorder (PTSD)

Resiliency

Simple Trauma

Trauma

Trauma-Focused (or
    Trauma-Specific)
    Interventions

Trauma-Informed Care
    (TIC)

Review Questions for Critical Thinking

1. From intake to discharge, how can we improve the ways in which we provide services to individuals across all ages, so that safety, empowerment, and collaboration with trauma survivors are key aspects of service delivery?

2. How can evidence-based practice rating systems be incorporated into the process of determining the most appropriate treatment techniques for individuals who have experienced trauma?

3. How is social work uniquely positioned to incorporate techniques of trauma-informed practice (TIP) within human service organizations?

4. What are the implications of trauma on future clinical practices and on how human service organizations are structured?

5. How might the proposed changes or recommendations for the *DSM-5* impact social work as well as clinical practices such as assessment, diagnostics, and treatment?

Online Resources

National Child Traumatic Stress Network (NCTSN): http://www.nctsn .org

Mission Statement: "To raise the standard of care and improve access to services for traumatized children, their families and communities throughout the United States."

Substance Abuse and Mental Health Services Administration (SAMHSA): National Registry of Evidence-Based Programs and Practices: http://nrepp.samhsa.gov

"NREPP is a searchable online registry of more than 220 interventions supporting mental health promotion, substance abuse prevention, and mental health and substance abuse treatment. We connect members of the public to intervention developers so they can learn how to implement these approaches in their communities."

National Center for PTSD: http://www.ptsd.va.gov

A "center of excellence for research and education on the prevention, understanding, and treatment of PTSD" that is provided through the United States Veterans Administration. Includes educational resources for the public and professional resources for practitioners and researchers, including a database of articles on PTSD, as well as assessment and treatment resources.

International Society for Traumatic Stress Studies (ISTSS): http://www.istss.org/

Mission Statement: "ISTSS is an international, interdisciplinary professional organization that promotes advancement and exchange of knowledge about traumatic stress." ISTSS also publishes the *Journal of Traumatic Stress*. The website also has an excellent pamphlet, *Childhood Remembered*, on the issues involved in memory and childhood trauma: http://www.istss.org/Content/NavigationMenu/Publications/Childhood Trauma/

International Society for the Study of Trauma and Dissociation (ISSTD): http://www.isst-d.org/

Vision Statement: "Social policy and health care will address the prevalence and consequences of chronic trauma and dissociation, making effective treatment available for all who suffer from the effects of chronic or complex trauma." Mission Statement: "ISSTD seeks to advance clinical, scientific, and societal understanding about the prevalence and consequences of chronic trauma and dissociation." ISSTD has many resources for practitioners, including online professional development opportunities and bibliographies and links to other web resources. This association also publishes the *Journal of Trauma and Dissociation*.

Living Proof Podcast Series on Social Work: http://www.socialwork.buffalo.edu/podcast/

Series of recorded "conversations with prominent social work professionals, interviews with cutting-edge researchers, and information on emerging trends and best practices in the field of social work" provided (at no charge) by the University at Buffalo School of Social Work. There are many interviews related to trauma and trauma-informed care which can be found by sorting the topics by category or by going to: http://www.socialwork.buffalo.edu/podcast/episode_category.asp?cat=Trauma%20|%20Trauma-Informed%20Care

References

American Psychiatric Association (2000). *Diagnostic and statistical manual of mental disorders* (4th ed., text rev.). Arlington, VA: Author.

American Psychiatric Association. (2010). *G 05 Posttraumatic stress disorder*. Retrieved from http://www.dsm5.org/ProposedRevisions/Pages/proposedrevision.aspx?rid=165

American Psychiatric Association. (2012a). Posttraumatic stress disorder. Retrieved from http://www.apa.org/topics/ptsd/index.aspx

American Psychiatric Association. (2012b). *Trauma- and stressor-related disorders*. Retrieved from http://www.dsm5.org/ProposedRevision/Pages/Traumaand StressorRelatedDisorders.aspx

Ayer, L. A., Cisler, J. M., Danielson, C. K., Amstadter, A. B., Saunders, B. E., & Kilpatrick, D. G. (2011). Adolescent posttraumatic stress disorder: An examination of factor structure reliability in two national samples. *Journal of Anxiety Disorders, 25*, 411–424.

Berkowitz, S. J., Stover, C. S., & Marans, S. R. (2011). The child and family traumatic stress intervention: secondary prevention for youth at risk of developing PTSD. *Journal of Child Psychology and Psychiatry, 52*, 676–685.

Bisson, J., & Andrew, M. (2009). Psychological treatment of posttraumatic stress disorder (PTSD) (Review). *The Cochrane Collaboration, 1*, http://www.the cochranelibrary.com

Bisson, J. I., McFarlane, A. C., Rose, S., Ruzek, J. I., & Watson, P. J. (2009). Psychological debriefing for adults. In E. B. Foa, T. M. Keane, M. J. Friedman, & J. A. Cohen, (Eds.). *Effective treatments for PTSD: Practice guidelines from the International Society for Traumatic Stress Studies* (2nd ed., pp. 83–105). New York, NY: Guilford Press.

Bloom, S. L., & Farragher, B. (2011). *Destroying sanctuary: The crisis in human services delivery systems*. New York, NY: Oxford University Press.

Bride, B. E. (2007). Prevalence of secondary traumatic stress among social workers. *Social Work*, FindArticles.com. Retrieved from http://findarticles.com/p/articles/mi_hb6467/is_1_52/ai_n29335754

Bride, B. E., Robinson, M. R., Yegidis, B., & Figley C. R. (2004). Development and validation of the Secondary Traumatic Stress Scale. *Research on Social Work Practice, 14*, 27–35.

Briere, J., Johnson, K., Bissada, A., Damon, L., Crouch, J., Gil, E., Hanson, R., & Ernst, V. (2001). The trauma symptom checklist for young children (TSCYC): Reliability and association with abuse exposure in a multi-site study. *Child Abuse and Neglect, 25*, 1001–1014.

Briere, J., & Scott, C. (2007). Assessment of trauma symptoms in eating-disordered populations. *Eating Disorders, 15*, 347–358.

Butler, L. D., & Wolf, M. R. (2009). Trauma-informed care: Trauma as an organizing principle in the provision of mental health and social services. *Trauma Psychology, 4*(3), 7–11.

Cahill, S. P., Foa, E. B., Hembree, E. A., Marshall, R. D., & Nacash, N. (2006). Dissemination of exposure therapy in the treatment of posttraumatic stress disorder. *Journal of Traumatic Stress, 19*, 597–610.

California Evidence-Based Clearinghouse for Child Welfare. (2009). *Scientific rating scale*. Retrieved from http://www.cebc4cw.org/ratings/scientific-rating-scale

California Evidence-Based Clearinghouse for Child Welfare. (n.d.). *Trauma treatment: Child and adolescent*. Retrieved from http://www.cebc4cw.org/topic/trauma-treatment-for-children

Cohen, J. A., Deblinger, E., Mannarino, A. P., & Steer, R. (2004). A multisite, randomized controlled trial for children with abuse-related PTSD symptoms. *Journal of American Academy of Child and Adolescent Psychiatry, 43*, 393–402.

Courtois, C. A., & Ford, J. D. (Eds.) (2009). *Treating complex traumatic stress disorders: An evidence-based guide*. New York, NY: Guilford Press.

Cusack, K. J., Frueh, B. C., & Brady, K. T. (2004). Trauma history screening in a community mental health center. *Psychiatric Services*, *55*, 157–162.

de Arellano, M. A., & Danielson, C. K. (2008). Assessment of trauma history and trauma-related problems in ethnic minority child populations: An INFORMED approach. *Cognitive and Behavioral Practice*, *15*, 53–66.

Elhai, J. D., Grubaugh, A. L., Kashdan, T. B., & Frueh, B. C. (2008). Empirical examination of a proposed refinement to *DSM-IV* posttraumatic stress disorder symptom criteria using the national comorbidity survey replication data. *Journal of Clinical Psychiatry* (February 20, 2008), e1–e6.

Ellis, B. H., Lhewa, D., Charney, M., & Cabral, H. (2006). Screening for PTSD among Somali adolescent refugees: Psychometric properties of the UCLA PTSD index. *Journal of Traumatic Stress*, *19*, 547–551.

Fallot, R. D., & Harris, M. (2002). The trauma recovery and empowerment model (TREM): Conceptual and practical issues in a group intervention for women. *Community Mental Health Journal*, *38*, 475–485.

Foa, E. B., Keane, T. M., Friedman, M. J., & Cohen, J. A. (Eds.). (2009). *Effective treatments for PTSD: Practice guidelines from the International Society for Traumatic Stress Studies* (2nd ed.) New York, NY: Guilford Press.

Fricker, A. E., & Smith, D. W. (2001). Trauma specific versus generic measurement of distress and the validity of self-reported symptoms in sexually abused children. *Journal of Child Sexual Abuse*, *10*(4), 51–66.

Friedman, M. J., Cohen, J. A., Foa, E. B., & Keane, T. M. (2009). Integration and summary. In E. B. Foa, T. M. Keane, M. J. Friedman, & J. A. Cohen (Eds). *Effective treatments for PTSD: Practice guidelines from the International Society for Traumatic Stress Studies* (2nd ed., pp. 617–642). New York, NY: Guilford Press.

Gearon, J. S., Kaltman, S. I., Brown, C., & Bellack, A. S. (2003). Traumatic life events and PTSD among women with substance use disorders and schizophrenia. *Psychiatric Services*, *54*, 523–528.

Gleiser, K., Ford, J. D., & Fosha, D. (2008). Contrasting exposure and experiential therapies for complex posttraumatic stress disorder. *Psychotherapy Theory, Research, Practice, Training*, *45*, 340–360.

Graham-Bermann, S. A., Howell, K., Habarth, J., Krishnan, S., Loree, A., & Bermann, E. A. (2008). Toward assessing traumatic events and stress symptoms in preschool children from low-income families. *American Journal of Orthopsychiatry*, *78*, 220–228.

International Society for Traumatic Stress Studies (ISTSS). (n.d.). What is traumatic stress? Retrieved from http://www.istss.org/Content/MainNavigationMenu ForthePublic/WhatisTrauma/What_is_Traumatic_Stress.pdf

Jensen-Doss, A., Cusack, K. J., & de Arellano, M. A. (2008). Workshop-based training in trauma-focused CBT: An in-depth analysis of impact on provider practices. *Community Mental Health Journal*, *44*, 227–244.

Kessler, R. C. (2000). Posttraumatic stress disorder: The burden to the individual and to society. *Journal of Clinical Psychiatry*, *61*(supplement 5), 4–12.

Kessler, R. C., Sonnega, A., & Bromet, E. (1995). Posttraumatic stress disorder in the national comorbidity survey. *Archives of General Psychiatry*, *52*, 1048–1060.

Kupfer, D. J., & Regier, D. A. (2011). Neuroscience, clinical evidence, and the future of psychiatric classification in *DSM-5*. *American Journal of Psychiatry*, *168*, 672–674.

Lehrer, J. (2012, February 17). The forgetting pill erases painful memories forever. *Wired*. Retrieved from http://www.wired.com/magazine/2012/02/ff_ forgettingpill

Lewis, C. S., Jospitre, T., Griffing, S., Chu, M., Sage, R. E., Madry, L., & Primm, B. J. (2006). Childhood maltreatment, familial violence, and retraumatization: Assessing inner-city battered women. *Journal of Emotional Abuse*, *6*(4), 47–67.

Mueser, K. T., Salyers, M. P., Rosenberg, S. D., Ford, J. D., Fox, L., & Carty, P. (2001). Psychometric evaluation of trauma and posttraumatic stress disorder assessments in persons with severe mental illness. *Psychological Assessment*, *13*(1), 110–117.

National Child Traumatic Stress Network. (2003a). *Effective treatments for youth trauma*. Retrieved from http://www.nctsnet.org/nctsn_assets/pdfs/effective_treatments_youth_trauma.pdf

National Child Traumatic Stress Network. (2003b). *What is child traumatic stress*. Retrieved from http://www.nctsnet.org/sites/default/files/assets/pdfs/what_is_child_traumatic_stress_0.pdf

National Child Traumatic Stress Network. (2005). *Empirically supported treatments and promising practices*. Retrieved from http://www.nctsnet.org/nctsn_assets/pdfs/promising_practices/NCTSN_E-STable_21705.pdf.

National Child Traumatic Stress Network. (n.d.a). *Types of traumatic stress*. Retrieved from http://www.nctsnet.org/trauma-types

National Child Traumatic Stress Network. (n.d.b). *Understanding child traumatic stress*. Retrieved from http://www.nctsnet.org/sites/default/files/assets/pdfs/understanding_child_traumatic_stress_brochure_9-29-05.pdf

National Child Traumatic Stress Network (n.d.c). *Complex trauma in children and adolescents*. Retreived from: http://www.nctsnet.org/trauma-types/complex-trauma

National Institute for Clinical Excellence (2005). *Posttraumatic stress disorder: The management of PTSD in adults and children in primary and secondary care*. Retrieved from http://www.nice.org.uk/CG26

Ohan, J. L., Myers, K., & Collett, B. R. (2002). Ten-year review of rating scales. IV: Scales assessing trauma and its effects. *Journal of the American Academy of Child and Adolescent Psychiatry*, *41*, 1401–1422.

Pignotti, M. & Thyer, B. A. (2009). Some comments on "Energy Psychology: A Review of the Evidence": Premature conclusions based on incomplete evidence. *Psychotherapy Theory, Research, Practice, Training*, *46*, 257–261.

Prigerson, H. G., Horowitz, M. J., Jacobs, S. C., Parkes, C. M., Aslan, M., Goodkin, K.,... Maciejewski, P. K. (2009). Prolonged grief disorder: Psychometric validation of criteria proposed for *DSM-5* and ICD-11. *PLoS Medicine*, *6*(8), 1–12. doi:10.1371/journal.pmed.1000121

Prince-Embury, S. (2007). *Resiliency Scales for Children and Adolescents: A profile of personal strengths*. Minneapolis, MN: Pearson.

Resick, P. A. (2001). *Stress and trauma*. New York, NY: Taylor & Francis.

Rivard, J. C., Bloom, S. L., Abramovitz, R., Pasquale, L. E., Duncan, M., McCorkle, D., & Gelman, A. (2003). Assessing the implementation and effects of a trauma-focused intervention for youths in residential treatment. *Psychiatric Quarterly*, *74*, 137–154.

Rosen, G. M., Spitzer, R. L., & McHugh, P. R. (2008). Problems with the posttraumatic stress disorder diagnosis and its future in the *DSM-5*. *British Journal of Psychiatry*, *192*, 3–4. doi:10.1192/bjp.bp.107.043083.

Runyon, M. K., Deblinger, E., & Schroeder, C. M. (2009). Pilot evaluation of outcomes of combined parent–child cognitive-behavioral group therapy for families at risk for child physical abuse. *Cognitive and Behavioral Practice*, *16*, 101–118.

Scheeringa, M. S., Salloum, A., Arnberger, R. A., Weems, C. F., Amaya-Jackson, L., & Cohen, J. A. (2007). Feasibility and effectiveness of cognitive-behavioral therapy for posttraumatic stress disorder in preschool children: Two case reports. *Journal of Traumatic Stress*, *20*, 631–636.

Silva, R. R., Cloitre, M., Davis, L., Levitt, J., Gomez, S., Ngai, I., & Brown, E. (2003). Early intervention with traumatized children. *Psychiatric Quarterly*, *74*, 333–347.

Silverman, W. K., Ortiz, C. D., Viswesvaran, C., Burns, B. J., Kolko, D. J., Putnam, F. W., & Amaya-Jackson, L. (2008). Evidence-based psychosocial treatment for children and adolescents exposed to traumatic events. *Journal of Clinical Child and Adolescent Psychology*, *37*, 156–183.

Smith, P., Yule, W., Perrin, S., Tranah, T., Dalgleish, T., & Clark, D. M. (2007). Cognitive-behavioral therapy for PTSD in children and adolescents: A preliminary randomized controlled trial. *Journal of American Academy of Child and Adolescent Psychiatry*, *46*, 1051–1061.

Smyth, N. J. (2011, January 9). Mobile devices in psychotherapy: Bane or benefit? [Web log post]. Retrieved from http://njsmyth.wordpress.com/2011/01/09/mobile-devices-in-psychotherapy-bane-or-benefit

Smyth, N. J. (2011, March 25). Virtual worlds as immersive treatment settings: The PTSD Sim [Web log post]. Retrieved from http://njsmyth.wordpress.com/2011/03/25/virtual-worlds-as-immersive-treatment-settings-the-ptsd-sim

Substance Abuse and Mental Health Services Administration (SAMHSA). (2011, May 3). *Helping children who have experienced traumatic events*. Retrieved from http://www.samhsa.gov/children/SAMHSA_Short_Report_2011.pdf

Substance Abuse and Mental Health Services Administration (SAMHSA): National Registry of Evidence-Based Programs and Practices. (2012). *Find an intervention*. Retrieved from http://nrepp.samhsa.gov/

Substance Abuse and Mental Health Services Administration (SAMHSA): National Center for Trauma Informed Care. (n.d.). Retrieved from http://www.samhsa.gov/nctic

Substance Abuse and Mental Health Services Administration (SAMHSA): Strategic Initiative #2: Trauma and Justice. (n.d.). Retrieved from http://store.samhsa.gov/shin/content//SMA11-4629/04-TraumaAndJustice.pdf

Welch, S. S., & Rothbaum, B. O. (2007). Emerging treatments for PTSD. In M. J. Friedman, T. M. Keene, & P. A. Resick (Eds.), *Handbook of PTSD science and practice* (pp. 469–496). New York, NY: Guilford Press.

Wethington, H. R., Hahn, R. A., Fuqua-Whitley, D. S., Sipe, T. A., Crosby, A. E., Johnson, R. L., . . . Chattopadhyay, S. K. (2008). The effectiveness of interventions to reduce psychological harm from traumatic events among children and adolescents: A systematic review. *American Journal of Preventive Medicine*, *35*, 287–313.

Chapter 3
Interviewing Skills

Francis J. Turner

> Are interview techniques different for every social worker who expresses social work values or can they be learned and implemented by all practitioners in a manner that permits their optimum effective use?

Introduction

Whomever we may be speaking with, their perception of a social worker would likely be of someone who *talks to their clients*. Whether or not this is a correct or full picture of today's social worker, it is true that much of his or her work involves talking to people about their problems or the problems of others.

But social workers are not the only people in the world who conduct interviews. In fact, no matter what our role may be in the complex situations in which most of us find ourselves, we need to be able to initiate conversations, to listen to others, to ask questions, to focus, to refocus, and to end the discussion. Probably we rarely think of our mundane, daily conversations as having all of these parts. However, if we studied them in detail we would find that indeed each of these facets of an interview is present. We would also notice that both we and the people with whom we converse implement the various tasks and roles of interviewing in a broadly differential, qualitative way.

What is so special about what we do in interviewing that sets social workers apart? One of the challenges we face as social workers is that so much of what we do in our interviewing activities, everybody else in the world does in one way or another. We differ in that we do these things in a more structured, targeted, and conscious manner with deliberate strategies and specific goals in mind.

But even when we talk about professional interviewing and attempt to distinguish it from our day-to-day interactions, for example, with the clerk at the corner market, there is still a great lack of clarity as to the specifics of interviewing.

It is commonly agreed that one can learn how to interview in a professional manner and can learn how to make an interview more effective.

A visit to any bookstore in the world will show that there are many self-proclaimed experts in professional interviewing in many different areas. This is evident in the wide range of "how-to" books: how to interview for a job, how to make a good impression, how to win friends and influence others, how to sell a car, how to talk to your physician, how to talk to your teenager, and so forth.

There is of an abundance of information about what makes for effective interviewing in social work. However, the majority of this material falls into the category of practice wisdom and is written by practitioners who are acknowledged to be good interviewers.

This is not to disparage practice wisdom as a source of knowledge. This is true especially when there is a high degree of consensus about interviewing between and among persons identified as skilled interviewers. The test of quality interviewing rests in the outcome of the interview. Do we for the most part attain the goals of our interviews in our practice? Are our clients more effective and satisfied human beings as a result of our verbal interactions with them?

Much research has been carried out on the effectiveness of social work intervention, and although there is still much to be done, the overall findings are that the interventions of social workers have an overall positive effect on their clients (Brothers, 2002; Thomlison, 1984). That is, social work *does* work. Social workers do help their clients—not in any absolute way, but in an overall way. Thus much of what we do in our interviews must be helpful. If we can begin with this understanding, then our task in this chapter is to try and identify how it is that we get positive results, that is, what makes for good or effective interviewing?

Definition

In beginning our discussion, we should first stop and identify, describe, or define just what we mean by a *social work interview*. We can define an interview as:

> *A verbal exchange between one or more clients and one or more social workers in which the social worker(s) involved draw(s) upon a fund of social work knowledge, skills, and techniques to better understand and determine the characteristics of the client(s) within a psychosocial perspective and, based on this understanding, seeks to assist the client(s) to enhance their psychosocial functioning.*

Of course, not everyone with whom a social worker is in an interview is a client in a technical sense. However we will use the term in our discussion here in a very broad sense to refer to anyone with whom a social worker is in verbal contact, either as a client or as someone who speaks on behalf of a particular client(s).

Interviewing as an Art

Effective, quality interviewing is not a science. Rather, it is an art in which we learn to make use of our knowledge, our skills, our techniques, and ourselves to attain the therapeutic goals that we and our clients seek. Much of what we know about interviewing comes from the gurus of our profession and other related professions, and our own observations of ourselves and others in practice.

The art of interviewing focuses on communications between people, both verbal and nonverbal. Since each of us is an individual, we bring to our verbal exchanges with other humans something of our individuality. However, it is important to remember that interviewing is an art based on knowledge and experience and practiced by professionals. Thus, as with other professional activities, there are things we can learn from each other that will help us to make our individual skills more creative and effective. Nevertheless, there will be differences in the way we make use of these skills.

Interviewer Challenges

One of the challenges facing us as we attempt to enhance our interviewing skills is to develop the ability to find a balance between spontaneity and very deliberative use of interviewing techniques. This skill comes from practice, just as practice for the athlete or artist results in skills that become spontaneous and automatic when they are competing or painting.

A further challenge facing anyone wishing to develop effective interviewing skills in social work is to develop that special kind of discipline that permits us to push the content and process of one interview from our consciousness and turn at once to another one just as complex, serious, and demanding as the one before.

An important component of this needed skill is to become adept at recording a brief summary immediately following an interview in which the essential data of the interview and our initial diagnostic thinking can be addressed, and including notes on the techniques we used. Rarely does it happen in practice that we go directly from one interview to the next without some kind of break, albeit a short one. Some practitioners find it useful to make use of short-term meditative skills that can be used between interviews. Such a process aids in helping to turn from a prior interview, to relax briefly to prepare for the next interview and to clear or refocus our attending skills.

Thus learning to listen is the *sine qua non* of interviewing, a skill often referred to as an attending skill. That is, not only must we hear what the client is telling us, or not telling us, but we must as well convey to the client that we are hearing what is being said or not being said. This ability to listen and to convey to the other that we are listening is one of the attributes of a professional interview that clearly separates it from many social conversations, in which much of what is said is not listened to or even heard.

The Helping Relationship

Interviewing in social work has frequently been described as the process of establishing, maintaining, and drawing upon the latent potential of "the helping relationship." The term *the helping relationship*, which is frequently found in the literature, is a concept endowed with great respect. The term indicates a belief and understanding of the power that is present in the social worker–client relationship. The goal of this relationship is to have the client experience the social worker as a safe, skillful, understanding, empathetic, knowledgeable person able to be helpful in a wide range of psychosocial situations.

Colleagues of a psychodynamic orientation view this helping relationship from the perspective of the concept of "transference." This is a Freudian term that describes the process in which the client begins to view and to respond to the therapist "as if" he/she were someone significant from their past, most frequently a parental figure, and presumes a broad range of potential unconscious wishes and desires (Coady, 2002, pp. 122–124; Perlman, 1971, pp. 76–78). Others minimize the importance or even the existence of transference and view the helping relationship as still powerful but viewed from a more present-centered reality perspective.

An author who contributed greatly to a helpful and clear understanding of how this process developed and the requisite factors for the success of this relationship was Dr. Carl Rogers, who was both a social worker and a psychologist. Dr. Rogers was very committed to research that examined therapeutic relationships with a view to identifying their essential qualities. Similar important work was done by both Helen Perlman and Florence Hollis (Hollis, 1973, pp. 57–85; Perlman, 1971, pp. 64–83). Within this work there is a remarkable degree of consensus about these qualities, usually described as Warmth, Acceptance, Empathy, Caring, Concern, and Genuineness. These six attributes are seen as the qualities that need to be present for the establishment of the helping relationship. They are not referred to as techniques. Techniques describe the ways and strategies we use to achieve these qualities.

It has long been taught that therapists need to learn to develop this profile of qualities in our work with clients and to find ways that lead the client to experience them. There is much that has been written about such things as eye contact, body language, being attentive, reflecting back an understanding of what has been said, offering support, and making use of mild challenges and the discreet use of opinion advice and authority.

Techniques or Values

An important issue that social work literature seems not to have viewed as important, or perhaps even avoided as heretical, in looking at the necessary qualities of the helping relationship is the matter of *authenticity*. The question is whether authentic feelings, attitudes, and qualities need to be actually present in the therapist or if it is sufficient for the client to feel or believe that these qualities are present. That is, does the social worker need to internalize all of these qualities? Do they need to be a part of his or her psyche? Or can the social worker feign them and yet still be effective?

Is it not sufficient that a profession holds a set of values to which its members subscribe and which they seek to demonstrate in their practice? However, it is strongly believed by many that to be an effective interviewer—that is, to be a helping therapist—this value set needs to be a part of each social worker.

One can also take the position that effective interviewing consists of a set of specific actions that can be learned and that are effective for the client. Our skill, and hence our effectiveness as practitioners, hinges on our ability to project the necessary qualities mentioned earlier, whether we feel them or subscribe to them in our own lives. Could a therapist, for example, thoroughly dislike a client and still be a highly effective therapist for him or her by utilizing a cluster of techniques that convey warmth, acceptance, empathy, and so forth?

Before we reject this position out of hand, we need to remember the power of the actor who can convey to us in a most convincing way virtually every human emotion, and from the stage can make us both love them and hate them in a very few minutes. We have all attended theatrical performances during which we were brought to tears by means of the skill of the actor or actress. We also hear from time to time of sociopathic therapists who have no feelings for their clients (apart from perhaps curiosity), who function as social workers or physicians and even when discovered still have strong support from their clients and patients.

This discussion is raised to bring added focus to the question of technique, which is a topic not considered of great importance in the social work literature. Although some research indicates that technique appears to contribute only minimally to the effectiveness of an interview (Coady, 2002), it may well be that we have underestimated to a great extent the fact that everything we do in an interview is a discrete and describable action, that is, a technique (Fischer, 1978, pp. 60–61). If so, and if we are interested in addressing more research to improving our interviewing effectiveness, we need to pay much more attention to the minutiae of our interventions—the complex yet varied actions that make up an interview. Otherwise, if we continue to see effective interviewing as the projection of a set of values and qualities, then anyone who had the desired set of attitudes and characteristics would make an effective interviewer and those without these values would be regarded incompetent interviewers, regardless of technique.

All of us know from our practice that conveying a positive attitude is important, but there is much to be learned about interviewing. We are aware that some colleagues are much more effective in working with certain kinds of clients. We know that there are techniques to be learned that facilitate the development of the relationship. We understand that particular problems and difficulties respond better to some types of intervention than others. Thus we know that it is important to devote much more time and attention than we have until now on studying how to make our interviewing more effective—that is, on how to enhance our technical skills.

An Ethical Issue

If it develops that we begin to put more emphasis on technique than on attitudes or values, then we will need to address an ethical issue related to the matter of research into interviewing techniques. Clearly, to ensure our effectiveness we have a responsibility to assess the differential impact of various techniques. However, this raises the question: How do I try out a technique that has not been tested or proven to be useful in practice? How do we find out if it is going to be effective without trying it out with patients?

We really have not addressed this in social work, principally because we have tended to see interviewing as a process between the social worker and the clients rather than seeing it as a series of identifiable individual actions or techniques. Our literature is replete with descriptions of the many techniques or activities that colleagues have used in their practices. These usually include descriptions of the presumed impact of the technique. It is in this way that the range of techniques expands in our profession. However, as mentioned earlier, there is often little evaluation of the effect of the technique apart from descriptions of its apparent impact as viewed by the author of the technique in regard to a specific group of clients or problems.

There are several kinds of evaluations of techniques. First, there is the evaluation of the expert—a well-known person in the profession who will comment on some interviewing technique and either support it as a positive contribution or challenge its usefulness and appropriateness. Second, there is the rare but highly necessary professional article that formally assesses the use of some techniques. Third, there is the response of the profession to the announcement or description of a new interviewing technique, the sociopolitical factor. In this way, there may be general acceptance of a technique, or there may be rejection of it as not being appropriate for the profession or not helpful to clients. Or there may be debate about it as practitioners express differing opinion as to the perceived utility and/or appropriateness of what is being suggested. As yet, however, there is no formal process that gives legitimization or approbation to individual techniques.

Certainly all of these evaluative methods for interviewing techniques are important. They do and will help us expand our knowledge of what makes for effective interviewing. However, encapsulated within this type of evaluation by experts in the profession is the need to address the ethical question mentioned earlier regarding how to establish whether a particular technique in interviewing is helpful without trying it out with clients. In the meantime, we will continue with our longstanding pragmatic approach, in which we try things out and see what happens, with the understanding that if it doesn't work or if it appears to be harmful in some situations, we will no longer use it.

At the same time, we need to keep foremost in our minds the need to move on two fronts: (1) we focus strong efforts on identifying the component parts of an interview, that is, the individual pieces of the interview from which the process is shaped and the techniques that are used; and (2) once we are clearer on the attributes of an interview, we focus our efforts on attempting to assess the differential impact of each piece. Already the study of interviewing is developing, as evidenced in the literature, which discusses the importance of such things as body position and eye contact in an interview.

Interviewing Modalities

Let us next look at the principal kinds of interviews in which we become involved as practitioners and comment very briefly on some differences between them. In this discussion, we will focus of the types of interviews in which there is only one social worker involved, with the understanding that there are situations when, for various therapeutic reasons, we would have more than one therapist conducting the interview.

From this perspective we can talk about one-on-one interviews, dyadic interviews in which there are two persons and one social worker involved, family interviews, and group interviews. Although there is much in common with each of these, there are differences, and it is important to discuss differences so as to make optimum use of each modality.

The One-on-One Interview

This is the type of interview of which we think most often when discussing interviewing. For the social workers, this interview allows the therapist to focus on only one person, although there may be "ghosts" of significant others in the room. Having a single client lets us adjust the setting to meet that client's preferences and needs regarding comfort, furnishings, sound, lighting, and so forth. The client can be assured of confidentiality, in that no one except the therapist will hear the content. The client can also be assured of privacy from the perspective of what is discussed as well as the emotional level and emotional response that may accompany any disclosure or content. As well, the client has the social worker all to his- or herself and need not share the worker's interest or attention, as can happen in other modalities. The worker can adjust the speed and content of the interview as well as the level of speech and intensity of content and direct the interview as appropriate to meet where the client is and where and when the client is ready to go or not go. As well, the therapist can elect to use techniques that are targeted to the individuality of the client.

However, there are limitations to this form of interviewing. With only one person present, the worker gets only a single presentation of a situation and a single perspective of its dimensions. As well, there is always the possibility that the client is misrepresenting a situation either deliberately, or as they view it or believe it to be. There is the further challenge that may come from the power in balance, in that the client may attribute a negative factor of power and control to the situation that inhibits his or her ability to invest fully into a therapeutic relationship.

The Joint or Dyadic Interview

The majority of the writing about this modality focuses on couple interviewing, that is, situations in which the clients know each other and are in some kind of relationship, and are more often than not married couples. However, there are many other dyadic situations where this type of interviewing could be and should be used, such as two siblings, two friends, two persons, or even two strangers who have gone through a similar experience or have something in common.

The advantages of this type of interviewing is that from the clients' perspective there can be a sense of enhanced power that minimizes the perceived power of the worker and gives them the ability to influence the relationship when it is a "two against one situation."

This is a somewhat different situation than when both persons in the interview are designated clients. Even here, both persons present may feel more at ease and more able to share material. There is as well the advantage of having two perceptions or viewpoints on the various presenting situations that may comprise the interview content. From the perspective of the therapist, the two sources can help him or her to better understand the situation. For the clients, the joint interview may present a different perspective on a situation that may be helpful both in understanding it and in seeking alternative solutions.

As with each methodology, there are limitations to the joint interview. First, as is known from experiences with group theory, triadic groups are difficult to manage, in that there is always the risk of two of the members pairing against the other. This could be the two clients in power struggles with the social worker; a more complex situation in which the social worker and one client form, or fall into, a relationship that excludes the other client; or one client assuming the role of assistant therapist. The struggle between the two clients need not be a power struggle but could reflect that each of the clients is vying for the attention of the worker; if this takes on elements of transference, the situation can become very complex. A further difficulty for the social worker is in keeping a balance between the attention given to the problems or wishes of each of the clients.

As mentioned earlier, one of the strengths of this type of interviewing is that it provides an opportunity for the two clients to mutually aid each other by sharing in understanding and finding mutually satisfying solutions. However, when this process goes off track, a great deal of the therapist's time and efforts can be taken up in keeping the relationship on track.

The Family Interview

One of the developments in social work practice that gained attention in the late 1950s was that of family therapy, a modality that involves having the whole family present for the interview. The theory and method draw heavily on systems theory and the idea of mutually influencing subsystems. This reflects the theoretical understanding that many problems clients brought to us involved difficulties in family dynamics and that these were best dealt with when all the family was present and all viewed as the client. As social workers became more comfortable with this form of treatment, it was found to be a powerful medium for family change.

On the positive side, it views the family as a system in which each member carries specific roles. Thus, by having all family members involved in the process of dealing with problems, much progress can be made. Everyone in the family can have an opportunity to speak and to hear how others view various family situations. This modality makes it difficult for individual family members or subsets of the family to hide, scapegoat, overinfluence the situation, or overblame other family members. The family interview provides a safe place where family matters can be discussed openly.

It is a type of interview that requires considerable comfort and discipline on the part of the interviewer. The family as a powerful unit can work to exclude the social worker from the family dynamics and family secrets, even though they state they want help with them. Family dynamics are very powerful, and a worker can feel very isolated by the family even though the family has sought help. Rivalries can develop within the family for the attention and approval of the worker, and such rivalries and power struggles can complicate the process of family healing. Nevertheless, many families have found family interviews to be helpful and useful.

Group Interviews

Working with groups has long been recognized as an essential part of social work practice. The group has long been known to be a powerful medium to achieve a broad range of objectives. These may be helping a group achieve a particular external goal or to help the members of a group in some personal, therapeutic, or educative way. For many persons, the possibility of working on a particular project with others is highly appealing.

The strengths of this type of interviewing are many. As a group begins to form its identity, there can quickly develop a strong sense of group loyalty and group support that can be extremely helpful to all its members. Within a group persons can learn much about themselves and their own potential in listening to others and in experiencing the power of the group. Clients can also find strength in themselves in being able to help others.

The skills required for successful group interviewing are an understanding of group processes and their complexities and an ability to assess the functioning of the group as well as the individual members of which it is composed. As group leader it is important to stress the development of the group process as the medium of growth and development and to avoid falling into or being pushed into roles that work against this.

Groups can have many goals and purposes and thus a constant challenge for the social worker leading a group is to be cognizant of the established goal of the group and to be aware that goals can change as the group develops. Such shifts in goal and purpose may be in a direction that is not acceptable to all its members. As with other forms of multiple client situations, individual members of the group or subsets of the group may develop complex relationships or power relationships with either the group leader or other group members. Thus there is an ongoing responsibility for the group leader to be observant of the relationship factors that are present and to ensure that individuals or subsystems are not being ignored or harmed. Not everyone is able to work with groups and a requisite skill for the social worker is to assess accurately his or her capability and level of interest in making use of it.

Other Interviewing Modalities

Interviews may be conducted in several ways. Telephonic interviewing is common, and some agencies are increasing their use of two-way video-based interviews, using systems such as Skype or even cell phones. Non-English-speaking persons are sometimes interviewed using an interpreter skilled in other languages, including signing for those who are deaf. These variations are presented in the following sections.

Telephone Interviewing

One other form of interviewing takes place through the medium of the telephone. In recent years, the spread of the availability of the phone on a worldwide basis has been dramatic. More and more of our interactions with others are by telephone. A ride on a city bus or subway train can expose anyone to the seemingly constant situation of being able to listen in on cell phone conversations (most of which we would prefer not to hear). In our practice, we find that many of our interactions with clients are on the telephone.

As with each interviewing modality, there are strengths and limitations to the use of the telephone and its allied technology. Clearly time is one advantage in that the phone can put the client and therapist in contact very quickly. This often permits issues to be dealt with in a prompt and convenient way for both parties. For some of our clients, there is an element of safety in using the phone. That is, the phone gives them an element of power and control in that they can terminate an interview at any time. As well, just as in our own lives, we know that some people are able to talk about very intimate or charged material by phone by talking from a comfortable setting surrounded by their various security objects, topics they are not able to talk about in a face-to-face interview situation. One other potential of the phone is that it can greatly facilitate involving more than one person in an interview, which may not be possible if we are trying to set up an in-office situation. It is even possible to have several persons involved in a conference call.

There are, of course, limitations to the telephone interview. Up until now, one of the realities about phone interviewing was that you could not see the client, and we know that many of our cues in treatment come from being able to observe the person(s) we are interviewing. However, this is changing: Virtually every teenager with whom I come in contact has a phone that permits you to see the person to whom you are speaking.

Neither does a phone interview permit you to control the setting in which the interview takes place, at least from the perspective of the client. This could result in situations in which the client is in a situation of high disruption, making the ability to discuss important matters or concentrate very difficult, if not impossible. Although for the most part I believe our preference is still for situations where we are in a face-to-face situation with our client, we should be very open to the potential of the phone as a modality of interviewing.

Video Interviews

A further type of interview involves phones with video capabilities. As with phone interviews, advances in technology have greatly facilitated the availability and cost of interactive video teleconferencing. This format of interviewing again allows us to interview individuals, dyads, families, and groups from a distance. In many situations, this is the only way that it is possible to be in contact with some clients. Experience has demonstrated that after one has experienced this form of interviewing, very quickly the sense of being in the direct presence of the client(s) develops and very intense and complex situations can be addressed.

Even with the enhanced capabilities and availabilities of this interview format, the reality is that the persons involved in the interview have to be present at a specific setting where the appropriate resources are available. This can mean that people are not in a therapeutic interviewing setting but rather, for example, in a studio. This raises the question of confidentiality in that technicians may be required, or if they are not actually present, the setting may nevertheless lack a sense of intimacy and confidentiality. With growing availability of the resources for video interviewing, we should develop and promulgate as much experience as possible about how to make maximum use of this modality.

Use of Interpreters

As our caseloads become increasingly diverse, we may find ourselves working with clients who do not speak a language in which we are fluent. Most of us at some time or another have had to conduct interviews through the medium of an interpreter. Most of us have found such interviews to be very unsatisfactory and difficult, for several reasons. Often persons we have called upon to serve in this role may indeed have the language ability that we need but not understand the role of the interpreter. However, as we know, some of the world's most sensitive issues are negotiated through the services of interpreters and it is possible to deal with the most complex and highly charged material in this format.

What is essential in interviewing through an interpreter is to recognize and understand that interpreting is a profession and when one conducts an interview with the assistance of a professional interpreter, much can be accomplished. It is probable that there are few situations with which we cannot deal with the assistance of a professional interpreter.

Unfortunately for many of us, the reality will be that professional interpreting services are not available and we will need to rely on persons who have language skills but not interpreting skills. In these situations, we need to make strenuous efforts to ensure that the person functioning as interpreter understands that they are to be our voice and the client's voice only, that they indeed are competent in the language skills sought, that they are acceptable to the client from a sociopolitical perspective, and that they understand they are to convey what is being said by you and the client without any embellishments, explanations, or side discussions, either with the worker or the client.

It is important as well that we understand the role of the interpreter and if we are in situations where this resource is needed, that we have at least consultation services available to us to assist in orienting persons with the language facility but not the interpreter skills.

As mentioned in the discussion of dyadic interviewing, one of the challenges of using an interpreter in a one-on-one client situation is the existence of a triadic situation and all the potential difficulties that go with it. Nevertheless, this format of interviewing is rapidly becoming a reality in all areas of practice and social work could well lead the way in developing therapeutic expertise in its use.

The Interview Setting

It is interesting that with more than one hundred years of experience in interviewing, we have still given minimal attention to the physical settings in which we interview. At least up to the present, there seems to have been an idea that since the essence of the interview was the establishment, maintenance, and utilization of the helping relationship through verbal interaction, this is where we need to focus. If we can do this well, then where we hold the interview and how we equip the place where we interview seems less important. This approach appears to reflect a professional presumptiveness that holds that if you are a good interviewer, you can interview anywhere.

This attitude is puzzling, for, as we said, one of the most human of activities is the process of conversation with others. We know that where we hold such conversations has a considerable impact on the quality and content of a conversation.

The following comments focus on the situation of a single client; however, they also apply to multiple client situations. As we know from our own lives, although we have conversations with one another in all kinds of settings and milieus, if we have a choice we prefer settings that are harmonious with our discussions. This seems obvious, but over the years I have seen such a range of uncomfortable chairs and settings in waiting rooms and interviewing rooms, leading me to conclude that for many therapists, these details are not important. Thus, as basic an aspect as the question of chairs needs to be considered. Since we are all different in our tastes and needs, I think it important that there be some choice of chairs for the client that provide different types of comfort for different people. There seems to be an attitude in some parts of the profession that where we practice and interview should not be too comfortable or attractive.

Another aspect of the interview that deserves important consideration is where we sit. In our culture, the across-the-desk position is often seen as a symbol of authority and hence is presumed to be uncomfortable for the client and thus to be avoided. Some therapists have prided themselves on getting rid of their desks, viewing them as barriers between themselves and the client and viewing their removal as a way of lessening any power issues that may be present, without fully appreciating the dimensions of this issue.

However, we need to be careful here and not set out a set of rules. Even though for some the desk can be a power symbol, it is also a safety barrier—and, indeed, a desired barrier for some clients, who need the protection of the desk until they at least have a better understanding of who we are and what the process is going to be like. One of the problems in any discussion of the "ideal" interviewing setting is that different positions have different meanings for different people. This is especially so in our increasingly differentiated client population, to the extent that a desk may be an expected and desired part of an interviewing space for some clients. For others, it may be an unwelcome symbol of authority.

I believe the answer to this and similar kinds of questions is that we have a variety of possible seating arrangements in our offices that permit a choice for the client. If we are uncertain about what the client would prefer, especially in regard to new cases, it is easier to begin with a formal setting and move to a less formal one, if desired, rather than the other way around.

The offices in which we interview should of course ensure privacy, confidentiality, and safety for both the social worker and the client. Thus, as simple a matter as not having client files on our desks or obvious to the client is a facet of this. (With more and more of our recordkeeping being in an electronic format, there is less risk regarding confidentiality). The color of the walls and pictures and overall décor should convey warmth, competence, security, and safety, as should all the furniture and furnishings. Washroom facilities should be convenient and private, and their location should be known to the client. Telephone resources need be present, but of course in a manner that will ensure there are no unnecessary interruptions. Coat racks, a mirror, writing equipment, necessary forms, and reference materials should all be easily accessible.

Both to assist in the requirements of privacy and also for its soothing and relaxing qualities, many practitioners like having appropriate background music as an office feature. Although there is abundant evidence that the proper music and the appropriate sound level does contribute to many persons being able to relax, there are those who find it distracting, unwelcome, and unprofessional, and thus it should be possible to turn it off when this is needed.

Therapists need also to be careful about having personal material in sight, such as family pictures. Some colleagues have suggested that, for example, having a picture of even one child available can create a security risk for workers. In this time of widespread violence, there should also be some unobtrusive way of calling for help, such as a panic button connected with a local security group or police station.

The lighting in our offices is also important, and considerable professional help is available to help us create the safe therapeutic mood that we seek in relation to our office size and shape. Once again, there should be a variety of lighting arrangements to set the tone we seek.

Overall, if we really wish to establish as therapeutic a setting as possible, then it behooves us as a profession to devote much more time and attention to a study of all the physical factors that contribute to this process and study in much more detail the effects of each.

Much more data are required to assess both the importance of the interview setting and how to vary the many aspects of an office setting to bring about the maximum desirable impact on the client.

In addition to the more formal office setting, there is another component of setting to which we need to give attention in seeking to enhance our interviewing skills, and that is where to conduct our interview. The majority of our discussion about setting relates to the formal offices where we practice. However, other choices are open to us as to where we may elect to interview, such as home visits, informal settings such as a coffee shop, or less structured settings such as a walk in the park or a visit to a museum. Often there are many such opportunities open to us that may serve for various therapeutic reasons. Each of these various settings offers us particular interviewing opportunities, yet each has its limitations.

The decision to make use of the *where* of an interview in each case is a strategic move on our part and needs to be carefully thought through. It is much more complex than a value issue on our part. For example, deciding to meet a client for a cup of coffee in a downtown restaurant could be an event of great positive importance to a client that could greatly strengthen the relationship in a manner that permits the client to develop a more relaxed and trusting attitude toward the relationship. However, it could be totally misunderstood by the client and reinforce their view of the relationship as being something more than it is, a sign from us that we want to go beyond the therapist/patient relationship and become friends.

One area to which we have given some formal attention came from our experience in family therapy. Especially in the early days of family therapy, the home visit was viewed as important. Seeing where the family lived and seeing how they interacted in their home was viewed as having diagnostic and assessment utility on the part of the therapist. The home visit, useful as it turned out to be for family work, has the same positive potential for other modalities, such as couple and individual work. However, this technique is not without its risks of being misunderstood. In some instance, a home visit puts an unnecessary burden on the client. It needs to be a strategic diagnostic decision rather than something we always choose to do or don't do.

Interviewing Techniques

As mentioned earlier, it is our view that, to date, we have tended to view interviewing as a process in which a discrete number of procedures are used to develop maintain and utilize the helping relationship. This stress on the process as the interaction between two people has led us to stress the responsibility of the workers to understand themselves, the effect of the client on them, and the tenor of the interaction. However, we need also to recognize that over the decades, in putting the stress that we have on the relationship, we have overlooked that what goes on between two people in an interview situation consists of a series of discrete actions between the persons involved, that is, a series of techniques (Fischer, 1978). This position leads us then to begin to consider interviewing as a series of actions that can be observed, individualized, manipulated, taught, and ultimately measured and assessed for impact.

The term *technique* assumes the use in practice of an ethical, observable action or object to achieve a particular therapeutic outcome. It is something that can be observed by others, can be replicated by others, and has received a level of professional approbation. Thus, we can view an interview as a series of such actions that are a series or combination of a cluster of techniques. In this way, we talk of such things as the empty chair, the use of games, food, music, gifts, reflection, advice, and so on. In considering techniques, the qualities and characteristics of each needs to be to understood to learn how to use them differentially. In so doing, we need to avoid a position that says if you want to accomplish this do this. Rather like the artist, we need to understand the potential of each technique and learn to use it in our own idiosyncratic way for the good of the client.

What is critical is for us to begin to focus on the concept that an interview is a series of diverse yet discrete acts, that is, techniques and to begin to identify these and focus more on evaluating their differential impact rather than only reporting on use of them in practice.

Conclusion

For more than one hundred years, social workers have been engaged in the process of professional interviewing. In this time, we have developed a rich repertoire of techniques and are skilled in their use. On the one hand we know a great deal. I suggest that the great majority of colleagues become skilled interviewers in a very short time. But we do so on almost a trial-and-error basis. Most of what we know is in the form of practice wisdom.

If we are going to become even more proficient and effective in the art and science of interviewing we need to become more precise and objective. This so that each of us is able to review our interviews and ask, What techniques did I use in this interview? Why did I interview in this way, and what was the result? As well, we need to become more comfortable in having others look at our interviewing skills to enhance our ability to identify the techniques we use in our interviews and the different effects they may have.

As stated earlier, since so much of the content of our work deals with the minutiae of our clients' everyday lives, we need to become more comfortable and skilled in making use of a much broader repertoire of the objects and processes of daily living. This to enrich our interviewing skills to assist individuals, couples, groups, and families to achieve their optimum potential as humans in the complex societies in which we all live.

Key Terms

Differential use of
    technique
Group interviewing
Family interviewing

Home visit
Interpreter
Interview
Setting

Techniques
Transference

Review Questions for Critical Thinking

1. How important is the physical setting in which we interview?

2. Describe an imaginary therapeutic situation in which you might chose to interview a client in a coffee shop for a therapeutic reason.

3. My relationship with a client is more important than the techniques I choose to use in an interview. (Discuss.)

4. It is possible to conduct an intensive clinical interview with the assistance of an interpreter. (Discuss.)

Online Resources

Interviewing Skills – I: http://www.youtube.com/watch?v = IiggMe4MgYA

A role-played interview between two social work students involving counseling a troubled college student.

Sample Social Work Interview: http://www.youtube.com/watch?v = zYoEdvEmUrU&feature = related

This sample interview illustrates the problem-solving process. A sex-worker is seeking help in finding alternative employment.

Motivational Interviewing: http://www.youtube.com/watch?v = nwlFUE N99OM

A 45-minute presentation on a special form of interviewing known as Motivational Interviewing.

Sample Interview with a Child: http://www.allencowling.com/intervew .htm

A transcript and discussion of some unacceptable and otherwise misleading interview techniques used with a child.

References

Brothers, C. (2002). The process of interviewing. In F. J. Turner (Ed.), *Social work practice* (2nd ed., pp. 191–203). Toronto, Canada: Prentice Hall.

Coady, N. F. (2002). The helping relationship. In F. J. Turner (Ed.), *Social work practice* (2nd ed., pp. 116–130). Toronto, Canada: Prentice Hall.

Fischer, J. (1978). *Effective casework practice: An eclectic approach.* New York, NY: McGraw-Hill.

Hollis, F. (1973) *Casework: A psychosocial therapy.* New York, NY: Random House.

Perlman, H. H. (1971). *Social casework: A problem-solving process.* Chicago, IL: University of Chicago Press.

Thomlison, R. J. (1984). Something works: Evidence from practice effectiveness studies. *Social Work, 29,* 51–58.

Chapter 4
Problem Identification, Contracting, and Case Planning

Sophia F. Dziegielewski

> Why is it important and what are the skills needed for all social workers and other human-service workers to be knowledgeable, competent, and skilled in problem identification, case planning, and accurate recordkeeping?

Introduction

With the rapid growth of behavioral-based or evidence-based care, social workers and other human-service workers employed in health and mental health settings are now expected to be keenly skilled in identifying, planning, and documenting the needs of clients (Rubin, 2008). This makes complete and accurate documentation and record keeping essential for effective practice (Dziegielewski, 2010a; Dziegielewski, Green, & Hawkins, 2002; Mumm, 2006). Furthermore, to keep these skills up to date all human-service professionals need specific exposure with subsequent application to the latest trends for documenting in the profession. This exposure allows the professional to further develop and refine problem-solving skills, thereby avoiding therapeutic setbacks and limited helping interventions. According to Dust (1996), when accurate records are prepared and utilized "...a clinician can examine the past and prepare for the future" (p. 50).

For the evidence-based practitioner, the most effective intervention plan is directly influenced by the need to measure the overall efficacy, necessity, and effectiveness of social services provided, while clearly ascertaining the variables that can be linked directly to outcome success and client change (Dziegielewski, 2004; Dziegielewski & Roberts, 2004; Rubin, 2008; Sheafor, 2011). Therefore, to avoid pitfalls in formulating the evidence-based or practice-based case plan, documentation is needed that clearly outlines the problem while explaining the actual differences between the intervention approaches utilized (Monette, Sullivan, & DeJong, 2005; Nugent, Sieppert, & Hudson, 2001). The individual treatment or intervention plans that are needed to address each situation can make it difficult to clearly establish the success of change efforts (Dziegielewski, 2010a, 2010b). The limitation rests in the fact that client or system change behavior and the resulting case plan can be seen as subjective. Controlling for subjectivity becomes even more complicated because client systems and identified problems are not constant and can change over time even without any therapeutic intervention. Regardless of the struggles inherent with achieving organized and complete client records, the impetus toward achieving evidence-based procedures remains unavoidably strong. Without clear progress records, helping professionals simply cannot accurately document the services that they provide (Kagle & Kopels, 2008; Sidell, 2011), nor can they stand behind the interventions that have been delivered. Furthermore, with the increased emphasis on accountability, documentation that cannot show evidence-based changes may result in system-related negative effects, such as the loss of insurance coverage from third-party payers (Dziegielewski, 2010a, 2010b).

In the human-service practice environment, workers are hired with the expectation that they have good problem identification, contracting, and case-planning skills. This expectation of pre-existing skill, however, may send a message to administrators that these employees already have all the necessary skills when hired. In difficult budgetary times when funds for staff development are tight, updating or refining skill development in this area may not be seen as a priority. Since agencies are not rewarded for providing training on case planning unless it is directly related to reimbursement practices, human-service workers may be forced to seek their own training. Or worse, when training is provided, the focus may be related directly to meeting agency standards rather than to enhancing quality care while improving service delivery. To assist in bridging this gap, this chapter provides tips for evidence-based intervention efforts that are based on sound case planning and the subsequent documentation of all problem-solving efforts.

Historical Background

According to Dziegielewski (2010a, 2010b) good documentation starts with identifying the treatment strategy and linking it to a clear treatment plan. As caseloads continue to grow in numbers, being accurate yet concise is paramount where client change behaviors are highlighted. This means measuring the amount of client change and relating it directly to the issues/problems in their lives that need to be addressed (Sheafor, 2011).

Furthermore, Kagle and Kopels (2008) believe that many social workers simply do not recognize the importance of keeping sound records. When a trial-and-error approach is used to document case-plan services, the link to the treatment plan gets lost as the worker may be uncertain about the nature, duration, and outcomes of the therapeutic encounter.

Developing a complete case plan can be hampered further by the methodological limitations inherent in most forms of time-limited interventions, especially when searching for the overall effectiveness of and between competing intervention approaches (Monette et al., 2005; Nugent et al., 2001). Methodological limitations such as clearly identifying the time needed to comprehensively assess the problem can hamper helping efforts.

In addition, some social workers may resist the extra time and effort needed to ensure that they have complete and accurate records. Oftentimes this resistance is related directly to their belief that this extra effort will result in less quality time spent with clients. At times, social service workers may place minimal importance on documentation because they do not consider this activity an integral part of the therapeutic process and, therefore, strengthening case recording skills becomes essential (Sidell, 2011). This resistance and subsequent anxiety can result in a strong desire by many social workers to postpone or defer documentation to a later time. To quell these fears, the service provider must recognize his or her current level of skill in this area, have the desire to improve, and be willing to focus attention on the importance of identifying and documenting behavioral outcomes, as well as involvement in using these outcomes to formulate and document intervention plans.

Importance of Evidence-Based Documentation Skills

Since service documentation remains an essential part of human-service work, learning to identify and record problem behaviors remains a basic requirement of all educational training efforts (Dziegielewski & Leon, 2001; Leon & Pepe, 2010). Yet, as the profession continues to struggle with establishing specific treatment goals and objectives, it is no surprise that evidence-based documentation continues to lag behind. Furthermore, since there are no national policies regarding documentation guidelines for many mental health conditions, professionals in the field often struggle with how best to document the case plan (APA Guidelines for Practitioners, 2012).

Given the importance of this type of skills training, many graduate and undergraduate human-service programs have been compelled to teach documentation from an evidence-based perspective. To develop this skill, the traditional approach may be for colleges and universities to offer a specific course on problem-focused documentation. This trend can be problematic, however, if it simply restricts this information to just one or two courses. Evidence-based documentation that includes treatment planning needs to be covered in conjunction with all courses across the curriculum, and limiting this exposure can result in a lack of emphasis on the direct application of these principles in the practice setting as well as disrupting the continuity of care (Leon & Pepe, 2010; Dziegielewski, 2005).

Furthermore, teaching this skill from such a limited perspective can result in beginning professionals having inadequate knowledge or limited skill in evidence-based documentation when they enter the workforce. Whether a human-services worker is involved in indirect practice (focusing on policy, planning, administration, and community organization) or direct practice (involving assessment, intervention, prevention, and alleviation of negative situations) with individuals, couples, families, or groups, the development of problem identification skills reflective of the case plan remains essential for quality intervention (Rubin, 2010).

Limited resources and specific program guidelines make it imperative that social workers remain responsive to growing expectations of accountability and improved program effectiveness. Despite this imperative, some educational programs still do not view integration of these principles across all practice courses as a critical component for achieving this. In our litigious society, documentation that is clear and concise protects the student social worker, the agency, and the client being served (Cumming et al., 2007).

Leon and Pepe (2010) highlight the need for this type of education, depicting research on the outcomes of providing a course on documentation skills to undergraduate social-work students. Their study included 101 students and utilized a pretest/posttest format regarding the acquisition of skills covered in an undergraduate documentation course. These authors found that students increased their knowledge in three essential areas: formatting, content, and writing skills. These authors argue for the importance of more courses and training in this area for efficiency and effectiveness in service provision as well as competitiveness in the job market.

According to Leon & Pepe (2010) the following seven recommendations are made:

> *1. Offer comprehensive courses or specific course content on documentation to undergraduate and graduate courses; 2. Train students on updated documentation formats currently used in the community; 3. Consider using adjunct faculty who are working daily with these formats to co-teach documentation content; 4. Integrate expertise from other disciplines, such as law, to understand documentation from different perspectives; 5. Facilitate collaboration and coordination between educators and field instructors on the rapidly changing documentation requirements; 6. Incorporate learning of actual documentation formats and forms in the classroom; and, 7. Use pretest and post-test designs to increase research on the scholarship of teaching and learning related to documentation skills. (pp. 374–375)*

With the influx and importance of evidence-based interventions, the inclusion of specific graduate and undergraduate training in documentation is important, as most human-service agencies will expect their new employees to know how to identify problems. When setting up case files it is essential to clearly document what is to be included to facilitate care (Kagle & Kopels, 2008).

When specifically addressing the needs of social workers, several articles and texts addressed the issue of how to clearly identify problem behaviors; however, few report specific data-based recommendations for specific training to be provided to practitioners and what has worked best. Several articles did, however, stress the importance of training professionals on documentation to prevent problems with managed care and accountability. In 1996, Kaczmarek and Barclay helped to address this need by conducting a study on documentation training. They asserted that accurate recordkeeping needed to include information such as clinical summaries, diagnosis, treatment plans, case progress notes, written contracts, and a termination summary. When they surveyed 235 psychologists about their record keeping practices, Kaczmarek and Barclay found great variability in the styles of client documentation reported. They attributed this variation to a lack of appropriate standards and training. According to Kaczmarek and Barclay, "in this age of rising malpractice litigation, managed care, and the need for professionals to demonstrate treatment outcomes, it is increasingly important that academic training programs provide more emphasis on client documentation" (p. 78). These authors advocated for more counselor training on documentation and urged that this content be covered in professional education. They suggested that the content be presented first in an introductory course and then built on and reinforced in all subsequent assessment and treatment courses.

In the introductory courses, they recommended that teaching techniques include: (a) reviewing current research on documentation to become familiar with new strategies in recording, (b) teaching at least one structured note system, (c) having students write notes on videotapes of counseling sessions, and (d) developing a diagnosis and a treatment plan from a vignette. These suggestions were intended to help students become familiar with current documentation strategies. In addition, Kaczmarek and Barclay suggested strategies that could be helpful for more advanced study, such as starting growth groups where poorly written case notes could be presented and improved. Kaczmarek and Barclay noted that: "academic training programs need to be proactive and incorporate more systematic skill training on client documentation within existing course work. Specific teaching strategies have been provided to implement more systemic training; however, research is needed to demonstrate their effectiveness" (p. 85). The absence of a systemic approach to documentation training could translate into inaccurate records and ineffective treatment interventions.

Although continuing education to provide human-service workers with evidence-based documentation training is assumed to be critical, there appears to be a paucity of controlled studies on this topic. Dziegielewski et al. (2002) engaged in a study to measure whether specific training could increase the human-service professionals' confidence in their documentation abilities after introducing options for specific evidence-based methods for measuring treatment effectiveness. Fifty-six professionals attended a 1-day, 6-hour seminar on social work recordkeeping, treatment planning, and documentation. All of the participants responded to pretest and posttest questions that measured their level of comfort and skill in documentation. Topics covered during the workshop included problem identification linked to evidence-based treatment planning and measurement, such as use of self-report instruments to support problem-solving efforts.

Information presented in the workshop addressed the professional changes based on reimbursement practices as well as skills for recordkeeping, treatment planning, and documentation. Workshop content stressed the knowledge and skills needed to develop specific treatment objectives and related interventions from a behaviorally based, managed care perspective. On completion of the workshop, the competencies to be enhanced included:

- Gain an understanding of the diversity, necessity, and limitations that can result from using specific preplanned treatment interventions.
- Become familiar with how to document and develop treatment plans reflective of the specific needs or identified problems of the client served.
- Describe the importance of, and be able to use, time-limited concrete intervention strategies that address specific behavioral treatment objectives.
- Be familiar with use of a multiaxis assessment system as a guide for concrete problem assessment and subsequent behavior change.
- Introduce the participant to a specific type of problem-oriented recordkeeping and considerations for how best to use this method.
- Understand the importance of clear documentation and appropriate intervention contracts (e.g., safety plans and no harm/no risk agreements) as part of the therapeutic process.
- Become familiar with several different models for concrete treatment planning that can be used to address common problems encountered in social work practice.

The pretest/posttest instrument revealed that these social workers wanted more training on problem identification, recordkeeping, treatment planning, and documentation. Because these professionals are required to document clinical records on a regular basis, participating in this continuing education seminar helped to provide them with an opportunity to improve both their comfort and skill when documenting the services provided. Although social workers initially reported feeling that documentation was important, their assessments of its importance increased after participating in the workshop. When examining the written comments, many of these social workers reported that they were not aware of how much was involved in defining behaviorally based goals and objectives and relating them to the appropriate intervention regimes. Nor were they aware of the degree to which standardized measures could support the acquisition of the case plan and practice effectiveness. This study, similar to the past study by Kaczmarek and Barclay (1996), found that social workers almost unanimously (97%) felt that professional educational training programs need to include more updated content and information on documentation and recordkeeping. Providing information on this content to human-service workers can only result in an improvement in their attitudes about its importance, in their confidence in their skills to document, and in their level of efficiency in recordkeeping activities.

Using Evidence-Based Principles in Problem Identification and Case Planning

Regardless of the population or the problem being identified, Bergin (1971) cautioned that one general premise that should always be applied is that "it is essential that the entire therapeutic enterprise be broken down into specific sets of measures and operations, or in other words, be dimensionalized" (p. 253). This ideal is still supported and considered essential in documenting evidence-based case planning resulting in a multifaceted assessment process (Rubin, 2010). In addition, the importance of individualizing all intervention efforts and basing all helping activity on this premise cannot be overestimated (Dziegielewski, 2005, 2006).

For the evidence-based practitioner, any discussion on problem identification, case planning, and documentation strategy must clearly relate to measuring treatment effectiveness (O'Hare, 2005). From a traditional standpoint, Kagle and Kopels (2008) reported that case records needed to focus on understanding the client in context, with a special emphasis on documenting the client's social history and current relationships and on describing and analyzing the process of intervention and change. This is somewhat different than evidence-based principles, where the focus starts and ends with direct observation, exploration, and intervention all related to the identified problem behavior(s). The evidence-based practitioner starts with the identification of the problem behavior and then links this behavior to the treatment plan (Berghuis & Jongsma, 2008; Jongsma, Peterson, McInnis, & Bruce, 2006; Klott & Jongsma, 2006; O'Leary, Heyman, & Jongsma, 2011). To start the process, it needs to be clear that understanding the problem is clearly related to ascertaining the variables that can be linked directly to client change (Dziegielewski, 2010a, 2010b; Dziegielewski & Roberts, 2004). From this perspective, the evidence-based practitioner identifies the problem as clearly and concisely as possible and relates the problem directly to the behavior change. When this connection is not clear, third-party reviewers who monitor records for quality control and service utilization may reject even the best-intended helping efforts. Furthermore, when problem behaviors are not clearly linked to positive behavior change, these reviewers have the power to terminate treatment on the basis that what is provided does not clearly reflect the continuity, effectiveness, and the need for continued services (Corcoran & Boyer-Quick, 2002). In this managed care environment, the documentation for continued care must clearly correspond with medical necessity (Wiger, 2005). Therefore, to avoid issues, all case plan progress must always reflect the evidence-based interventions being implemented and link these interventions to whether the services are medically necessary.

This clear linkage between problem intervention and outcome connects the relevance of the intervention to the problem, creating a pathway for the acknowledgment and achievement of intervention success. The social worker must clearly identify in each record the client's problem(s), the need for service, goals and objectives to be achieved, plans to be achieved, service attitudes, activities, and the impact of the situation on the client. Although this newer approach to case planning and recordkeeping may be unfamiliar to many social workers, it is imperative for developing new and innovative approaches for ensuring practice effectiveness.

In viewing client problems from an empirical standpoint, the various dimensions of the intervention experience need to be treated as a complex network of functional relationships within which there occurs a series of interactions among the primary factors (i.e., the independent and dependent variables). Simply stated, in any functional relationship, the independent variables operate as presumed causes and dependent variables operate as the presumed effects (Kreuger & Newman, 2005). Therefore, when documenting a client problem, an important first step in the evaluation process is to sort out what is believed to be the causal connection operating in any given problem situation. This involves identifying a series of interdependent problem-solving steps that logically flow from the presenting problem (Rubin, 2008). It is at this point that the social worker needs to ascertain which of the problem behaviors need to be addressed in order to yield the most relevant and important therapeutic gain. The identified behaviors to be addressed must also be part of a mutually negotiated plan.

Creating the Problem Statement

Embedded in the logic of this problem identification and solving process is an implied hypothesis that can be stated as follows:

> In problem situations, if X is employed as an intervention strategy (i.e., the independent variable), then it is expected that Y (i.e., obtain desired functioning level) will be the predicted outcome (i.e., the dependent variable).

Evidence-based documentation is based on identifying and linking the problem statement in this way. In this format, the problem statement is clearly related to the implied hypothesis. This requires stating clearly what it is that he or she intends to do with or on behalf of the client, as well as the expected consequences of those actions. To do this, the identified problem statement must correspond to both the case plan and the outcome; and all must be defined in operational or measurable terms. To start the process, generating research statements that can define the problem and how to best measure the changes that result, becomes essential. To accomplish this, vague concepts such as "emotional support will result in enhanced client self-esteem" need to be avoided. Although on the surface this statement may appear very important for guiding practice strategy, when stated in such global terms, it simply cannot adequately operationalize testable hypotheses or identified problem statements. Evidence-based practice documentation requires that vague concepts be linked to constructs that involve the measurement of self-esteem and how an increase of this concept will be obtained.

Although the task of operationally defining concepts is not easy, many researchers concur that it is essential to the effective evaluation of the intervention, regardless of one's theoretical orientation (Bloom, Fischer, & Orme, 2009; Monette et al., 2005). Furthermore, the value and subsequent recognition of our clinical practice efforts will prove to be only as good as the empirical observations on which they are based. This makes the use of measurement instruments designed to help operationalize this concept central. Picking a standardized instrument to assist with identifying problem behaviors will help to achieve greater accuracy and objectivity in measuring some of the more commonly encountered clinical problems.

Measuring the Problem Behavior

The most notable development in assisting the evidence-based practitioner has been the emergence of numerous brief pencil-and-paper assessment devices known as rapid assessment instruments (RAIs). These types of instruments and the measurements that result can assist with focusing on a client's strengths (Poulin, 2010). As standardized measures, RAIs share a number of characteristics. These measurements are brief, relatively easy to administer, score, and interpret, and require very little knowledge of testing procedures on the part of the clinician. For the most part, these self-report measures can be completed by the client, usually within 15 minutes, RAIs are independent of any particular theoretical orientation, and as such, can be used with a variety of intervention methods (Dziegielewski & Powers, 2005). These instruments provide a systematic overview of the client's identified problem(s) and can be used to stimulate discussion related to the information elicited by the instrument itself. The score that is generated provides an operational index of the frequency, duration, or intensity of the problem. Most RAIs can be used as repeated measures and thus are adaptable to the methodological requirements of both research design and goal assessment purposes. In addition to providing a standardized means by which change can be monitored over time with a single client, RAIs can also be used to make equivalent comparisons across clients experiencing a common problem (e.g., marital conflict).

RAIs can assist in providing information concerning reliability and validity (Fischer & Corcoran, 2007a, 2007b). Reliability refers to the stability of a measure and whether the questions mean the same thing to the individual answering them at different times, as well as whether different individuals interpret like questions similarly. Unless an instrument yields consistent data, it is impossible for it to be valid. But even highly reliable instruments are of little value unless their validity can also be demonstrated. Validity speaks to the general question of whether an instrument does in fact measure what it purports to measure. Although both are important, validity tends to be a little more elusive than reliability. There are several different approaches to establishing validity (Babie, 2011; Dziegielewski & Powers, 2005), each of which is designed to provide information regarding how much confidence we can have in the instrument as an accurate indicator of the problem under consideration. While levels of reliability and validity vary greatly among available instruments, it is very helpful to the social work professional to know in advance the extent to which these issues have been addressed. Information concerning reliability and validity, as well as other factors related to the standardization process (e.g., the procedures for administering, scoring, and interpreting the instrument), can help the professional make informed decisions concerning the appropriateness of any given instrument.

The key to selecting the best instrument for the intervention is knowing where and how to access the relevant information concerning potentially useful measures. This requires working on skills for identifying client needs and communication skills (Oliver & Margolin, 2009). Once client need is assessed and identified, the best instrument can be selected. Fortunately, there are a number of excellent sources available to the clinician to help facilitate this process. One such compilation of standardized measures is *Measures for Clinical Practice and Research: A Source Book*, a two-volume set by Fischer and Corcoran (2007a, 2007b). This set provides adult assessment strategies as well as family measures. This reference set can serve as a valuable resource for identifying useful rapid-assessment instruments suited for the kinds of problems most commonly encountered in clinical social work practice. In the beginning of the books there is a list of health and mental health related variables and guidelines for their use with different types of practice-related problems. In addition to an introduction to the basic principles of measurement, these books discuss various types of measurement tools, including the advantages and disadvantages of RAIs. These books also provide some useful guidelines for locating, selecting, evaluating, and administering prospective measures. The availability of these, as well as numerous similar references related to special interest areas, greatly enhances the social work professional's options with respect to monitoring and evaluation practice. Overall, the RAIs can serve as valuable adjuncts for the social work professional's evaluation efforts.

Another type of measurement used to enhance documentation that helps to record a client's functioning level are the therapist-directed rating scales provided in the *DSM-IV-TR* on Axis V (Generalized Assessment of Functioning [GAF]). The scale provides individual rating scores for each client served. In this method, ratings of a client's functioning are assigned at the outset of therapy and again on discharge. The scales allow for assigning a number that represents a client's behaviors. The scales are designed to enable the worker to differentially rank identified behaviors from 0 to 100, with higher ratings indicating higher overall functioning and coping levels. By rating the highest level of functioning a client has attained over the past year and then comparing it to his or her current level of functioning, helpful comparisons can be made. Utilizing this scale can help professionals to both quantify client problems and document observable changes that may be attributable to the counseling relationship. This allows the worker to track performance variations across behaviors relative to client functioning. See the *DSM-IV-TR* published by the American Psychiatric Association (2000) for a copy of the scale and Dziegielewski (2010a) for a way to utilize these scales in practice.

Also, in the *DSM-IV-TR* "Criteria Sets and Axes Provided for Further Study," there are two scales that are not required for the formal multiaxial diagnosis yet can provide a format for ranking function that might be particularly helpful to social work professionals. The first of these optional scales is the relational functioning scale termed the Global Assessment of Relational Functioning (GARF). This index is used to address the status of family or other ongoing relationships on a hypothetical continuum from competent to dysfunctional. The second index is the Social and Occupational Functioning Assessment Scale (SOFAS). With this scale, the individual's level of social and occupational functioning can be addressed (American Psychiatric Association, 2000). The complimentary nature of these scales in identifying and assessing client problems is evident in the fact that all three scales, the GAF, GARF, and SOFAS use the same rating system. The rankings for each scale range from 0 to 100, with the lower numbers representing more severe problems. The uses of all three of these tools have been encouraging for obvious reasons. Collectively, they provide a viable framework within which human-service workers can apply concrete measures to a wide variety of practice situations. They also provide a multidimensional perspective that permits workers to document variations in levels of functioning across system sizes, including the individual (GAF), family (GARF), and social (SOFAS) perspectives.

In summary, tools to help document client change are essential in problem identification and case planning and these measures can help to quantify the resultant progress and reporting of these accomplishments. To further address use of these measurement tools, specific concrete goals and objectives need to also incorporate a number of direct behavioral observation techniques that are identified by the self-administered RAIs or other types of therapist-directed rating scales. Space limitations do not permit a more thorough discussion of these methods in this chapter. However, there are a number of excellent sources available that discuss in detail the kinds of information one would need in order to make informed decisions regarding their selection and application to specific cases (Bloom et al., 2009). To further supplement these efforts, scales such as the GAF, GARF, and SOFAS can be used to assist in behavioral-based outcome measures. Overall, once the problem behavior is identified, case plan development can use this wide array of measures to operationally define the various dimensions of the intervention process.

Developing the Service or Case Plan

Once the problem statement is outlined and how it will be assessed has been developed, the task now becomes integrating the problem behavior with the appropriate service or case planning strategies. This integration needs to encompass a seamless and synergistic bond (Dziegielewski, 2010a, 2010b). In evaluating the service or case planning, evidence-based practice dictates that the problem statement, the behavioral-based goals and objectives, and the accompanying intervention plan coincide completely. For the new practitioner, coordinating all of these parts into an integrated whole can be both frustrating and confusing. Therefore, to effectively implement such a case plan, the process must be clearly linked to the outcome. And, this linkage must occur in an informed and sensitive manner, where the practitioner is well versed in the following procedures.

In selecting the practice strategy, it must be firmly based within the reality of the environment. This can present a particular problem for the evidence-based practitioner, as the pressure to select a method of intervention may be influenced by and subsequently trapped within a system that is driven by social, political, cultural, and economic factors. It is obvious to the social worker that the bottom line is most often cost reduction and containment (Franklin, 2002). In conjunction with cost-saving strategy, the guidelines and practices developed through quality improvement programs can also be used as pre-established criteria for service delivery. These pre-established criteria for practice delivery can limit the treatment plans and types of case planning strategy utilized (Dziegielewski, 2004).

This is further complicated by the need to individualize each case plan so that it reflects the unique symptoms and needs the client is experiencing. When the case plan clearly delineates the intervention plan, families and friends of the client may feel more at ease and may actually agree to participate and assist in any behavioral interventions that will be applied. Factors that influence the case plan strategy are numerous with the most important being the general use of traditional methods of time-limited intervention, lack of a formal space for counseling, and time and/or agency constraints. A further complication when selecting a structure for practice intervention is defending the type of intervention in the best interest of the client. In the practice environment, reality dictates the duration of most therapeutic sessions, regardless of the intervention used or the orientation of the social worker. In social work practice, most of these therapeutic encounters generally range from 6 to 8 sessions to as many as 20 sessions. Generally speaking, the least number of sessions is 1, and the greatest number is 20. For the evidence-based practitioner, an intervention plan carried out in one session and monitored periodically over time can provide attraction for funding sources.

It is beyond the scope of this chapter to review all possible modes of practice strategy that can be implemented to support the case plan. Yet regardless of the method used, all helping efforts must include a viable time-limited approach with mutually negotiated concrete and realistic goals, a clear problem statement, and a plan for measuring effectiveness, as well as a specific time frame for conducting and completing the service (Dziegielewski, 2010a). Furthermore, regardless of the method selected, in the *initial phase* of the case plan, a hopeful environment is created where the client begins to feel confident that his or her problem can and will be addressed. The role of the social worker is clear in helping the client to break down problems into practical terms and establish the groundwork for the development of concrete goals and objectives. For the evidence-based practitioner, a written case plan that shows a clear understanding of what will transpire is essential. If measurement scales are not implemented to serve as a baseline, an initial ranking to compare client functioning at the beginning and end of intervention is suggested.

At the root of this process is the establishment of a positive and supportive working relationship with the client and therefore building rapport is considered part of the process of problem identification. This process is greatly facilitated by the articulation of a set of mutually nego-tiated, realistic, and specific time-limited goals and objectives. When the problem behavior is clearly articulated, the objectives can flow accordingly and ambiguousness and confusion on expectations and/or outcomes is controlled. These goals and objectives should be clearly outlined in relation to a client's identified needs and capacities and this in turn creates a func-tional relationship between the independent variables and the dependent variables (Kreuger & Neuman, 2005). Furthermore, social workers need to remain mindful of the personal, cultural, and environmental circumstances that can directly or indirectly affect the problem behavior and how these dynamics may impact the problem-solving process. This awareness correlates nicely with recognizing the person in his or her environment or situation creating a comprehensive case plan. From this perspective, the social worker's role is one of action and direction, particularly when individuals are in the early phases of problem identification. It is essential to realize that for individuals, the problem impairment can result in a type of crisis where frustration and an inability to start the process are prominent. At times, especially in the beginning of the problem-solving process, clients may seek the input of the social worker for help in seeing the connection between the problem behaviors and the outlined behavior change. Once identified, the case plan (often referred to as the treatment or intervention plan) is formulated. This initial phase ends with an agreed-on time frame for service provision, and in the initial phase, the measurement of effec-tiveness will be finalized. It is here that the social worker must decide and plan for implementation of how she or he will measure the effectiveness of the intervention strategy employed.

The *main phase of intervention* is generally based on the model and format chosen in the initial phase. This is the most active of the stages because this is when concrete problem solving actually occurs. In this phase, individualized case plans reflect the concrete efforts to address the problem. It is here the foundation is made for the case plan and the bench-marks for completion to be linked. According to Whitlock, Orleans, Pender, and Allan (2002), the case plan should always clearly identify the five A's (assess, advise, agree, assist, and arrange). In this main phase of the inter-vention, the treatment plan needs to be formulated and applied (Jongsma & Peterson, 2006).

First, in developing the treatment plan problem behaviors, which are interfering with functioning, must be identified or selected. Second, once selected, the problems must be defined (Klott & Jongsma, 2006). The role of the social worker is to *assess* and *advise* along therapeutic lines. In practice, it is considered essential that the client and his or her family *agree* to participate and assist in this selection process as much as possible in terms of identifying the issues, problem behaviors, and coping styles that are either causing or contributing to the client's discomfort. Of all the problem behaviors a client may be experiencing, it is important to clearly select the ones that should receive the most attention—the behaviors that impair independent living skills, cause difficulties in completing tasks of daily living, or impair usual occupational or social functioning.

The role of the human-service professional is clear in helping to *arrange* a course of action and to help the client to complete the tasks assigned. The third step is goal formulation and development, coupled with an objective interpretation of the problem. To measure progress in the case plan, the social worker must start with clear and behaviorally specific goals. The more precisely these goals are defined in measurable terms, the easier it is to verify if and when they are achieved. Identification of the goals allows for further refinement in terms of more specific immediate, intermediate, and long-term objectives. When the problem behavior has been clearly identified, the case plan flows from it. Once all related factors have been identified, the reported problems are then prioritized so that goals, objectives, and action tasks may be developed. This step constitutes the basis for the case plan. Furthermore, these goals must be broken down into specific objective statements that reflect target behaviors to be changed and ways to measure the client's progress on each objective. As subcomponents to the objectives, the case plan needs to include the action tasks that clearly delineate the steps to be taken by the client and the helping professional to ensure successful completion of each objective. For example, if the problem behavior is ambivalent feelings that impair general task completion, the main goal may be to help the client reduce feelings of ambivalence. An objective that clearly articulates a behavioral definition of ambivalence is discussed, along with the ways that the ambivalence will be decreased (Dziegielewski & Powers, 2005). This approach provides the mechanisms used to determine whether the behavior has been changed. For example, a client is able to demonstrate the ability to express his or her feelings toward a significant other. In this case, the therapeutic intervention involves assisting the client to develop specific and concrete tasks that are geared toward increasing this behavior and consequently meeting the objective. The outcome measure simply becomes establishing whether the task was completed.

Fourth, once the goals and specific objectives are identified and the social worker and the client have mutually agreed on them, the intervention strategy must be selected. To start this process, a partnership of mutual respect needs to be formed. In this relationship, agreement and support starts with the belief that the client will succeed, and the practitioner can help provide the necessary foundation for progress within the case plan. Basically, no matter what evaluation strategy is selected, it is likely to be meaningful only if it is initiated early and brought to closure fairly quickly (Dziegielewski & Powers, 2005). In addition, the methodology itself should not be experienced by the client as being in any way intrusive to the helping process. Ideally, the purposes of both the intervention and the evaluation should be compatible and mutually supportive, making all efforts at establishing a treatment plan a team effort. Once the client agrees, the client can determine whether the goals and objectives sought are consistent with his or her own culture and values. The responsibility of developing the structure and intervention strategy rests with the practitioner; however, emphasis on mutuality is a joint effort between the practitioner and the client, where the practitioner may take an active role in the beginning.

Measurement is an important aspect of problem identification but the importance of practice wisdom when creating the case plan cannot be underestimated. To facilitate effective planning, the human-service worker must be aware of what is likely to work for a particular client, and possess the theoretical knowledge necessary to justify the selection and application of appropriate techniques. Theory informs practice by providing a plausible framework within which critical intervention and evaluation issues can be simultaneously raised and interpreted. Therefore, the more we know about the theoretical underpinnings of any given problem-solving focused counseling strategy, the better informed we will be in our efforts to document what is predicted and/or explained. As stated earlier, practice wisdom often dictates how best to proceed in helping a client, given the specific nature of the situation and the surrounding circumstances. It can also help the practitioner decide when to apply and/or withdraw the various components of the treatment package throughout the course of the intervention process.

One technique that can aid the evidence-based practitioner is *summarization*. In summarization, regardless of the model chosen, each session is planned in advance and reviewed in the session, remaining open and flexible if renegotiation needs to occur in regard to the problem-solving process. In this phase, regardless of how many sessions are being implemented, the summarization should be incorporated into each session (Dziegielewski, 2004). In this process, each formal encounter is dedicated to the client actually stating the agreed-on problem statement and objectives to be addressed. This allows both client and social worker to quickly focus on the task at hand. Summarization should also be practiced at the end of each session. This allows the client to recapitulate what she or he believes has transpired in the session and how it relates to the stated objectives. Clients should use their own words to summarize what has transpired. In acknowledging and summarizing the content and objectives of the session, (a) the client takes responsibility for his or her own actions, (b) repetition allows the session accomplishments to be highlighted and reinforced, (c) the client and the social worker ascertain that they are working together on the same objectives, and (d) the therapeutic environment remains flexible and open for renegotiation of contracted objectives.

Last, after the problem behavior has been identified, the goals and/or objectives of intervention have been established, and practice strategy has been determined, the difficult task becomes evaluating the clinical intervention in standardized or operationally based terms. Now outcomes will need to be articulated in terms of realistic goals that can be easily converted to operationally defined objectives that avoid vague and nebulous language. As stated earlier, this is a much easier task when subjective terms such as stress, anxiety, and depression, which are often used to describe important facets of a client's social/psychological functioning, have been assessed beyond their usual subjective connotations. Specific definitions are essential, because when semantic elusiveness exists, it makes it very difficult to establish reliable measures of change (Whitlock et al., 2002).

In the *final phase* of the intervention process, follow-up contact is established. Here the social worker either meets the client in person for intermittent sessions or arranges for telephone communication to review and evaluate current client progress and status. A recommended time lapse of no more than 1 to 4 months is recommended (Dziegielewski, 2004). The social worker should prepare in advance for this meeting to continue and reaffirm previous measurement strategies. In this final phase, measuring practice effectiveness and reaching the stated outcomes typically involves a process designed to determine whether or to what extent mutually negotiated goals and objectives have been met. These changes need to be documented through concrete measurement that is indicative of client progress. Dziegielewski, Green, and Hawkins (2002, 2004) suggest that this process can be greatly facilitated by establishing clear-cut treatment contracts with clients who, in turn, provide a viable foundation for a variety of individual and/or group evaluation designs. Once the treatment agreement is in place, standardized instruments can be used as repeated measures to gather consistent data from baseline through termination and follow-up.

In summary, it is important to note, however, that no case plan is designed to be all-inclusive. Rather, each case plan is designed to provide the guidelines for effective documentation of the assessment and intervention process. Each case plan must be individualized for the client, outlining the specific problem behaviors and how each of these behaviors can be addressed. Once problems are identified and a case plan is being formulated, input from the client's support system needs to be included. This input can enhance communication between the client and his or her family members. Involving the family and support system in treatment plan formulation and application can be especially helpful and productive because at times individuals experiencing mental confusion and distortions of reality may exhibit bizarre and unpredictable symptoms. If support systems are not included in the intervention planning process, and the client's symptoms worsen, the client–family system environment may become characterized by increased tension, frustration, fear, blame, and helplessness. To avoid support systems that withdraw from the client, thereby decreasing the available support, family members and key support system members need to either be involved or at a minimum made aware of the treatment plan goals and objectives that will be utilized if the client consents to their involvement. Family education and supportive interventions for family and significant others can be listed as part of the treatment plan for an individual client. It is beyond the scope of this chapter to discuss the multiple interventions available to the family members; however, interested readers are encouraged to study the applications described in the remainder of this book.

RecordKeeping and the Problem-Oriented Record

Sound documentation is at the root of intervention success and clear problem-oriented case recording can facilitate this process. Traditionally, one of the most popular types of recording formats has been the problem-oriented recording (POR) (Dziegielewski et al., 2002, 2006). Still often used widely in health care or medical settings, this type of recording was originally formulated to encourage multidisciplinary and interdisciplinary collaboration and to train medical professionals (Dziegielewski, 2004). What most professionals report is that for multidisciplinary or interdisciplinary teams, helping professionals find that problem-oriented case documentation enables them to maintain documentation uniformity while remaining active within a team approach to care. For the evidence-based practitioner, this focus on the problem along with the clear outlining of attempts to bring about change fits well within this data-based framework.

To use POR from an evidence-based perspective, it must clearly emphasize accountability through brief and concise documentation of client problems, services, or interventions as well as client responses. Although there are numerous formats for problem-oriented case recording, the underlying principle is always to keep comments brief, concrete, measurable, and concise. This approach provides a relevant practitioner-friendly format that corresponds well to making connections to increased client caseloads, the use of rapid assessment instruments to measure problem behaviors, and implementing time-limited treatment options. Brief and problem-focused notes help to provide detailed summaries of the intervention progress. Generally, use of the POR is often based on agency choice as well as the need for accountability.

One element that all POR formats share is that all formats start with a problem list that is clearly linked to the behavioral-based biopsychosocial interventions (Dziegielewski, 2010a, 2010b). Data-based documentation related directly to the identified problem helps guide the case plan, allowing the social worker to focus on the strategies needed to address presenting problems and coping styles. Maintaining a clear focus on all documentation efforts helps to limit abstractions and vague clinical judgments. In addition, an inventory that reflects the current active problems to be addressed needs to be periodically updated. Therefore, when a problem is resolved, it can be crossed off the list with the date of resolution clearly designated. Note that the behavioral-based objectives that the evidence-based practitioner uses to describe the client problem are considered the basic building blocks for POR.

Although numerous POR formats for progress note documentation can be selected, the subjective-objective-assessment-plan (SOAP) is the most commonly used. The SOAP first became popular in the 1970s. In this format, the **S** (subjective) records the data relevant to the client's request for service and the things the client says and feels about the problem (Dziegielewski et al., 2002, 2004). This section allows some degree of clinical judgment and skilled diagnostic impression that may not be based on clear data. Some professionals prefer to document this information in terms of major themes or general topics addressed, rather than making specific statements about what the practitioner thinks is happening. Generally, in this section, intimate personal content or details of fantasies and process interactions should not be included. When charting in this section of the SOAP, the social worker needs to examine whether his or her statements could be open to misinterpretation. If statements are in fact vulnerable to misinterpretation or resemble a personal rather than professional reaction to the problem identified, these comments should not be included. For the evidence-based practitioner, this section will probably be the shortest and is provided to introduce the objective information to follow.

The **O** (objective) includes observable and measurable criteria related to the problem. These are symptoms, behaviors, and descriptors related to the client-focused problems observed directly by the worker during the assessment and intervention process. Here the independent and dependent variables are identified and described. In addition, some agencies, clinics, and practices have started to include client statements in this section as well. If a client statement is to be utilized as objective data, however, exact quotes must be used. For example, if in the session a client states that he will not harm himself, the practitioner must document exactly what the client has said and in the client's exact words how it relates to the behavioral outcome. What is said must be enclosed within quotation marks.

This section may also include the introduction of standardized assessment instruments designed to measure psychological or social functioning. As the notes progress, it makes sense to also include the results of these measures as well.

In each part of the objective section, clearly defined goals and objectives need to be linked to clear descriptors of what is happening. The frequency, intensity, and duration of each behavior are highlighted.

The **A** (assessment) includes the therapist's assessment of the underlying problems, which in the mental health setting might include a *DSM-IV-TR* multi-axial system. Since application of this framework is beyond the scope of this chapter, please see Dziegielewski (2010a) for more detail.

In **P** (plan), the practitioner records how treatment objectives will be carried out, areas for future interventions, and specific referrals to other services needed by the client. A clear behavioral assessment is needed to establish the plan to follow. The plan must also provide a method for follow-up or for tracking changes and time frames. This will allow the evidence-based practitioner to clearly document the changes and the time frames in which the changes occurred.

The traditional format of the SOAP has been extended in some settings to answer issues related to implementation and evaluation. To address this, new areas have been added to the original SOAP format (Dziegielewski 2010b). This extension, referred to as SOAPIE, identifies the first additional term as **I**, which stands for the *implementation* considerations of the service to be provided. Exactly how, when, and who will implement the service is explained.

In the last section, an **E** represents service provision *evaluation* (Dziegielewski, 2010a). This has become a popular addition to treatment plan formulation and development that can be tracked on the service note. Specific actions are evaluated that relate to the progress achieved after any interventions are provided. When treatment is considered successful, specific outcomes-based objectives established early in the treatment process are documented as progressing or checked off as attained.

In some agencies, a modified version of the SOAPIE has been introduced, referred to as SOAPIER. In this latest version, the **R** stands for the client's *response* to the intervention provided.

The SOAP is only one type of POR, yet regardless of the type of POR used, the same principles should always be applied. A second type of POR is the data, assessment, and plan (DAP) format. The DAP identifies only the most salient elements of a practitioner's client contact. Using the **D** (data), objective client data and statements are recorded that relate to the presenting problem and the focus of the therapeutic contact. The **A** is used to record the diagnostic assessment intervention from the multiaxial format, the client's reactions to the service and intervention, and the human-service worker's assessment of the client's overall progress toward the treatment goals and objectives. Specific information on all tasks, actions, or plans related to the presenting problem and to be carried out by either the client or the helping professional is recorded under **P** (plan). Also recorded under **P** (plan) is information on future issues related to the presenting problem to be explored at the next session, and the specific date and time of the next appointment (Dziegielewski, 2010a). Again, similar to the SOAP, the DAP format has undergone some changes. For example, some counseling professionals who generally use the DAP are now being asked to modify this form of recordkeeping to add an additional section. This changes the DAP into the DAPE and adds a section where documentation under the **E** reflects what type of educational and evaluative services have been conducted.

Two other forms of problem-based case recording formats often used in health and mental health setting are the problem, intervention, response, and plan (PIRP) and the assessed information, problems addressed, interventions provided, and evaluation (APIE). Similar to the SOAP and the DAP, a comparison structure is employed. All four of these popular formats of problem-oriented case recording have been praised for supporting increased problem identification and the standardization of how client behaviors and coping styles are reported. In effect, the formats provide a greater understanding of health and mental health problems and the various methods of managing them. This type of problem-oriented record brings the focus of clinical attention to an often neglected aspect of recording that involves the recognition of a client's problems by all helping professionals to quickly familiarize themselves with a client's situation. Utilizing a problem-focused perspective must go beyond merely recording information that is limited to the client's problems, because when the focus is limited to gathering only this information, important strengths and resources that clients bring to the therapeutic interview may not be validated. Furthermore, partialization of client problems presents the potential risk that other significant aspects of a client's functioning will be overlooked in treatment planning and subsequent practice strategy. Therefore, problem-oriented forms of case recording need to extend beyond the immediate problem, regardless of whether insurance reimbursement requires it (Dziegielewski, 2010a).

As the use of computer-generated notes continues to become more common, varying forms of problem-oriented case recording will be linked directly into computerized databases (Gingerich, 2002). In terms of convenience, this can mean immediate access to fiscal and billing information as well as client intervention strategy, documentation, and treatment planning. When working with computerized records, Hartsell and Bernstein (2008) suggest the following: (a) always address the difficulty of maintaining confidentiality when using electronic communications; (b) be aware that when recording client information on a hard drive or disk it needs to be stored in a safe and secure place; (c) use encryption software when possible; (d) discuss the possibility of electronic failure and what that means for record retrieval. Also, when working with electronic data systems, always maintain a secure backup system and be clear as to how the sanctity, privacy, and confidentiality of the records will be maintained. All practitioners should take the potential of computer theft or crash seriously and implement a safeguard policy in case this should ever happen. The convenience of records and information now being easily transmitted electronically produces one major concern. Since clinical case records are so easy to access and are portable, there is a genuine problem represented by the vulnerability of unauthorized access of the recorded information, and every precaution should be taken to safeguard the information that is shared. In addition, since clinical records are kept for the benefit of the client, access to the record by the client is generally allowed. When engaging in any type of disclosure or transfer to either the client or third parties, however, a written client consent form is usually obtained.

In closing, documentation in the case plan should always be clearly sequenced and easy to follow. If a mistake occurs, never change a summary note or intervention plan without acknowledging it. When changes need to be made to the clinical case record, the intervention plan, or any other type of case recording, clearly indicate that a change is being made by drawing a thin line through the mistake and dating and initialing it. Records that are legible and cogent limit open interpretation of the services provided. In addition, the mental health practitioner will always be required to keep clinical case records (including written records and computerized back-up files) safeguarded in locked and fireproof cabinets; often, after a service is terminated, many health and mental care facilities prefer to use archival types of storage systems such as microfiche or microfilm to preserve records and maximize space.

Conclusion

Helping human-service practitioners to become better equipped with problem identification and case-planning skills by utilizing an evidence-based perspective allows for a higher level of comfort and confidence with their ability to be efficient, effective, and accountable. This in combination with service coordination will help to provide standardization across the "boundaries of multiple systems on behalf of clients with serve and multiple service needs" (Bunger, 2010, p. 398). In addition to providing a clear record of the intervention, clear and concise documentation serves to protect the client, the professional worker, and the human-service agency. Since practitioners assist a variety of social and human-service agencies as well as other professionals with the treatment of clients, identifying client problems and providing clearly articulated case plans are critical because it is this written record that is often used to justify treatment for the clients served.

The evolution of evidence-based practice has changed the expectations of what should be contained in the case plan and the subsequent documentation effects that follow. Evidence-based practice principles go beyond general theoretical approaches and provide a procedural framework that uses scientific methodology along with qualitative and quantitative practice methods. Professional training in this area is essential, and practice application highlights the importance of uniting problem identification with the case plan using a process that clearly leads to the outcome.

Key Terms

Case plan

Global Assessment
   of Relational
   Functioning (GARF)

Global Assessment of
   Functioning (GAF)

Identified problem

Problem-oriented
   Record (POR)

Rapid Assessment
   Instrument (RAIs)

Reliability

SOAP note

Social and
   Occupational
   Functioning
   Assessment Scale
   (SOFAS)

Subjectivity

Treatment Plan:
   Treatment
   Objectives

Validity

Review Questions for Critical Thinking

1. Identify the key elements needed for effective documentation; what type of information should be included in a client's record?

2. Why is it imperative that social workers and other human-service workers utilize effective documenting skills in recordkeeping?

3. How is the service plan developed as an evidence based practitioner? Describe the steps for effective practice.

Online Resources

American Psychological Association: APA Style

This site is a valuable resource providing links and tutorials for those not familiar with APA style writing.

http://www.apastyle.org/index.aspx

This site offers specific guidelines (PDF) for documentation.

http://www.apa.org/practice/guidelines/record-keeping.pdf

National Association of Social Workers (NASW): http://www.naswdc .org/

This website has a wealth of information for the professional social worker.

http://www.naswdc.org/practice/clinical/default.asp

A list of links about documentation from the NASW site.

The National Institute of Mental Health: http://www.nimh.nih.gov/index .shtml

This website provides access to information regarding multiple sources in medical affairs, included but not limited to medical conditions, medications, patient resources, current and latest health news, and free web-based tools.

The Menninger Clinic: http://www.menningerclinic.com

The Menninger Clinic provides mental health information regarding treatment and interventions materials, education for graduate and advanced students in mental health, and educational materials for families and caregivers of people suffering from mental disorders.

Podcast

The Social Work Podcast: http://www.socialworkpodcast.com/socialwork podcast.xml

The site serves as a multifunctional and updated informational setup where current information can be obtained, utilizing multimedia functions, including Podcasts, where connection to iTunes (utilizing MP3) provides lectures on topics such as social work practice and psychopathology.

References

American Psychiatric Association. (2000). *Diagnostic and statistical manual of mental disorders* (4th ed., text rev.).Washington, DC: Author.

APA Guidelines for Practitioners. (2012). American Psychological Association (APA) Online. Available from http://www.apa.org/practice/guidelines/index.aspx

Babie, E. (2011). *The basics of social research* (5th ed.). Belmont, CA: Wadsworth, Cengage Learning.

Berghuis, D. J., & Jongsma, A. E. Jr., (Series Ed.). (2008). *The severe and persistent mental illness progress notes planner* (2nd ed.). Hoboken, NJ: Wiley.

Bergin, A. E. (1971). The evaluation of therapeutic outcomes. In A. E. Bergin & S. L. Garfield (Eds.), *Handbook of psychotherapy and behavior change* (pp. 217–270). New York, NY: Wiley.

Bloom, M., Fischer, J., & Orme, J. (2009). *Evaluating practice: Guidelines for the accountable professional* (6th ed.). Boston, MA: Allyn & Bacon.

Bunger, A. C. (2010). Defining service coordination: A social work perspective. *Journal of Social Service Research*, *36*, 385–401.

Corcoran, K., & Boyer-Quick, J. (2002). How clinicians can effectively use assessment tools to evidence medical necessity and throughout the treatment process. In A. R. Roberts & G. J. Greene (Eds.), *Social workers' desk reference* (pp. 198–204). New York, NY: Oxford University Press.

Cumming, S., Fitzpatrick, E., McAuliffe, D. McKain, S., Martin, C., & Tonge, A. (2007). Raising the Titanic: Rescuing social work documentation from the sea of ethical risk. *Australian Social Work*, *60*, 239–257.

Dust, B. (1996). Training needs. *Training and Development*, *50*, 50–51.

Dziegielewski, S. F. (2004). *The changing face of health care social work: Professional practice in managed behavioral health care*. New York, NY: Springer.

Dziegielewski, S. F. (2005). *Substance addictions: Assessment and intervention*. Chicago, IL: Lyceum Books.

Dziegielewski, S. F. (2006). *Psychopharmacology handbook for the non-medically trained*. New York, NY: Norton.

Dziegielewski, S. F. (2010a). *DSM-IV-TR in action*. Hoboken, NJ: Wiley.

Dziegielewski, S. F. (2010b). *Social work practice and psychopharmacology*. Hoboken, NJ: Wiley.

Dziegielewski, S. F., Green, C. E., & Hawkins, K. (2002). Improving clinical record keeping in brief treatment: Evaluation of a documentation workshop. *Brief Treatment*, *2*(1), 1–10.

Dziegielewski, S. F., & Leon, A. (2001). Time-limited case recording: Effective documentation in a changing environment. *Journal of Brief Therapy*, *1*, 51–56.

Dziegielewski, S. F., & Powers, G. T. (2005). Procedures for evaluating time-limited crisis intervention. In A. Roberts (Ed.), *Crisis intervention handbook* (3rd ed., pp. 742–774). New York, NY: Oxford University Press.

Dziegielewski, S. F., & Roberts, A. R. (2004). Health care evidence-based practice: A product of political and cultural times. In A. R. Roberts & K. R. Yeager (Eds.), *Handbook of practice-focused research and evaluation* (pp. 200–204). New York, NY: Oxford University Press.

Fischer, J., & Corcoran, K. (2007a). *Measures for clinical practice and research: A source book, Vol. 1: Couples and families and children* (4th ed.). New York, NY: Oxford University Press.

Fischer, J., & Corcoran, K. (2007b). *Measures for clinical practice and research: A source book: Vol. 2: Adults* (4th ed.). New York, NY: Oxford University Press.

Franklin, C. (2002). Developing effective practice competencies in managed behavioral health care. In A. R. Roberts & G. J. Greene (Eds.), *Social workers' desk reference* (pp. 3–10). New York, NY: Oxford University Press.

Gingerich, W. J. (2002). Computer applications for social work practice. In A. R. Roberts & G. J. Greene (Eds.), *Social workers' desk reference* (pp. 23–28). New York, NY: Oxford University Press.

Hartsell, T. L., Jr., & Bernstein, B. E. (2008). *The portable ethicist for mental health professionals: A complete guide to responsible practice* (2nd ed.). Hoboken, NJ: Wiley.

Jongsma, A. E., & Peterson, L. M. (2006). *The complete adult psychotherapy treatment planner* (4th ed.). Hoboken, NJ: Wiley.

Jongsma, A. E., Jr., (Series Ed.), Peterson, L. M., & McInnis, W. P. M., & Bruce, T. J. (Contributing Author). (2006). *The child psychotherapy treatment planner* (4th ed.). Hoboken, NJ: Wiley.

Kaczmarek, P., & Barclay, D. (1996). Systematic training in client documentation: Strategies for counselor educators. *Counselor Education and Supervision, 36,* 77–85.

Kagle, J. D., & Kopels, S. (2008). *Social work records* (3rd ed.). Long Grove, IL: Waveland Press.

Klott, J., & Jongsma, A. E. (2006). *The co-occurring disorders: Treatment planner.* Hoboken, NJ: Wiley.

Kreuger, L. W., & Neuman, W. L. (2005). *Social work research methods: Qualitative applications.* Boston, MA: Allyn & Bacon.

Leon, A. M., & Pepe, J. (2010). Utilizing a required documentation course to improve the recording skills of undergraduate social work students. *Journal of Social Service Research, 36,* 362–376.

Monette, D. R., Sullivan, T. J., & DeJong, C. R. (2005). *Applied social research: A tool for human services.* Belmont, CA: Books/Cole-Thompson Learning.

Mumm, A. M. (2006). Teaching social work students practice skills. *Journal of Teaching in Social Work, 26*(3/4), 71–89.

Nugent, W. R., Sieppert, J. D., & Hudson, W. W. (2001). *Practice evaluation for the 21st century.* Belmont, CA: Brooks/Cole-Thomson Learning.

O'Hare, T. (2005). *Evidence-based practices for social workers: An interdisciplinary approach.* Chicago, IL: Lyceum Books.

O'Leary, K. D., Heyman, R. E., & Jongsma, A. E., Jr., (Series Ed.). (2011). *The couples psychotherapy treatment planner* (2nd ed.). Hoboken, NJ: Wiley.

Oliver, P. H., & Margolin, G. (2009). Communication/problem-solving skills training. In W. T. O'Donohue & J. E. Fisher (Eds.), *General principles and empirically supported techniques of cognitive behavior therapy* (pp. 199–206). Hoboken, NJ: Wiley.

Poulin, J. (2010). *Strengths-based generalist practice: A collaborative approach* (3rd ed.). Belmont, CA: Wadsworth, Cengage Learning.

Rubin, A. (2008). *Practitioner's guide to using research for evidence-based practice.* Hoboken, NJ: Wiley.

Rubin, A. (2010). *Statistics for evidence-based practice and evaluation* (2nd ed.). Belmont, CA: Brooks/Cole.

Sheafor, B. W. (2011). Measuring effectiveness in direct social work practice. *Social Work 41,* 25–33.

Sidell, N. L. (2011). *Social work documentation: A guide to strengthening your case recording.* Washington, DC: NASW Press.

Whitlock, E. P., Orleans, T., Pender, N., & Allan, J. (2002). Evaluating primary care counseling interventions: An evidence-based approach. *American Journal of Preventive Medicine, 22,* 267–284.

Wiger, D. E. (2005). *The psychotherapy documentation primer.* Hoboken, NJ: Wiley.

Chapter 5
Case Management

Valerie Holton and Joseph Walsh

> The profession of social work is said to be uniquely positioned to undertake the challenges of case management, given its holistic perspective and its biopsychosocial framework for assessment. Is it possible for social work to develop a recognized professional expertise when dealing with such broad concerns?

While there is not a single, generally accepted definition of the term, *case management* can be defined as an approach to social service delivery that attempts to ensure that clients with multiple, complex problems and disabilities receive the services they need in a timely, appropriate fashion (Rubin, 1992). It is practiced in such fields as mental health, child welfare, aging and long-term care, alcohol and drug treatment, health care, and the public welfare system. Case managers, who may be social workers, nurses, psychologists, and members of other health care professions, may work independently or as members of coordinated teams. Service objectives in case management include continuity of care, accessibility, accountability, and efficiency. Many years ago, Roberts-DeGennaro (1987) observed that case managers must possess the traditional social work practice skills of casework, group work, and community organization, because any of these may take priority with clients in community systems. The concept of case management emerged in mental health literature during the 1970s, but the practice can be understood as the modern application of social casework techniques that have a century-old tradition in social work and nursing.

The case manager is responsible for service coordination and helping the client hold elements of the service system accountable for adequate service delivery. Two driving principles of case management practice are that clients tend to get lost or frustrated and may drop out of treatment without a central point of integration, and that the community contains many resources that can meet the needs of clients. These two principles sometimes conflict because improving the quality of care for vulnerable populations may be at odds with controlling the costs of such care (Frankel & Gelman, 2004).

The National Association of Social Workers (NASW; 2006) has established standards for case management that stress the importance of the case

---
The authors would like to thank Jessica Cann, MSW, for contributing her example of case management brokerage.

manager's appropriate knowledge base, educational background, and skill level. The case manager should work for the benefit of the client, involve the client in all levels of the case management process, hold client information as confidential, and participate in all levels of the service delivery system, including advocating for appropriate service delivery and evaluating services.

While case management can be utilized with a variety of client populations, the remainder of this chapter focuses on its uses with clients who have serious mental illnesses.

Models of Case Management

Case management can be organized in a variety of ways, depending on the nature of the client population, the host agency, and the financial and staff resources available. Moxley (1996) differentiates *system-driven* from *consumer-driven* case management. System-driven case management may be practiced in areas where practitioners must rely on limited outside services (such as medical care, job training, and recreation), whereas consumer-driven case management may be exercised in areas where many services are available in coordination with the practitioner's agency, and clients can choose from among them. In either situation, clients can be helped to experience *service empowerment*, or participation in service decisions and reciprocity in their relationships with case managers (Crane-Ross, Lutz, & Roth, 2006). Research has shown that service empowerment is a significant predictor of recovery outcomes across all models of case management.

Strengths-based case management focuses on needs assessments and goal setting that empower the client (Rapp, 2002). The focus is on client strengths rather than pathology. For example, people with major mental illnesses are valued as people who can continue to grow, learn, and reach goals, and interventions are based on client self-determination. The community is seen as providing a wealth of resources, and aggressive outreach is the preferred mode of intervention. The most important part of strengths-based case management is the engagement and relationship with the client. The relationship should be based on the social work value of unconditional positive regard and include the qualities of empathy, genuineness, and positive reinforcement. Rapp (1998) states that the case manager–client relationship must be purposeful, reciprocal, friendly, trusting, and empowering. It helps if the social worker meets the client in natural settings of the client's choice, maintains a conversational focus, jointly attends to concrete tasks, and delineates the roles that each member will play in the relationship. In this model, purposeful self-disclosure is viewed as being helpful in establishing a trusting relationship, as is modeling the appropriate expression of emotion, providing alternate views of how challenging situations can be handled, and normalizing the client's feelings or concerns. Accompanying clients to first-time appointments and helping them with new tasks can also alleviate anxiety and demonstrate the case manager's commitment to helping clients.

Person-centered planning is an approach to case management that is considered a promising practice for people with long-term needs due to mental illness, addiction, and developmental disabilities (Centers for Medicare and Medicaid Services, 2004). However, it is increasingly being used in services targeted to those with developmental disabilities (such as intellectual disability, autism spectrum disorders, and cerebral palsy). Like the strengths-based case management, person-centered planning focuses on assessments and goal setting that empower the client. The assessment identifies the strengths, capacities, preferences, needs, and goals of the client. The process is client-directed and involves family members and other supporters in establishing goals and identifying interventions and services to help achieve those goals. The key aspects of person-centered planning include community presence (the sharing of ordinary places that define community life), choice (in all matters), competence (the opportunity for the client to perform meaningful activities), respect, and community participation (Claes, Van Hove, Vandevelde, van Loon, & Schalock, 2010).

Consumer case management, also referred to as peer support, is a rapidly developing area of client-centered services (Craig, Doherty, & Jamieson-Craig, 2004). It occurs when "consumers" or "peers" (in this case, persons with mental illness) are employed as full-fledged case managers or aides for clients to assist them with obtaining needed social, vocational, financial, and other supports. The use of peers provides gainful employment for clients and also taps into the expertise of persons who have a unique appreciation for the challenges faced by persons with mental illness. In these programs, peers usually work under the supervision of another professional.

Some researchers and theorists have specified models of case management. While there is variety in how the models are described and differentiated, we summarize them into the following four models:

- The Broker Model
- Assertive Community Treatment
- Intensive Case Management With Individual Case Managers
- Clinical Case Management

The Broker Model

In the broker model, which is the most "basic" type of case management, individual case managers are responsible for connecting their clients to appropriate resources in the community. Case manager tasks include assessment, planning, linking, monitoring, and perhaps advocacy on behalf of the client (Walsh, 2002). Case managers who operate under the broker model do not have financial responsibility for clients and so may not assume responsibility for how well their referrals will result in desired service delivery (Austin & McClelland, 2002). For instance, a case manager might refer a client to receive therapy services; however, the client may not have a clear working relationship with the therapist and thus may have no influence on how that referral might be implemented. Nor does the case manager have the authority to negotiate the cost of that service.

Case Example: Hospital Broker

Jessica works in a university medical center as a hospital social worker in the spinal cord rehabilitation unit where there is a team of physical therapists, occupational therapists, recreation therapists, speech therapists, rehabilitation psychologists, nurses, doctors, and social workers. The role of the social worker is to help patients prepare for life outside of the unit. When the patient leaves the unit, the team needs to make sure his or her support system is in place to ensure safety and well-being. Jessica's job as a social worker/case manager involves planning for a patient's discharge by linking the patient and family with ongoing rehabilitative and medical resources in the community. To achieve this, Jessica completes a biopsychosocial assessment during the initial interaction to find out what the patient has in place and what is needed. Prior to discharge, Jessica checks in with the patient and family to see how they are mentally preparing for the next step and if there are any concerns about being able to follow through with any of her referrals. She offers to help clients and families if they have any difficulty with referral sources after discharge, but has no scheduled contacts with them.

Assertive Community Treatment

Assertive community treatment (ACT) is carried out in multidisciplinary teams with five or more members who share a caseload of clients with serious mental illness (Hangan, 2006). This model was initially developed in the late 1970s by Leonard Stein and Mary Ann Test in Madison, Wisconsin (Lehman et al., 2003; Test & Stein, 1985). Their initial experiment essentially moved the treatment team of the state hospital into the community setting. Rather than connecting their clients with services in the community, ACT staff attempt to provide the majority of the services themselves. All members are cross-trained to the extent possible and provide services to their clients in the community as opposed to meeting in office settings. Additionally, all team members are equally responsible for working with all the clients. It is a model of direct, intensive, and aggressive outreach to clients. The model emphasizes a person's strengths in adapting to community life and providing consultation and support to a person's natural support networks, including families, employers, peers, friends, and community agencies (Lehman et al., 2004; McReynolds, Ward, & Singer, 2002).

King (2006) lists the following as key features of ACT programs:

- A clear program identity and structured program processes;
- Team-based service delivery and responsibility for ensuring continuity and effectiveness;
- Mobile responsive services delivered in the home or local environment of the client;
- Extended hours service response and capacity to deal with crises at any time;
- High contact frequency (usually several times per week) that is not dependent on client initiative;

- Clinical, rehabilitation, and social support needs are closely integrated; and

- Close liaison with family members and other client supports.

The ACT model's philosophy of intervention has remained fairly constant over the years, although staff, client ratios, and resources vary across programs. The terms *programs of assertive community treatment* (PACT) and *assertive community treatment* (ACT) are frequently used interchangeably to describe this model; other terms include *enhanced community management* and *mobile intensive treatment* (NAMI, 2007).

Case Example: Community Treatment Team

Vicki, the mental health agency's treatment team leader, began her Monday as usual, calling the five-member team meeting to order at 8:30. Vicki had a master's degree in social work and was especially skilled at client assessment and linkage with financial aid services in the midwestern city. She maintained a highly professional demeanor and was known as the "best" team member with the administrative tasks of meeting other service providers, helping them understand the needs of clients, and emphasizing the cooperative relationship they could expect with the team. Paul was the housing specialist. Barbara, a registered nurse, conducted health assessments and had good relationships with medical personnel and pharmacists in the area. Jeff had a background in vocational counseling. Abby was the team's recreational specialist and loved to organize social activities for members of the team's caseload.

On this Monday morning, the team reviewed client "events" over the weekend. It had been Jeff's turn to be on call and he reviewed the six clients whom he had visited over the weekend, and how he had dealt with their needs, which ranged from needing cooking appliances to having lost a bottle of psychotropic medication. He had coordinated several of his activities with staff at the nearby hospital emergency services unit. Following this update, Vicki informed the team about the new referrals that were expected from the psychiatric hospital this week, and she made assignments to the team members regarding who would assume primary responsibility for entering those clients onto the team caseload and making the first community contacts. Barbara would arrange for their initial appointments with the agency physician. Before the meeting ended, Abby reminded staff of the picnic that was planned for later that week and for all staff to invite their clients to attend. When the meeting ended, all of the team members left the agency in their cars to begin making client home visits. Six clients would be transported that day to scheduled appointments in the community at the housing authority and social services departments.

Intensive Case Management With Individual Case Managers

This model of intensive case management (ICM) bears similarities to the ACT model except that it is delivered by one case manager rather than a team (King, 2006). This model may be utilized in agencies with relatively small numbers of overall staff, or in communities where there is not a high number of clients with mental illness. It goes well beyond the broker role in that the case manager is responsible for spending much time with clients, including being available, or arranging for another contact person's availability during evenings and weekends. The case manager also works primarily in the community to help clients successfully establish themselves in stable life structures. Using King's (2006) characteristics of ACT as a basis, ICM provides the same range of services except there is no team and the case manager cannot provide as many services to the clients himself or herself. Referrals are more common within this model, although unlike the broker model, the case manager will spend much time developing relationships with referral sources and following clients through their referral processes.

Case Example: "Mobile Home" Visitor

Family preservation services (FPS) provides time-intensive in-home counseling and case management services to families who have been identified as "at risk" for serious health, mental health, or social functioning problems. Social workers go to clients' homes three or four times per week, spending time with all family members to help them with problems that are considered to be serious and potentially long-term. An average visit is 2 or 3 hours long, and the full intervention process can take 6 months or more. Andy worked with the McCurdy family for a full year. The mother, her live-in boyfriend, two adolescent sons, and adolescent daughter came to the attention of several legal and human service agencies because of their physical violence with one another. The mother had filed assault charges against each of her sons, but she also initiated fights with them and with her daughter. The family had recently moved from another state into a small, two-bedroom trailer in an isolated rural area. The family members were estranged from each other and disconnected from the nearby community. FPS hoped to teach them alternative ways to work out conflicts.

The entire family was ambivalent about Andy's visits, which is typical of FPS clients. In-home services are highly invasive, so the social worker's engagement and relationship-building skills are essential. Andy's clinical assessment skills were also important in developing an intervention plan that would address each family member's psychosocial as well as material needs. The McCurdys made good progress during the months that followed through Andy's teaching, conflict mediation, cognitive-behavioral interventions, role-playing, and modeling activities. Andy also made decisions about appropriate social, educational, and vocational referrals to make for various members of the family. The McCurdys' use of violence fell markedly and they seemed to increase their sense of contentment with each other. They were able to step back and think about their behaviors more clearly and became better at controlling their impulses. Reports from the referring agencies, with whom Andy kept in regular contact, were positive. During the final months, Andy initiated a "step-down" process, in which he gradually reduced his amount of contact with the family.

Clinical Case Management

One type of case management that is closely associated with the individual intensive model is clinical case management. Clinical case management integrates elements of clinical social work and traditional case management practices, and is generally provided by a single professional (Walsh, 2000, 2002). The social worker combines the interpersonal skill of the psychotherapist with the creativity and action orientation of the environmental architect. The practice gives priority to the quality of the relationship between the client and social worker as a prerequisite for the client's personal growth. Further, due to the inherent problems with role confusion and authority in traditional case management, the client is considered to be best served if the worker functions as the primary therapeutic resource. Clinical case management draws in part on psychodynamic theories that help the social worker attend to transference, countertransference, and boundary issues, but also utilizes other intervention perspectives that draw from cognitive, behavior, and social support theories.

Clinical case management includes the following 13 activities within four areas of focus:

1. *Initial phase* — engagement, assessment, and planning.
2. *Environmental focus* — linking with community resources, consulting with families and caregivers, maintaining and expanding social networks, collaboration with physicians and hospitals, and advocacy.
3. *Client focus* — intermittent individual psychotherapy, independent living skill development, and client psychoeducation.
4. *Client-environment focus* — crisis intervention and monitoring. (Kanter, 1996a)

The client/case manager relationship provides a context in which the full range of medical, rehabilitative, educational, and social interventions can be effectively implemented (Buck & Alexander, 2006). The other clinical skills needed for long-term work with clients having mental illness include the ability to:

- Make ongoing judgments about the intensity of one's involvement with a client.
- Assess and recognize a client's fluctuating competence and changing needs.
- Titrate support so as to maximize a client's capacity for self-directed behavior.
- Differentiate the biological and psychological aspects of mental illness.
- Help family members cope with their troubled relative.
- Appreciate the effects of social factors on a client's sense of competence.
- Understand how clients both shape and internalize their environments.
- Appreciate a client's conscious and unconscious motives for behavior.
- Develop a longitudinal view of the client's strengths, limitations, and symptoms. (Harris & Bergman, 1988; Kanter, 1995, 1996a)

With this overview of current models of case management, we now consider how the modality has evolved over the past century.

Historical Background of Case Management

In many ways, social casework was the hallmark intervention of early social work practice. Over time, casework took on a pronounced mental health emphasis. In the late 1970s, a shift occurred, moving the field in the direction of community-based case management, stimulated in part by a concern over controlling the spiraling costs of caring for the chronically mentally ill. This led to an expansion of more proactive methods, such as assertive community treatment, which have proved to be more effective in promoting the enhanced functioning of the mentally ill. These developments are reviewed in the following sections.

Social Casework

Between 1890 and 1920, social casework was the hallmark of the young social work profession, which was then focused on alleviating the urban problems of poverty and illness. Its mediating and linkage functions included any activities designed to influence behavior and improve client welfare (Lubove, 1965). Mental health became a field of social work practice at this time as well due to the crowding of the large public institutions that had once held the promise of "curing" mental maladies. With the influence of Freud's writings during the 1920s, however, the treatment of mental illness in social work became more psychoanalytic and less social (Ehrenreich, 1985). Practitioners invested more of their professional energy into working with clients in the community who could benefit from long-term analytic therapies. The most seriously impaired clients still spent much time in state hospital facilities, and these were not well coordinated with community services (Fellin, 1996).

Since World War II, however, partly in response to demands for mental health care for war veterans, social welfare policy has been characterized by a gradual shift from the hospital to the community as the preferred locus of care for persons with mental illness (Grob, 1991). Federal initiatives culminated in the 1963 Community Mental Health Centers Act. Reformers anticipated that these centers would make effective mental health intervention accessible to all who needed it, with far less reliance on state hospitals. The appeal to economy, however, was equally strong in the evolution of community care. State hospitals were viewed as anachronistic institutions and drains on the public purse. There was hope that the mental health centers would result in public savings.

Until the mid-1970s, there was federal support for community mental health center development through matching grants with local communities. However, states and communities did not participate to the extent planned, and eventually the federal formula policy was terminated after fewer than half the projected 1,500 centers were established (Levine, 1981). The mental health centers came under attack from some professionals and family advocacy groups for serving clients with relatively minor emotional problems. As late as 1975, only 20% of mental health center clients had ever been hospitalized, and from 1970 to 1978 the percentage of persons with schizophrenia served by agencies actually dropped from 19% to 10% (Mechanic, 1999). Thus, community and state hospital systems coexisted without a mandate for a unified system of care. This resulted in a lack of central planning, organizational barriers, service duplications, and service gaps, despite community center availability, the new availability of psychotropic medication, increased attention to patients' rights, and the new federal money for persons with disabilities (Medicaid, Medicare, and Social Security Disability funds). By 1989, the average daily state hospital population was 130,000, but the rate of admissions had declined by only 10% since 1970, indicating a "revolving door" phenomenon (Mechanic, 1999).

Policy makers who valued the idea of community care became disillusioned with the ongoing difficulties clients with mental illness faced in trying to become established in their communities. By 1980, enthusiasm about the mental health centers was waning (Grob, 1991). Some of this was related to President Reagan's desire to reduce the scope of the federal government and institute discretionary state block grants for social services. Community mental health centers became a lower priority among state legislators because they were costly and voters demanded lower taxes.

Still, federal policy continued to be influential in addressing the perceived inadequacies of community mental health centers. The assumption that community care was more effective and less expensive than hospital care persisted. In 1963, 96% of public funding for persons with mental illness came from the states, but by 1985 only 53% was state provided, with 38% coming from federal programs (Torrey, 1988). Seventy percent (70%) of public mental health resources remained in hospitals, despite emerging research on the comparable effectiveness of community-based treatment alternatives.

Emergence of Community-Based Case Management

The emergence of community-based case management was spurred in part by National Institute of Mental Health policies introduced in 1978 to make support services available for clients who were not being adequately served through traditional agency systems (Turner & TenHoor, 1978). Community care problems at the time included a lack of clarity of mental health service system goals, fragmentation of responsibility for client interventions, the lack of a systematic approach to financing, inadequate agency commitments to clients, and a need for government leadership in planning for mental health service delivery. Case management was identified as a means of enhancing assistance to clients with mental illness, including greater access to entitlements, crisis stabilization services, psychological rehabilitation and other support services, medical care, support to families and friends, and protection of clients' rights.

The Community Mental Health Centers Act had bypassed state governments, but by 1981 most control of programs was returned to the states in the form of block grants. The Omnibus Budget Reconciliation Act, a product of President Reagan's antifederalist inclinations, expanded the state's power to make choices about how certain federal funds would be allocated (Rochefort & Logan, 1989). Community centers became more dependent on state funding policies. By 1991, 64% of center funds were coming from the states in the form of revenues, block grants, Medicaid, and user fees. These developments made the enhancement of service for persons with mental illness, with the hope of cost reductions, the top priority of state mental health directors (Ahr & Holcomb, 1985). Financial incentives were expected to reduce state mental hospital use, resulting in innovative case management programs at the local level.

Innovative program developers, such as Test and Stein (1985) in Wisconsin, demonstrated that community-based programs characterized by assertive case management could reduce psychiatric hospitalizations and improve the social functioning of persons with mental illness, allegedly at a lower cost. Their interventions acknowledged the chronic nature of mental illness and focused on rehabilitation rather than cure. Service goals focused on normalizing the lives of clients by providing them with case management support in securing jobs, housing, socialization opportunities, and access to medical care. This approach was implemented in other sites across the country.

Many state departments, impressed by the efforts of community support programmers and faced with the need to reduce hospital costs, turned over considerable budgeting and planning responsibility to community agencies. The State Comprehensive Mental Health Service Plan Act of 1986 was a federal initiative requiring states to develop and implement plans for achieving an organized system of community-based care for persons with mental illness. A 1990 amendment required the same coordination of children's services (Davis, Yelton, Katz-Leavy, & Lourie, 1995).

With the policy shift to community care, case management gained momentum as a favored treatment modality, with its potential to help clients develop productive lifestyles. Through case management, clients could be linked with informal supports (friends, neighbors, recreation centers, etc.) as well as with formal systems. The social value of community care was one rationale for shifting money from the state to the community mental health centers; such care was also ostensibly less expensive. Early experiments in community care tended to confirm this, but later the issue of reduced cost was challenged (Mechanic, 1999). Case managers came under pressure from administrators to keep out of the hospital even those clients who might benefit from a short in-patient experience. In geographic areas with few alternative funding sources, agencies had difficulty providing supportive services to clients even when hospital stays were reduced. Still, by 1996 there were 397 ACT programs in the United States (Mueser, Bond, Drake, & Resnick, 1998). As described earlier, other kinds of case management programs shared some characteristics of the ACT model.

The Present

Mental illness continues to represent a major social problem in the United States as evidenced by the numbers of people who experience it and who endure its associated costs. The precise prevalence of mental illness is unknown, but the National Institute of Mental Health (National Institute of Mental Health, 2006a, 2006b) estimates that 26.2% of Americans over 18 years old suffer from a diagnosable mental disorder (not including substance abuse). In 2004, 57.7 million people suffered from a mental health disorder. The most significant burden of mental illness is experienced by the 6% of the adult population who suffer from a serious mental illness. Each year, about 6.7% of adults (14.4 million) suffer from Major Depressive Disorder and 2.6% (5.7 million) suffer from Bipolar Disorder. About 18% (40 million) of adults experience Anxiety Disorders, and these frequently co-occur with depressive and substance abuse disorders. Additionally, 1.1% (2.4 million) adults suffer from Schizophrenia in a given year. Nearly half (45%) of those with any mental disorder meet criteria for two or more co-occurring disorders. One in 10 children suffer from a mental disorder severe enough to cause some level of impairment.

The concept of managed care has also advanced in response to this problem. Managed care refers to organizational arrangements that alter treatment decisions that would otherwise be made by clients or providers (Mechanic, Schlesinger, & McAlpine, 1995). Its goals are to contain costs, efficiently allocate resources, monitor care, and improve the quality of care. All models of managed care seek to control *who* shall receive *what services* with *what frequency*, over *what duration* and from *what providers* (regarding discipline and experience), in pursuit of *what outcomes* (Sherman & Dahlquist, 1996). In an ideal situation, the client receives the best care for the fewest dollars. The philosophy of managed care is quite consistent with, and supportive of, the service modality of case management.

The primary reason for the shift of public mental health systems toward forms of managed care is Medicaid program cost increases (Edgar, 1996). Although 16% of Medicaid recipients have physical or mental disabilities, they account for 32% of Medicaid costs. Elders and disabled people make up 30% of recipients and 70% of costs, with the largest proportion of funds going to nursing homes. Certain underinsured groups might also benefit from managed care strategies. For example, persons with mental illness who live in rural areas face difficulties in receiving adequate mental health care because they have limited access to service providers. Health care reform may benefit these clients, as consolidating services within a benefits package might encourage their use of alternative treatment to crisis care (Shelton & Frank, 1995).

Case management interventions with persons having mental illness have the capacity to streamline service delivery in keeping with managed care objectives. Managed care providers support only short-term hospitalization and greater client use of community support or recovery groups when warranted (Davis, 1996). The modality can ration service while efficiently using formal and informal resources. The case manager's involvement of significant others (friends and family) in a client's treatment is another way of reducing the amount of professional service that must be provided. Further, the process of carefully coordinating intervention plans with clients and other professionals can reduce projected costs of treatment (Kanter, 1996b).

Cost control is not synonymous with low-quality care, but the ability to provide high-quality service in a managed care context is another argument for skilled case management. Costs should not override the value of helping clients achieve a decent overall quality of life, defined as one's life satisfaction, living situation, daily activities, family and social relations, financial status, occupation, safety, and physical and mental health status (Lehman, 1988). Some policy makers assert that there should be special managed care corporations for persons with mental illness based on case management models of intervention (Scheffler, Grogan, Cuffel, & Penner, 1993). Eligibility for such an HMO would be determined by criteria including diagnosis, level of disability, and duration of illness. In this way, case managers, working individually or on teams, might successfully integrate services and provide effective continuity of care for the most disabled clients.

A recent trend toward cost containment and expanded service quality is the privatization of case management (Merrick, Horgan, & Garnick, 2006). Historically, case management has been provided through public agencies and staff through "purchase of service" agreements. However, in some states Medicaid dollars now "follow the client" rather than being given directly to agencies, enabling private case management agencies to compete with public providers. Many people consider this a positive development because competition is promoted.

There has been an increased focus on integrating mental health care with care of other chronic conditions. Chronic conditions are those that last a year or more and require ongoing medical attention or limit activities of daily living and include physical medical conditions (e.g., arthritis, asthma, chronic respiratory conditions, HIV, and hypertension) as well as substance abuse and addiction disorders, mental illness, cognitive impairment disorders, and developmental disabilities (U.S. Department of Health and Human Services, 2010). More than one in four Americans have two or more chronic conditions (Anderson, 2010). Those with multiple chronic conditions account for much of the growth in health care spending—66% of total health care spending is directed towards the approximately 27% of those with multiple chronic conditions (Anderson, 2010). In response, the Patient Protection and Affordable Care Act encourages the use of case management and care coordination as a means to contain costs and expand service quality, particularly for those with chronic conditions and multiple chronic conditions. At this time, it is not clear what impact the new law will have on case management services, but it is expected that it will facilitate the development and evaluation of new approaches to case management services (Meek, 2012; U.S. Department of Health and Human Services, 2010).

Case management, then, has "face validity" as a practice that can maximize clients' adaptations to community life and also contain the costs of health care. In the next section, we see if these goals in fact are achieved.

Summary of Current Evidence-Based Information on Case Management

Given the enthusiasm for case management programs among policy makers, it is not surprising that government and academic organizations have sponsored much evaluation research on the modality. The focus of these evaluations is both on the process of implementation and client outcomes. Appropriate research questions include the following:

- What clients can be best served with case management?
- How can its implementation be assessed?
- Which of its many components are most crucial?
- How can it be modified to meet the needs of special populations?
- Is it more effective than other models of service?
- Can clients eventually move from more to less intensive forms of care? (Drake & Burns, 1995)

Implementation Research

Process evaluation is important because administrators need to know whether the services provided match those that are prescribed. For example, case managers do not always function in the ways program developers intend because of the unpredictable effects of the service environment on practice (Floersch, 2002). Perhaps the most intensive evaluation of a community support system program to date was made through the Robert Wood Johnson Foundation Program on Chronic Mental Illness, conducted in nine major cities across the United States in the late 1980s and early 1990s. The program's five goals were to ensure continuity of care, create a flexible financing system, develop a range of housing options, provide a range of psychosocial and vocational rehabilitation supports, and improve client outcomes (Morrissey et al., 1994). This was primarily a service system intervention, focused on the development of local mental health authorities.

The research team concluded that a local authority can be created, and the continuity of case management improved in all sites, but it was more difficult to document improvements in client outcomes (Lehman, Postrado, Roth, McNary, & Goldman, 1994). They found that structural change reforming mental health services for persons with serious mental illness was not sufficient by itself to produce improvements in clients' quality of life (Goldman, Morrissey, & Ridgely, 1994). That is, no direct correlation exists between case management program implementation and improved quality-of-life outcomes. Devising strategies for helping clients achieve their goals requires ongoing financial investments from administrators and policy makers, as well as the creative ideas of skilled case managers.

Outcome Research

Research on the effects of case management on client outcomes dates back to the early 1980s. Initially, case management services were compared with "traditional," or office-bound, interventions. Draine (1997) reviewed eight experimental studies conducted between 1981 and 1993 and noted that while early studies of case management focused on broad models of community care, research over time has focused on narrower applications of the modality, including those for special populations. Case management has advanced from a generic approach to a range of different applications to special client circumstances. By 1999, the comparative impact of types of case management programs became more of a focus for study. This is because of the great variability found in programs with regard to staffing, types of clients, and resources (Mueser et al., 1998). In all instances, results have been mixed for a variety of outcome indicators such as costs, use of hospitals, client vocational status, and life satisfaction. These results do not necessarily reflect on the value of case management; rather, they suggest that researchers need to refine methodologies and distinguish between the activities of case managers in different sites.

Several meta-analyses have found encouraging results for all types of case management. Gorey, Leslie, Morris, Carruthers, John, and Chacko (1998) conducted a meta-analysis of 24 studies published between 1980 and 1996 and concluded that 75% of clients who participate in case management programs do better than clients who do not. Positive outcomes were noted in the areas of functional status, rehospitalization, quality of care, cost of care, range of services received, emergency room visits, intervention compliance, social networks, and jail time. They found no differences, however, among models. In a recent review of 75 studies, Marshall and Lockwood (2003) found that both ACT and other types of case management were more effective than other forms of intervention in helping clients stay in contact with services, spend fewer days in the hospital, secure employment, and express life satisfaction. There were no clear differences, however, in measures of mental status and social functioning. Case management was superior to other interventions with regard to client use of hospitalization, but differences were not clear on the other measures.

Reviewers have tended to find that client gains persist only as long as comprehensive services are continued. This raises the question as to whether clients are acquiring skills and resources that promote permanent improvement or are showing short-term gains reflective of intensive support. We now look more closely at evaluations of particular types of case management programs and their impact on clients.

Assertive Community Treatment/Intensive Case Management

Studies have consistently demonstrated the efficacy of the ACT model in both improving the living conditions for persons with mental illness and reducing symptoms and the length of hospitalizations (Bond, Drake, Mueser, & Latimer, 2001; Lehman, Dixon, Kernan, DeForge, & Postrado, 1997). Gains in both quality of life and functional status are also frequently reported as outcomes (Dixon, 2000). A recent systematic literature review of 38 studies by Dieterich, Irving, Park, & Marshall (2010) concluded that clients receiving ACT services were significantly more likely to remain in treatment, experience improved general functioning, find employment, not be homeless, and experience shorter hospital stays. There was also a suggestion that such clients had a lesser risk of death and suicide. In an earlier review of 75 studies, Marshall and Lockwood (2003) found that both ACT and case management were more effective than other forms of intervention in helping clients stay in contact with services, spend fewer days in the hospital, secure employment, and experience life satisfaction. There were no clear differences, however, in measures of mental status and social functioning. ACT was superior to case management in client use of hospitalization, but differences on the other measures were not clear. Phillips and colleagues (2001) found similar results: that ACT improves the quality of life and increases housing stability for people experiencing the most severe and persistent forms of mental illness.

Mueser et al. (1998) reviewed the literature on ACT programs with serious mental illness, including 75 studies that were either comparative studies or single programs with pre- and posttest measures. Increased housing stability was indicated in 9 out of 11 studies. A decrease in the amount of time spent in the hospital occurred in 14 of 22 studies. Few of the studies compared models with each other. Case management was effective in reducing hospital time, improving housing stability, and, to a lesser degree, reducing symptoms and improving quality of life. It had little effect on social functioning, arrests, time in jail, and vocational functioning. The available evidence for ACT also suggests that it is a less costly intervention for high mental-health-service users, and participants report high levels of satisfaction with services (Mueser & McGurk, 2004; Lauriello, Bustillo, & Keith, 1999). Less evidence exists for demonstrating ACT's impact on social functioning and competitive employment (Lauriello, Lenroot, & Bustillo, 2003).

Rapp and Goesha (2004) examined 21 case management studies employing quasi-experimental or experimental designs to identify the common denominators of intervention that produced statistically significant positive outcomes for people with psychiatric disabilities, including persons with schizophrenia. They concluded that the strengths model of case management demonstrated desired impacts on nonhospitalization outcomes, such as symptoms, housing, social functioning, vocational, quality of life, leisure time, and social contacts. They found the simpler broker model of case management, which relies only on indirect service coordination, to be ineffective.

While ICM has been widely considered to be an research-based and cost-effective form of service to people struggling with severe mental health disorders, recent studies have begun to show a decrease in its effectiveness. King (2006) used a narrative analytic procedure to analyze five independent studies from the United States, United Kingdom, Australia, and the Netherlands. Surprisingly, he found that none of the studies reported significant differences in frequency of acute hospital admission between ICM and usual care. He also found that an additional three studies found mixed results regarding the impact of ICM on service costs. Overall, King asserts that while the first and second generation of studies found benefits for the use of ICM, more current studies are finding lesser effects. Similarly, program costs are either not significantly different or are more costly than usual care unless usual care includes lengthy hospital admission. In conclusion, King encourages the use of ICM for clients who consume about 50 days or more of hospitalization per year, when standard case management does not allow for flexible and assertive treatment, and when resources from inpatient services can be shifted to ICM.

Clinical Case Management

When compared to standard care, clinical case management has shown mixed results. When compared with no case management, clinical case management is more effective for people who have been hospitalized but are not dependent on substances (Havassy, Shopshire, & Quigley, 2000). Another set of researchers found that clinical case management significantly improved the substance-dependent client outcomes on alcohol use, medical status, employment, family relations, and legal status (McLellan et al., 1999). The addition of clinical case management to other therapy services has also been shown to be beneficial. For instance, Miranda, Azocar, Organista, Dwyer, and Areane (2003) found that the use of clinical case management with cognitive-behavior treatment for impoverished, depressed patients improved retention rates and outcomes, especially for the Spanish-speaking clients.

Ziguras and Stuart (2000) conducted a meta-analysis to study the effectiveness of case management based on 44 published studies between 1980 and 1998, specifically to compare clinical case management and ACT outcomes. For both modalities, similar positive outcomes were reported with regard to family satisfaction with services, family burden, and cost of care, compared to other interventions.

Specialized Programs

Since people who are experiencing addiction problems often have multiple other problems in their lives that need to be addressed concurrently with their addiction, case management is receiving growing attention in substance abuse services. Research has shown that case management increases retention that is associated with better outcomes (SAMHSA, 1998, 2005;

Vanderplasschen, 2006). One model of case management used in substance abuse services is Reinforcement-Based Treatment (RBT). Under that module, case management is intensive, comprehensive, features outreach, and emphasizes direct skill building. It also involves a strong therapeutic relationship that adapts a nonconfrontative motivational stance. Additionally, at least 25% of the case management activities are conducted outside of the office and there is greater structure in the beginning of treatment. The effectiveness of case management in substance abuse services, regardless of the model, depends on staff training, effective communication between the case managers and other professional staff, regular supervision, administrative support to clients for case management services, and use of tested protocols (Tuten, Jones, Schaeffer, & Stitzer, 2012).

There has been an increased focus on case management for those who have co-occuring severe mental illness and substance use disorders. The Substance Abuse and Mental Health Services Administration (SAMHSA) reports that 20% of those with a mental illness in 2011 also met the criteria for substance dependence or abuse (as compared with 6.1% among those without a mental illness). The rate of co-occurring substance abuse disorders is even higher for those with a serious mental illness (25.2%) (SAMHSA, 2012). In a meta-analysis of 15 empirical studies of interventions with clients who have dual diagnoses of mental illness and substance abuse, it was found that intensive case management was associated with the greatest effect size, and that smaller effect sizes were found for standard practices (Dumaine, 2003). Interestingly, there were no correlations found between levels of practitioner training or staff-to-client ratios and client outcomes. Jerrell and Ridgely (1995) compared the effectiveness of a 12-step, behavioral skills management program with a case management program for persons with the dual disorders of mental illness and substance abuse. While clients in the behavior skills intervention functioned best overall, both programs offered useful interventions and could be effectively combined.

Several case management models have been used effectively in interventions for people who have mental illness and are homeless. Calsyn (2003) found that a modified ACT intervention was more effective in finding stable housing for homeless individuals who were mentally ill than the drop-in center, outpatient treatment, and brokered case management. Those clients also expressed greater satisfaction with the ACT intervention. In the NIMH McKinney Project, 894 homeless mentally ill adults in four cities were exposed to rehabilitation, assertive community treatment, or intensive case management services, depending on which model was offered in each city (Shern et al., 1997). Though the specific intervention models differed, all of them used teams of case managers and assertive outreach. The project report noted a 47.5% increase in individuals living in community housing among those who received the intervention. Additionally, 78% of clients had been housed in permanent sites by the end of the program. While the focus of this study was on housing outcomes for those who were homeless, the multisite project did a randomized experimental design in concluding that the services were effective. As with other studies of case management, residential stability, independence, and daily life functions seemed to improve with the duration of service provision.

In a review of 16 controlled outcome evaluations of housing and support interventions for people with mental illness who have been homeless, Nelson, Aubry, & Lafrance (2007) found that all were able to reduce homelessness and psychiatric hospitalizations as well as support people in getting connected to and utilizing other services. The best outcomes for housing stability were found in programs that combined housing with supports (often referred to as supportive housing), followed by ACT alone, and then ICM programs alone. Studies of ACT alone and ICM alone reported a greater impact on quality of life and overall well-being than supportive housing programs.

Housing First is an intervention for people who have mental illness and who are homeless. It combines scattered-site, community-based housing, with support services through ACT. A unique feature of the module is that there are no prerequisites for sobriety. Evaluation studies have found that participants in Housing First programs are placed in housing at higher rates and demonstrate greater housing stability than those in the standard-care programs (Padgett, Gulcur, & Tsemberis, 2006; Stefanic & Tsemberis, 2007; Tsemberis, Gulcur, & Nakae, 2004).

Macias, Kinney, Farley, Jackson, and Vos (1994) studied the combined effects of case management and psychosocial rehabilitation services (including scheduled daily activities, staff assistance with social activities, and counseling) to case management alone, and found that the experimental group demonstrated better mental and physical health, fewer mood or thought problems, a higher sense of well-being, and less family burden. The two types of service were mutually supportive. Walsh (1994) compared two variations of a single case management program (in one clients received group interventions, and in the other they received individual interventions) with regard to natural social support outcomes. The clients receiving group interventions developed more extensive friendship networks.

The literature also includes examples of consumers working as advocates or peer specialists on case management teams. Solomon and Draine (1995) report on the 1-year outcomes of a randomized trial of consumer case management with 91 clients with serious mental illness using a pre- and posttest experimental design. They found that consumers who received services from a consumer case management team had the same outcomes as consumers who received services from a nonconsumer team on quality of life and various clinical and social outcomes such as housing, homelessness, size of social network, and level of functioning, and behavioral symptoms. Dixon, Krauss, and Lehman (1994) reported on the experience of employing two full-time consumer advocates as part of an experimental ACT team that provided services to persons who were homeless and had a severe mental illness. Consumer-advocates served as role models for recovery and played an important role in the engagement of clients, and sensitizing team staff to consumer experiences. Felton et al. (1995) examined 104 clients served by teams that included these peer specialists and found a reduction in the number of major life problems experienced and greater improvement in multiple areas of quality of life.

Cost Containment

Policy makers and agency administrators are concerned with how well case management services achieve the goals of cost containment and service quality. Scott and Dixon (1995) reviewed 13 major studies conducted between 1981 and 1994 and concluded that assertive community treatment clearly reduces the rates and duration of hospitalization, and may be less costly over the short-term than other service approaches. Still, client improvements in community functioning and resource access were not achieved in all studies, and program costs seem to increase in the long run. Research findings across sites may differ because programs are modified when transferred from one setting to another. One theme across studies is that, with new programs, the amount of time required to make significant differences in the lives of clients may be 2 years or more. The authors recommend that family well-being be adopted as an additional outcome indicator, and that researchers include the perspectives of the client, family, and case manager as data sources.

A recent study examined the impact of ICM in reducing the rates of psychiatric rehospitalization and costs among high-risk patients within 6 months of discharge from a psychiatric hospital. Those who received ICM were significantly less likely to be hospitalized during that time period (22% of the ICM group as compared to 50% of the control group). Inpatient psychiatric costs were $4,982.90 lower for those who received ICM than the control group. Significant savings were also found for inpatient substance abuse costs and psychiatric emergency department costs. After factoring in program costs, it was estimated that the ICM services contributed to approximatly $1,500,000 in cost savings over the 6-month period (Kolbasovsky, Reich, & Meyerkopf, 2010).

Several studies have demonstrated that "capitated" case management programs can control health care costs for persons with mental illness. In a New York study, clients in one program used the psychiatric hospital less than a control group of clients receiving free-for-service case management, with no observed differences in symptoms or functional status (Cole, Reed, Babigham, Brown, & Fray, 1994). Differences in case manager behavior in the two groups appeared to result from the flexibility in client care made possible by the capitation system. That system inspired case managers to develop new services, and case managers became more adept at crisis intervention. Program costs were reduced by 13.8% in year 1 and 14.5% in year 2 of the capitated program. In a New Hampshire study, fee-for-service case management was compared with an approach that confined capitation with fee-for-service schemes to evaluate the impact of flexibility on community-based treatment (Clark, Drake, McHugo, & Ackerson, 1995).

Results indicated a shift from office to community-based practice in the capitation group, although total case management time provided by the groups did not differ. It was not apparent whether these changes had an impact on client outcomes. McCrone, Beecham, and Knapp (1994) compared case management costs with those in a more traditional community psychiatric nursing service in Britain. They identified short-term savings (on hospital care, community health and mental health services, education, law enforcement, social care services, employment services, and housing) with the innovative program, but these did not persist beyond 6 months, implying that the institution of new community services is not inexpensive.

Limitations of the Evidence

Several methodological limitations are evident in the previous studies. First, the independent variable of case management is difficult to define clearly enough to make comparisons across studies. Given the reliance on links with other service providers, the case managers, the programs, or the adjunctive community service, it might be useful to evaluate each of these components distinctly. Further, researchers have tended to overlook the impact of individual case manager's skill on service outcomes. Because case management was initially conceptualized rather generically, and is frequently delivered in teams, it is not often considered that differences in outcomes may be due to individual case managers. The work of Ryan, Sherman, and Judd (1994) is one exception to this trend. They studied the implementation of three community support programs and found that, while all were effective, case managers themselves significantly influenced client outcomes when the type of service was controlled.

One critique of the PACT approach suggests that the research is biased by study authors who support the program philosophy, and that evaluators may be confusing workers' efforts for clients' efforts. That is, some positive outcomes may be due to administrators refusing some services such as hospitalization to clients as an option, and practitioners may be coercing clients to behave in ways that are consistent with program values. In summary, ACT programs and other forms of intensive community intervention for persons with schizophrenia do produce positive outcomes, but some questions remain as to the influence of resource availability (fewer hospital beds, more short-term crisis residences) and the more pervasive presence of case managers in clients' lives.

Implications for Social Work on Micro, Mezzo, and Macro Levels

Based on the previous research review, we now outline some implications for case management at three systems levels. The micro level of practice refers to direct service delivery to clients. The mezzo level reflects operations at the agency or local system level, while the macro level refers to the larger policy level.

Micro Level

Because the practice of case management involves many services provided by many agency practitioners in distinctive community service systems, it is difficult to confidently generalize findings from one program to another program. For this reason, it is important to acknowledge the role of the individual case manager in helping programs meet overall objectives and helping clients to meet their goals. In short, people deliver services, not programs. At the micro level, it is important to utilize highly skilled case managers who will have access to ongoing supervision, training, and continuing education opportunities. Case managers also need to be given the flexibility to titrate their activities to address the particular characteristics of their clients and community systems (Floersch, 2002).

Mezzo Level

Agency administrators need to be aware that case management practice is often stressful, frustrating, and conflict-riddled. Administrators need to be able to provide their case managers with an agency atmosphere that is supportive of their work, concretely values their work (via salaries, benefits, recognition, advancement opportunities), and actively deals with the possibility of worker burnout. While the benefits to clients and public budgets are clear, the short half-life of case managers is also well known (Frankel & Gelman, 2004). Administrators can help to support the work of case managers by offering competitive compensation packages, agreeable working conditions, adequate agency material supports, close access to referral providers such as agency physicians, reasonable caseload sizes, and opportunities for professional advancement. Recently, Glisson, Dukes, and Green (2006) have developed an availability, responsiveness, and continuity organizational intervention strategy to minimize caseworker turnover and improve the working climate and cultures in one case management system.

Macro Level

All policy makers hope that their case management programs are effective across a range of client goals that include quality of life, and that those programs are cost-effective in comparison to treatment alternatives. Given the various ways in which case management programs "play out" in different service systems, it is still hard to understand *what works* for *what clients* under *what circumstances*. Further, when a program is implemented, it cannot be assumed that it will unfold in precisely the manner that the policy makers have intended. Policy makers should ensure that case management programs are available in all localities for persons with mental illness, but they should be hesitant about promoting "exact" replications from one service setting to another. Further, the interests of cost containment and quality of life may best be achieved if policy makers allow for competitive markets to develop along the lines of privatization as well. It seems that this can be best achieved if the dollars follow the client, rather than being provided to various providers in purchase of service agreements.

Limitations

Case management is thriving as a method of service delivery that spans many client populations, but it does seem to have several inherent limitations. Case managers possess only a modest level of authority in some community service systems. If the case manager is responsible for linking clients with a variety of service providers, it follows that he or she should have some authority over how those services are delivered, including decision making about which are adequate. But though case managers generally have college degrees in a variety of human service professions, many do not have graduate degrees, which tends to limit their recognized authority in interdisciplinary work. For example, a case manager might decide that a certain vocational counselor's work with a given client is for some reason inappropriate. Should the case manager approach the counselor about changing the treatment modality? Many providers would question whether a professional with lesser credentials should make judgments about the quality of his or her work, but the case manager's monitoring and evaluation of services are considered to be essential roles.

Other limitations of the approach include unclear expectations for job performance and problems with attrition (McClelland, Austin, & Schneck, 1996). The case management modality risks failure because of such issues as role ambiguity, inadequate resources, a lack of administrative authority, and low salaries. Case managers function best when their roles are clearly delineated, and opportunities for professional growth and advancement within their positions might enhance retention and job satisfaction.

Caseload size is often cited as a determining factor of the nature of case manager activity. Caseloads generally range from 15 to 50 clients per worker (Rothman & Sager, 1998). Rose and Moore (1995) point to the irony that as the complexity of client needs increases, caseload size also tends to increase, and educational standards for employment are lowered.

Conclusion

The practice of case management has become a professionally and politically preferred means of providing and coordinating social services to clients with multiple needs. Even as social service delivery becomes more streamlined and unified, there will always be a need for professionals who are adept at assessing client's broad needs and knowing how to pull together those services in complex social environments. The profession of social work has always been uniquely positioned to undertake the challenges of case management, given its holistic perspective on people and its biopsychosocial framework for assessment. Developing systems of care that are specifically effective with clients of various needs in various service systems will always be a challenge for programmers and administrators, and clients will be best served if social workers are at the forefront of those processes.

Key Terms

Assertive community treatment

Broker model

Clinical case management model

Consumer case management

Strengths-based case management

Review Questions for Critical Thinking

1. Is it possible for a social worker to be equally skilled in attending to a consumer's micro, mezzo, and macro concerns?

2. It is sometimes said that for effective interprofessional practice to be delivered to a consumer, the case manager must be the focal point of all professional activities. Is this realistic, given social work's status as a profession? How can social workers develop such a central role in different settings?

3. What are some of the benefits and limitations (if any) of consumer case management?

4. What are some practical ways that social workers can evaluate the quality and effectiveness of their own (or their team's) case management practices?

Online Resources

National Association of Social Workers (2012)—NASW Standards for Social Work Case Management: www.socialworkers.org/practice/standards/sw_case_mgmt.asp

Includes definitions, goals, tasks, functions, and 10 standards for practice.

Social Work Best Practice Healthcare (2012): Social Work Best Practice Healthcare Case Management Standards

www.sswlhc.org/docs/swbest-practices.pdf

Includes information about definitions, education and training, the scope of services for case management, and quality of care indicators.

The Case Management Society of America (2012): http://www.cmsa.org

This is a leading membership association providing professional collaboration across the health care continuum to advocate for clients' well-being and improved health outcomes by fostering case management growth and development. The association provides evidence-based tools and resources.

The Substance Abuse and Mental Health Services Administration (2012): http://www.samhsa.gov

SAMHSA works to improve the quality and availability of substance abuse prevention, alcohol and drug addiction treatment, and mental health services. The site includes many links to literature on case management interventions and programs.

References

Ahr, P. R., & Holcomb, W. R. (1985). State mental health directors' priorities for mental health care. *Hospital and Community Psychiatry, 31*, 47–52.

Anderson, G. (2010). *Chronic care: Making the case for ongoing care.* Princeton, NJ: Robert Wood Johnson Foundation.

Austin, C., & McClelland, R. W. (2002). Case management with older adults. In A. Roberts & G. Greene (Eds.), *Social workers' desk reference* (pp. 502–506). Oxford, U.K.: Oxford University Press.

Bond, G. R., Drake, R. E., Mueser, K. T., & Latimer, E. (2001). Assertive community treatment for people with severe mental illness: Critical ingredients and impact on clients. *Disease Management and Health Outcomes, 9*, 141–159.

Buck, P. W., & Alexander, L. B. (2006). Neglected voices: Consumers with serious mental illness. *Administration and Policy in Mental Health and Mental Health Services, 33*, 470–481.

Calsyn, R. J. (2003). A modified ESID approach to studying mental illness and homelessness. *American Journal of Community Psychology, 32*, 319–331.

Centers for Medicare and Medicaid Services Brief, Promising Practices in Home and Community-Based Services. (2004). *Michigan—Person-Centered Planning for People with Mental Illness, Addiction Disorders, and Developmental Disabilities*, updated December 16, 2004, available at: https://www.cms.gov/Promising Practices/Downloads/mipcp.pdf

Claes, C., Van Hove, G., Vandevelde, S., van Loon, J., & Schalock, R. L. (2010). Person-centered planning: Analysis of research and effectiveness. *Intellectual and Developmental Disablities, 48*, 432–453.

Clark, R. E., Drake, R. E., McHugo, G. J., & Ackerson, T. H. (1995). Incentives for community treatment: Mental illness management services. *Medical Care, 33*, 729–738.

Cole, R. E., Reed, S. K., Babigham, H. M., Brown, S. W., & Fray, J. (1994). A mental health capitation program, Vol. I: Patient outcomes. *Hospital and Community Psychiatry, 45*, 1090–1096.

Craig, T., Doherty, I., & Jamieson-Craig, R. (2004). The consumer-employee as a member of a mental health assertive outreach team, vol. I: Clinical and social outcomes. *Journal of Mental Health, 13*(1), 59–69.

Crane-Ross, D., Lutz, W. J., & Roth, D. (2006). Consumer and case manager perspectives of service empowerment: Relationship to mental health recovery. *Journal of Behavioral Health Services and Research, 33*, 142–155.

Davis, K. (1996). *Managed care and social work practice.* Richmond: Virginia Commonwealth University School of Social Work.

Davis, M., Yelton, S., Katz-Leavy, J., & Lourie, I. S. (1995). Unclaimed children revisited: The status of state children's mental health service systems. *Journal of Mental Health Administration, 22*, 147–166.

Dieterich, M., Irving, C. B., Park, B., & Marshall, M. (2010). Intensive case management for severe mental illness. The Cochrane Library, DOI:10.1002/14651858.CD007906.pub2

Dixon, L. (2000). Assertive community treatment: Twenty-five years of gold. *Psychiatric Services, 51,* 759–765.

Dixon, L., Krauss, N., & Lehman, A. F. (1994). Consumers as service providers: The promise and challenge. *Community Mental Health Journal, 30,* 615–625.

Draine, J. (1997). A critical review of randomized field trials of case management for individuals with serious and persistent mental illness. *Research on Social Work Practice, 7,* 32–52.

Drake, R. E., & Burns, B. J. (1995). Special section on assertive community treatment: An introduction. *Hospital and Community Psychiatry, 46,* 667–668.

Dumaine, M. L. (2003). Meta-analysis of interventions with co-occurring disorders of severe mental illness and substance abuse. *Research on Social Work Practice, 13,* 142–165.

Edgar, E. (1996). Managed care basics. *NAMI Advocate, 18*(2), 6–16.

Ehrenreich, J. H. (1985). *The altruistic imagination: A history of social work and social policy in the United States.* Ithaca, NY: Cornell University Press.

Fellin, P. (1996). *Mental health and mental illness: Polices, programs, and services.* Itasca, IL: Peacock.

Felton, C. J., Stastny, P., Shern, D., Blanch, A., Donahue, S. A., Knight, E., & Brown, C. (1995). Consumers as peer specialists on intensive case management teams: Impact on client outcomes. *Psychiatric Services, 46,* 1037–1044.

Fiorentine, R., & Grusky, O. (1990). When case managers manage the seriously mentally ill: A role-contingency approach. *Social Service Review, 64,* 79–93.

Floersch, J. (2002). *Meds, money, and manners: The case management of severe mental illness.* New York, NY: Columbia University Press.

Frankel, A. J., & Gelman, S. R. (2004). *Case management* (2nd ed.). Chicago, IL: Lyceum.

Glisson, C., Dukes, D., & Green, P. (2006). The effects of the ARC organizational intervention on caseworker turnover, climate, and culture in children's service systems. *Child Abuse and Neglect, 30,* 855–880.

Goldman, H. H., Morrissey, J. P., & Ridgely, M. S. (1994). Evaluating the Robert Wood Johnson Foundation program on chronic mental illness. *Milbank Quarterly, 72*(1), 37–47.

Gorey, K. M., Leslie, D. R., Morris, T., Carruthers, W. V., John, L., & Chacko, J. (1998). Effectiveness of case management with severely and persistently mentally ill people. *Community Mental Health Journal, 34,* 241–250.

Grob, G. (1991). *From asylum to community: Mental health policy in modern America.* Princeton, NJ: Princeton University Press.

Hangan, C. (2006). Introduction of an intensive case management style of delivery for a new mental health service. *International Journal of Mental Health Nursing, 15,* 157–162.

Harris, M., & Bergman, H. C. (1988). Clinical case management for the chronically mentally ill: A conceptual analysis. In M. Harris & L. Bachrach (Eds.), *Clinical case management* (pp. 5–13). San Francisco, CA: Jossey-Bass.

Havassy, B. E., Shopshire, M. S., & Quigley, L. A. (2000). Effects of substance dependence on outcomes of patients in a randomized trial of two case management models. *Psychiatric Services, 51,* 639–644.

Jerrell, J. M., & Ridgely, M. S. (1995). Comparative effectiveness of three approaches to service people with severe mental illness and substance abuse disorders. *Journal of Nervous and Mental Diseases, 183,* 566–576.

Kanter, J. (Ed.). (1995). *Clinical issues in case management.* San Francisco, CA: Jossey-Bass.

Kanter, J. (1996a). Case management with long-term patients. In S. M. Soreff (Ed.), *Handbook for the treatment of the seriously mentally ill* (pp. 259–275). Seattle, WA: Hogrefe & Huber.

Kanter, J. (1996b). Case management and managed care: Investing in recovery. *Psychiatric Services, 47*, 699–701.

King, R. (2006). Intensive case management: A critical reappraisal of the scientific evidence for effectiveness. *Administration and Policy in Mental Health and Mental Health Services Research, 33*, 529–535.

Kolbasovsky, A., Reich, L., & Meyerkopf, N. (2010). Reducing six-month inpatient psychiatric recidivism and costs through case management. *Case Management Journal, 11*(1), 2–10.

Lauriello, J., Bustillo, J., & Keith, S. J. (1999). A critical review of research on psychosocial treatment of schizophrenia. *Biological Psychiatry, 46*, 1409–1417.

Lauriello, J., Lenroot, R., & Bustillo, J. R. (2003). Maximizing the synergy between pharmacotherapy and psychosocial therapies for schizophrenia. *Psychiatric Clinics of North America, 26*, 191–211.

Lehman, A. F. (1988). A quality of life interview for the chronically mentally ill. *Evaluation and Program Planning, 11*, 51–52.

Lehman, A. F., Buchanan, R. W., Dickerson, F. B., Dixon, L. B., Goldberg, R., Green-Paden, L., & Kreyenbuhl, J. (2003). Evidence-based treatment for schizophrenia. *Psychiatric Clinics of North America, 26*, 939–954.

Lehman, A. F., Dixon, L. B., Kernan, E., DeForge, B. R., & Postrado, L. T. (1997). A randomized trial of assertive community treatment for homeless persons with severe mental illness. *Archives of General Psychiatry, 54*, 1038–1043.

Lehman, A. F., Kreyenbuhl, J., Buchanan, B. W., Dickerson, F. B., Dixon, L. B., Goldberg, R.,...Steinwachs, D. M. (2004). The schizophrenia Patient Outcomes Research Team (PORT): Updated treatment recommendations 2003. *Schizophrenia Bulletin, 30*, 193–217.

Lehman, A. F., Postrado, L. T., Roth, D., McNary, S. W., & Goldman, H. H. (1994). Continuity of care and client outcomes in the Robert Wood Johnson Foundation program on chronic mental illness. *Milbank Quarterly, 72*(1), 105–122.

Levine, M. (1981). *The history and politics of community mental health.* New York, NY: Oxford University Press.

Lubove, R. (1965). *The professional altruist: The emergence of social work as a career, 1880–1930.* Cambridge, MA: Harvard University Press.

Macias, C., Kinney, R., Farley, O. W., Jackson, R., & Vos, B. (1994). The role of case management within a community support system: Partnership with psychosocial rehabilitation. *Community Mental Health Journal, 30*, 323–339.

Marshall, M., & Lockwood, A. (2003). Early intervention for psychosis. *Cochrane Database of Systematic Reviews, 2*, Article CD004718.

McClelland, R. W., Austin, C. D., & Schneck, D. (1996). Practice dilemmas and policy implications in case management. In C. C. Austin & R. W. McClelland (Eds.), *Perspectives on case management practice* (pp. 257–278). Milwaukee, WI: Families International.

McCrone, P., Beecham, J., & Knapp, M. (1994). Community psychiatric nurse teams: Cost-effectiveness of intensive support versus generic care. *British Journal of Psychiatry, 165*, 218–221.

McLellan, A. T., Hagan, T. A., Levine, M., Meyers, K., Gould, F., Bencivengo, M.,...Jaffe, J. (1999). Does clinical case management improve outpatient addiction treatment? *Drug and Alcohol Dependence, 55*, 91–103.

McReynolds, C. J., Ward, D. M., & Singer, O. (2002). Stigma, discrimination, and invisibility: Factors affecting successful integration of individuals diagnosed with schizophrenia. *Journal of Applied Rehabilitation Counseling, 33*, 32–39.

Mechanic, D. (1999). *Mental health and social policy: The emergence of managed care.* Boston, MA: Allyn & Bacon.

Mechanic, D., Schlesinger, M., & McAlpine, D. D. (1995). Management of mental health and substance abuse services: State of the art and early results. *Milbank Quarterly, 73*(1), 19–55.

Meek, J. A. (2012). Affordable Care Act: Predictive modeling challenges and opportunities for case management. *Professional Case Management, 17*, 15–21.

Merrick, E. L., Horgan, C. M., & Garnick, D. W. (2006). Managed care organizations' use of treatment management strategies for outpatient mental health care. *Administration and Policy in Mental Health and Mental Health Services Research, 33*, 101–114.

Miranda, J., Azocar, F., Organista, K., Dwyer, E., & Areane, P. (2003). Treatment of depression among impoverished primary care patients from ethnic minority groups. *Psychiatric Services, 54*, 219–225.

Morrissey, J. P., Calloway, M., Bartko, W. T., Ridgely, M. S., Goldman, H. H., & Paulson, R. I. (1994). Local mental health authorities and service system change: Evidence from the Robert Wood Johnson program on chronic mental illness. *Milbank Quarterly, 72*(1), 49–80.

Moxley, D. P. (1996). *Case management by design: Reflections on principles and practices.* Chicago, IL: Nelson-Hall.

Mueser, K. T., Bond, G. R., Drake, R. E., & Resnick, S. G. (1998). Models of community care for severe mental illness: A review of research on case management. *Schizophrenia Bulletin, 24*, 37–70.

Mueser, K. T., & McGurk, S. R. (2004). Schizophrenia. *Lancet, 363*, 2063–2072.

National Alliance on Mental Illness. (2007). *Assertive Community Treatment (ACT).* Retrieved from http://www.nami.org/Template.cfm?Section = ACT-TA_Center/

National Association of Social Workers (NASW). (2006). *NASW standards for the practice of clinical social work.* Silver Spring, MD: Author.

National Institute of Mental Health. (2006a). *NASW standards for social work case management.* Retrieved from www.socialworkers.org/practice/standards/sw_case_mgmt.asp

National Institute of Mental Health. (2006b). *The numbers count: Mental disorders in America.* Retrieved from http://www.nimh.nih.gov/publicat/numbers.cfm#Intro/

Nelson, G., Aubry, T., & Lafrance, A. (2007). A review of the literature on the effectiveness of housing and support, assertive community treatment, and intensive case management interventions for persons with mental illness who have been homeless. *American Journal of Orthopsychiatry, 77*, 350–361.

Padgett, D. K., Gulcur, L., & Tsemberis, S. (2006). Housing first services for people who are homeless with co-occurring serious mental illness and substance abuse. *Research on Social Work Practice, 16*, 74–83.

Phillips, S., Burns, B., Edgar, E., Mueser, K. T., Linkins, K. W., Rosenheck, R. A.,... McDonel Herr, E. C. (2001). Moving assertive community treatment into standard practice. *Psychiatric Services, 52*, 771–779.

Rapp, C. (1998). *The strengths model: Case management with people suffering from severe and persistent mental illness.* New York, NY: Oxford University Press.

Rapp, C. (2002). A strengths approach to case management with clients with severe mental disabilities. In A. Roberts & G. Greene (Eds.), *Social workers' desk reference* (pp. 486–489). New York, NY: Oxford University Press.

Rapp, C., & Goesha, R. J. (2004). The principles of effective case management of mental health services. *Psychiatric Rehabilitation Journal, 27,* 319–333.

Roberts-DeGennaro, M. (1987). Developing case management as a practice model. *Social Casework, 68,* 416–420.

Rochefort, D. A., & Logan, B. (1989). Mental illness and mental health as public policy concerns. In D. A. Rochefort (Ed.), *Handbook on mental health policy in the United States* (pp. 143–167). Westport, CT: Greenwood.

Rose, S. M., & Moore, V. L. (1995). Case management. In R. L. Edwards & J. G. Hopps (Eds.), *Encyclopedia of social work* (19th ed., pp. 335–340). Washington, DC: National Association of Social Workers.

Rothman, J., & Sager, J. S. (1998). *Case management: Integrating individual and community practice.* Boston, MA: Allyn & Bacon.

Rubin, A. (1992). Case management. In S. M. Rose (Ed.), *Case management and social work practice* (pp. 5–24). New York, NY: Longman.

Ryan, C. S., Sherman, P. S., & Judd, C. M. (1994). Accounting for case manager effects in the evaluation of mental health services. *Journal of Consulting and Clinical Psychology, 62,* 965–974.

Scheffler, R., Grogan, C., Cuffel, B., & Penner, S. (1993). A specialized mental health plan for persons with severe mental illness under managed competition. *Hospital and Community Psychiatry, 44,* 937–942.

Scott, J. E., & Dixon, L. B. (1995). Assertive community treatment and case management for schizophrenia. *Schizophrenia Bulletin, 21,* 657–668.

Shelton, D. A., & Frank, R. (1995). Rural mental health coverage under health care reform. *Community Mental Health Journal, 31,* 539–552.

Sherman, P. S., & Dahlquist, B. L. (1996). Managed care viewpoint. *NAMI Advocate, 18*(1), 4–6.

Shern, D. L., Felton, C. J., Hough, R. L., Lehman, A. F., Goldfinger, S., Valencia, E., . . . Wood, P. A. (1997). Housing outcomes for homeless adults with mental illness: Results from the second-round McKinney program. *Psychiatric Services, 48,* 239–241.

Solomon, P., & Draine, J. (1995). Consumer case management and attitudes concerning family relations among persons with mental illness. *Psychiatric Quarterly, 66,* 249–261.

Stefanic, A., & Tsemberis, S. (2007). Housing first for long-term shelter dwellers with psychiatric disabilities in a suburban county: A four-year study of housing access and retention. *Journal of Primary Prevention, 28,* 265–279.

Substance Abuse and Mental Health Services Administration. (1998). *Comprehensive case management for substance abuse treatment.* Treatment Improvement Protocol (TIP) Series, Number 27. HHS Publication No. (SMA) 08–4215. Rockville, MD: Author.

Substance Abuse and Mental Health Services Administration. (2005). *Substance abuse treatment for persons with co-occurring disorders.* Treatment Improvement Protocol (TIP) Series, Number 42. HHS Publication No. (SMA) 08–3992. Rockville, MD: Author.

Substance Abuse and Mental Health Services Administration. (2012). *Results from the 2010 National Survey on Drug Use and Health: Mental health findings,* NSDUH Series H-42, HHS Publication No. (SMA) 11–4667. Rockville, MD: Author.

Test, M., & Stein, L. (Eds.). (1985). *The training in community living model: A decade of experience. New directions for mental health services, 26.* San Francisco, CA: Jossey-Bass.

Torrey, E. F. (1988). *Nowhere to go: The tragic odyssey of the homeless mentally ill.* New York, NY: Harper & Row.

Tsemberis, S., Gulcur, L., & Nakae, M. (2004). Housing first, consumer choice, and harm reduction for homeless individuals with a dual diagnosis. *American Journal of Public Health, 94,* 651–656.

Turner, J., & TenHoor, W. (1978). The NIMH community support program: Pilot approach to a needed social reform. *Schizophrenia Bulletin, 4,* 319–334.

Tuten, L. M., Jones, H. E., Schaeffer, C. M., & Stitzer, M. L. (2012). The role of case management in substance abuse treatment. In L. M. Tuten, H. E. Jones, S. M. Schaeffer, & M. L. Stitzer (Eds.), *Reinforcement-based treatment for substance use disorders: A comprehensive behavioral approach* (pp. 121–144). Washington, DC: American Psychological Association.

U.S. Department of Health and Human Services (2010, December). *Multiple chronic conditions—A strategic framework: Optimum health and quality of life for individuals with multiple chronic conditions.* Washington, DC.

Vanderplasschen, W. (2006). Research note: Implementation and evaluation of case management for substance abusers with complex and multiple problems. *European Journal of Social Work, 9,* 259–261.

Walsh, J. (1994). Social support resource outcomes for the clients of two community treatment teams. *Research in Social Work Practice, 4,* 448–463.

Walsh, J. (2000). *Clinical case management with persons having mental illness: A relationship-based perspective.* Pacific Grove, CA: Wadsworth-Brooks/Cole.

Walsh, J. (2002). Clinical case management. In A. Roberts & G. Greene (Eds.), *Social workers' desk reference* (pp. 472–476). New York, NY: Oxford University Press.

Ziguras, S. J., & Stuart, G. W. (2000). A meta-analysis of the effectiveness of mental health case management over 20 years. *Psychiatric Services, 51,* 1410–1421.

Chapter 6
Advocacy

Malabika Misty Das, Cheryl Hiu-Kwan Chui, and Cecilia Lai-Wan Chan

> How can we integrate advocacy as a core value and a practical tool to meet the needs of social workers in contemporary times?

Social workers of today are facing a global crisis in which massive human suffering, exploitation, unnecessary hunger and preventable diseases, and natural and manmade disasters are prevalent. In order to ensure justice, it is critical that social workers strengthen our advocate identity. Advocacy for human rights and social justice is a unique feature of the social work profession. The National Association for Social Work (NASW) Code of Ethics strongly emphasizes that all social workers participate in social justice advocacy by engaging in social action for disadvantaged groups and influencing policy change (Swenson, 1998). As social workers, we have a moral and professional obligation to fight for, and ensure justice (Cleaveland, 2010).

This chapter critically reflects on the current discourse of advocacy in the social work profession. We ask students and practitioners the overarching question found at the beginning of this chapter: *How can we integrate advocacy as a core value and a practical tool to meet the needs of social workers in contemporary times?* Through an examination of social work advocacy's role, strengths, and challenges, we reclaim advocacy as a fundamental pillar of practice and provide suggestions for integration and application. We share key terms and definitions, questions for critical thinking, and resources for further study.

Advocacy and Social Work

Advocacy has always been taken as part of professional social work practice, including social workers' contribution and participation in networking, capacity building, resource mobilization, advocacy of rights without neglect of responsibilities, policy change, and attitude change among the public. However, there are intense debates in the profession regarding a fundamental reexamination of social workers' role in advocacy and system change (Beresford & Harding, 1993; Dominelli, 1996).

Definitions and Classifications

Despite previous attempts to define social work advocacy, it seems an exact definition of social work advocacy does not exist (Freddolino, Moxley, & Hyduk, 2004). Schneider and Lester (2001) consider it as "the exclusive and mutual representation of a client(s) or a cause in a forum, attempting to systematically influence decision making in an unjust or unresponsive system(s)" (Schneider and Lester, 2001, p. 65). They compiled 11 key dimensions of social work advocacy as:

1. Pleading or speaking on behalf of others
2. Representing another
3. Taking action
4. Promoting change
5. Accessing rights and benefits
6. Serving as a partisan
7. Demonstrating influence and political skills
8. Securing social justice
9. Empowering clients
10. Identifying with the client
11. Establishing a legal basis (adapted from Schneider and Lester, 2001)

The profession has historically classified and differentiated advocacy into level and system categories such as "micro and macro," "case, class, and cause," and "clinical and political." Davidson and Rapp (1976) suggest three levels of advocacy intervention: (1) individual, (2) administrative, and (3) policy.

1. The *individual level* usually entails a case-based advocacy method. It promotes the rights of marginalized individuals. It may involve certain individuals experiencing ongoing or one-time service barriers or injustice.
2. The *administrative level* usually entails persuasion of decision-makers to change particular bureaucratic procedures. For instance, domestic violence advocates may argue for social work assistance for the survivor of abuse preceding police and legal procedures.
3. The *policy level* advocates aim to change the nature of laws and policies. An example would be attempting to change the eligibility criterion for social welfare assistance (Sosin & Caulum, 1983).

Although these definitions and classifications have provided a useful foundation and descriptor of social work advocacy, these delineations do not seem to fully express the nature of advocacy, its efforts, or its distinction from typical job activities. We challenge the current limiting distinctions and suggest adopting a holistic advocacy lens integrating and promoting advocacy at all levels and aspects of social work. Advocacy can be conceptualized as an ethical value as well as a strategic tool for social justice.

Creating Advocacy Culture

Social workers are historically linked to orchestrating changes in people's lives through collective action, advocacy for effective social policy, empowerment through community development, and fostering communication through family interventions and individual casework. Ezell (1994) evaluated the nature of and time spent on advocacy for 353 social work respondents. Although 90% indicated participation in advocacy, the time spent per week on advocacy was quite minimal. Brill (2001) identified a great discrepancy between what is stated in the NASW Code of Conduct and actual professional practice. The social work profession has claimed to care for the "at risk population," but there seems to be less concern for social injustice, inequity, and oppression.

It seems that "the profession has been ambiguous in its definition of advocacy, and ambivalent in its commitment which has contributed to a lack of integration of this aspect of practice" (Faust, 2008, p. 296). Mitchell and Lynch (2003) suggest that contemporary social workers are not equipped for legal and political advocacy in the 21st century. Increasing *knowledge* of oppression, the *will* to engage in and the *desire* to collectively advocate could enable the profession to manifest its social justice aims (Mitchell & Lynch, 2003). Now, more than ever, creating an *advocacy culture* through social work education, training, practice, and research will enable the profession to fully realize and utilize advocacy's potential for social justice. It can also enable collective social work action in the face of multilevel oppression under the globalization of world economies.

CHEERS Model of Attributes for Social Work Advocacy

Social work advocates have been entrusted with titles such as "champion," "reformer," "fighter," and "defender" (Sosin & Caulum, 1983). Such labels can be limiting or even intimidating. Instead, we suggest that social workers strive to attain the key attributes listed in Figure 6.1 to strengthen their advocate identity and execute successful advocacy work.

The acronym CHEERS describes a positive attitude for an advocate. These attributes serve as a foundation for any social worker to be a successful advocate.

Advocacy Education

Within social work education, an emphasis on social justice advocacy can ground emerging social workers in this fundamental pillar of practice. Increased education and training around advocacy is imperative since it

Figure 6.1

CHEERS model of attributes for social work advocacy.

Commitment	Social workers have a strong commitment to those they are serving. This often entails an invested commitment. Social change is often a process that occurs incrementally over the long-term.
Holistic	Social workers can develop a holistic approach and perspective towards advocacy. Advocacy work is contextualized and should consider a range of bio-psycho-social-spiritual, socioeconomic, cultural, and political contexts and norms. They can work in interdisciplinary advocacy teams with other professional arenas.
Empowerment	Social workers can strive to facilitate empowerment for themselves, as well as for clients and underpriviliged communities to raise their voices. They can help educate clients in understanding their individual and structural oppression. They can play the roles of informers and educators of the public and policymakers to raise awareness of injustices experienced by vulnerable individuals and groups.
Empathy	Social workers can engage and align themselves with the clients and communities through an emphatic attitude. Empathy will enable a deeper understanding of the needs and issues for which advocacy is required. It can ignite a motivation to bring about change.
Resilient	Social workers can be resilient in the face of multilevel and structural oppression to increase political pressure and effectuate change. Through resiliency they can invest in advocacy efforts for the long term, as is often the case with systemic and policy changes. Through this investment, resiliency of the cause and stakeholders can also be increased.
Strengths Focus	Social workers can use their own strengths to foster, identify, and assist others to recognize their strengths. They can facilitate leadership, confidence, and awareness for individuals or groups in their efforts to promote advocacy. A strengths focus can harness energy, inspiration, and collective action.

is understood that not all social workers are natural advocates. Spicuzza (2003) argues that there is untapped potential in social work students and that social work education may be missing opportunities to build social work advocates and leaders. Building leadership skills is often emphasized for clients, but is also necessary for social work students and practitioners. Dynamic opportunities in and outside of the classroom will foster these two characteristics in emerging social workers. This idea is compatible with most social work curriculums since there is usually a combination of classroom and fieldwork education.

Often advocacy education is limited to macro level courses such as community development or organizing, but could instead be promoted through active and experiential learning within the diversity of social work curriculums. For example, using *problem-based learning* (PBL), a dynamic approach to student-centered learning, could be a way to integrate advocacy training ranging from community organization to mental health courses. PBL fosters self-directed learning and problem solving through active learning by doing. Students experience learning scenarios with structural problems and are encouraged to think creatively in building practical and achievable multilevel solutions. Through working in groups, students develop teamwork, communication, leadership, and reasoning skills. Building these skills will strengthen their advocate identity.

Experiential learning can prepare students for advocacy in their future professional roles. Suggestions include "testifying at in-case mock congressional hearings, developing media campaigns, field organizing, working with coalitions and grassroots, volunteering for political campaigns, attending political meetings and debates, and writing op-eds, letters to the editor, position papers, and policy briefs" (Ritter, 2007, p. 355). Social work emerged because of problems in society that needed solving and is quite congruent with PBL and experiential learning. A comprehensive integration of advocacy into social work core curriculums can ensure that new generations of social workers are equipped and committed to seek sociopolitical justice locally, regionally, and globally.

Professional Advocacy Training

The lack of systematic training on advocacy and system change may contribute to the discomfort among social workers with advocacy and interacting with politicians and legislators (Haynes & Mickelson, 1992). Ritter (2007) found that social networks and psychological engagement with politics were factors in explaining social workers political participation. For practitioners, advocacy training and building core CHEERS attributes can strengthen their advocacy identity and commitment to social justice work.

Professional organizations can emphasize advocacy's importance and establish platforms to enable social and political changes. An example is the Association of Oncology Social Work website that provides an "Advocacy Toolbox" to share strategies and information on advocacy for cancer patients in hospitals and the community. Agencies can adopt a holistic perspective toward social justice advocacy to enable it to become a distinct part of agency culture. Transforming misconceptions of advocacy as radical or antiestablishment will assist in facilitating staff and client empowerment. This can foster support, ignite collective action toward social change, and shift oppressive policies. Building community partnerships and networks can assist agency advocacy efforts throughout all levels.

Advocacy Research and Evaluation

Compared to research in the clinical domain of practice, advocacy and policy change research is still very limited (Donaldson & Shields, 2008). McNutt (2010) poses that the lack of evaluation of advocacy deters the effectiveness of impact and assessing the economic costs of activities and efforts.

New evaluation tools such as the *Policy Advocacy Behavior Scale* seek to help in this dilemma and have demonstrated promise to inform social work research integrating policy advocacy methods (Donaldson & Shields, 2008).

With identity being defined by settings or methods of intervention, for example, a hospital, child welfare, clinical, or community social worker, most social workers find advocacy a challenge. Advocacy should actually be a generic and core task for social workers. Social workers should adopt a dynamic and holistic approach "from case to policy" and vice versa.

We can start with the needs of a client, getting to know them, and then we mobilize them to contribute toward helping their fellow sufferers as well as carrying out policy advocacy. We can also start with a community organization while paying attention to the needs of individuals (Chan & Ng, 2004, p. 316).

This paradigm emphasizes the importance of three key components of the profession: practice, research, and education. Thus, social workers can serve as a practitioner–researcher–educator role to promote awareness of needs of clients, mobilize resources, facilitate communication and understanding among various interest parties, and collect evidence of effective intervention and contribution to problem prevention.

Advocacy in Clinical Social Work

Clinicians work in community mental health agencies, hospitals, local and international NGOs, educational institutions, professional organizations, the government sector, lobbying groups, and, of course, private practice. Within the multitude of settings, clinical social workers can be advocates not only for fighting for the benefits of the clients, but also to transform the oppressive systems of society that have directly and indirectly contributed to their client's issues.

More and more clinicians are finding themselves working in multidisciplinary teams and conducting advocacy. In hospital settings, clinicians advocate for the psychosocial needs of patients and their rights to service among an interdisciplinary team of professional care providers. Within forensic social work and legislative casework, clinicians may be working with legal advocates, the police force, and, in the larger judicial systems, providing micro- and macro-level advocacy for individual clients.

In a study of social justice advocacy, McLaughlin (2009) identified three primary domains of advocacy efforts in which clinical social workers engaged, from micro- to macro-level advocacy. These are: (1) instrumental, (2) educational, and (3) practical.

1. *Instrumental approaches* include: liaison between services (micro); demonstrations (mezzo); and professional association in standard setting and advocacy (macro).
2. *Educational approaches* include: educating individuals about their rights to services, options, or choices available in the system (micro);

committee work (mezzo); and public health awareness as well as pre-vention strategies (macro).

3. *Practical approaches* include: accompany clients to appeals or inter-views (micro); volunteer on a crisis line (mezzo); and run for political office (macro). (Adapted from McLaughlin, 2009)

International Clinical Social Justice

Clinical social work practice is largely practiced in more developed coun-tries; however, there is a stronger urgency for the promotion of mental health around the world. Clinical social workers in international settings are challenged with a great opportunity to serve as change agents for the advancement of holistic psychosocial services, research, and education. Working alongside community members and stakeholders, clinicians can identify gaps, generate actions, and alter structural oppression to promote access to mental health and psychosocial services where they are often lim-ited or nonexistent.

In disaster relief as well as political and humanitarian crises, social workers can be great resources on the organizational or ground level, pro-viding therapeutic services, training the trainers, or informing policy mak-ers on necessary and appropriate actions. Clinicians can provide culturally competent and tailored therapeutic services to address the multiple levels of trauma and to ensure sustainable systemic improvements in service deliv-ery and training in local communities. Here, advocacy can occur at multiple levels. Chan, Chan, and Ng (2006) suggest advocates to focus on facilitating posttraumatic growth and resiliency of those affected.

In her work with Christian Action's Chungking Mansions Service Cen-ter for Refugees and Asylum Seekers in Hong Kong, Das adopted a collab-orative and multimodal clinical social work approach serving refugees and asylum seekers. On the micro level, she helped to develop psychosocial structures to remove barriers to therapeutic services. Using action research methods, she worked at the mezzo level to identify organizational gaps and build capacities and skills to improve team efficacy. At the macro level, she focused on strengthening community partnerships to decrease structural inefficiencies and public discrimination.

Evolving Clinical Social Work Advocacy

Slowly but surely clinical social work is reclaiming its advocacy roots. More clinical social workers are developing creative strategies of advocacy for their clients and service users. Through advocacy, clinicians can reconnect with the profession's social justice goals, and it is this advocacy path that uniquely distinguishes social work from other mental health professions (McLaughlin, 2009). Ultimately, clinical social workers have a good oppor-tunity to provide multilevel advocacy from "case to cause."

"Clinical social justice works also includes planning and advocating for services that decrease clients' relative deprivation in political, economic, social, spiritual, and psychological spheres" (Swenson, 1998, p. 535). Psychotherapy has been criticized for client relationship power imbalances and for disengaging from advocacy work with disenfranchised communities. Helping clients understand the larger structural and power imbalances that influence their circumstances may help rectify these imbalances (Dietz, 2000). If clinicians can connect clients to relevant larger movements, their supports will increase and they may feel compelled to advocate for structural change.

Aware of this dichotomy between the micro- and macro-level practitioners, Vodde and Gallant (2002) offer a narrative–deconstruction method merging micro and macro social work practices into one practice model. Vodde and Gallant (2002) cited a typical method of White and Epston (1990) with anorexic clients by asking whether the client would like to know stories of other anorexic patients and to connect the client with those who are also suffering from anorexia. Raising this question effectively modifies the role of the practitioner from the one who "'helps clients defeat a problem" to "one who facilitates the connection to others who resist oppression'" (Vodde & Gallant, 2002, p. 445). Connecting people who are suffering from similar forms of oppression or problems can be empowering and can foster self-help. This breaks the isolation that is often associated with clinical cases and gives the story a "political character."

Clinicians can also advocate for structural balance within the mental health systems. Clinicians, who are increasingly restricted by organizational constraints and advised to help clients accept limitations caused by insufficient resources, instead could form coalitions or networks through their professional groups that can bring about change in the unjust sociopolitical system outside the context of their service agency. They can facilitate access to therapeutic services for vulnerable groups by volunteering at community mental health agencies, initiating or supporting psychosocial programming for communities in need, and educating themselves and their colleagues to become culturally competent and sensitive service providers. On a macro level, clinicians may want to become involved with larger national and international movements to promote mental and behavioral health access and dialogue.

Advocacy in Macro Social Work

The social work profession is criticized for the lack of advocacy and political participation. Social workers seem to emphasize their casework efforts and neglect broader social and economic factors affecting their clients. For instance, O'Brien (2011) argues that social workers tend to view disability through a diagnostic lens and largely neglect efforts to eradicate oppression of this community. Rome and Hoechstetter (2010) found a high prevalence of social workers' unwillingness to participate in campaigns for the well-being of vulnerable groups. Likewise, Ritter (2007) found less than half of social work respondents were active in political engagement for clients.

Such hesitation to advocate for disadvantaged populations and facilitate empowerment of users has ignited debates in the profession for reform (Beresford & Harding, 1993; Dominelli, 1996).

Contrary to these somewhat disheartening findings, there are exemplary role models of social workers advocating for political and social change. One of most renowned social workers, Celia B. Wiseman, who advocated against anti-Semitism and undesirable human conditions, influenced policy decision throughput most of her life. In her role as an executive committee member of the IFSW and that organization's representative to the UN, she organized annual Social Work Days in the United Nations. Wiseman held public lectures worldwide, attracting thousands of social work professionals. An inspiration for many, her efforts have produced many positive social impacts on the local and international arenas. She serves as an example of social workers taking on active international political action in pursuit of social justice.

Macro Practice Strategies

Advocacy is often seen as part of macro social work practice. Some argue that inequalities are influenced by complex factors that only a thorough adjustment at the structural level can resolve. For instance, the mitigation of health inequities may require advocacy for fundamental changes in social and economic policies that lead to such disparities (Israel et al., 2010; Warnecke, Oh, & Breen, 2008). Effective advocacy strategies can produce desirable social impact. However, advocates are usually faced with a string of unforeseen obstacles, from political opponents to economic barriers to moral hurdles. Nevertheless, there are ways in which advocacy can be propelled in a more effective manner. Sosin and Caulum (1983) advise social workers to ask themselves three basic questions:

1. Who is the target for change?
2. What should the level of advocacy be?
3. What strategies should be used in a specific case?

The decision makers in the legislature and governmental and nongovernmental organizations in the process of change will have to be identified right from the start of the advocacy action design phase. With a clear understanding of the persons, processes, and systems of change, appropriate strategies of advocacy can be selected. Hence, social work advocates should develop a keen awareness of powerful and influential characters within their advocacy issue.

Social workers can adopt a holistic perspective of advocacy to examine all levels for application. From advocating for one distinct client to a group facing systemic oppression, strategies at a micro, mezzo or macro level can be developed accordingly. Using a holistic perspective can lessen missed opportunities for multilevel and multimodal advocacy. Sosin and

Table 6.1 **Selection of Advocacy Strategies and Tactics According to the Stance of Public Opinion and Policy Makers**

Community and Policy Makers' Stance on the Issue	Agreeable	Neutral	Opposition
Strategies	Normative	Bargaining and Negotiation	Confrontation
Case Examples	MADD	AMI	GLAD
Tactics	Education and awareness campaigns	Education and awareness campaigns	Education and awareness campaigns
	Research and evaluation	Research and evaluation	Research and evaluation
	Mass media and advertisement	Political lobbying	Litigation and judicial actions
	Case studies	Petitions	Collective action
	Lobbying for legislation change	Lobbied with pharmaceutical companies	Political persuasion

Caulum (1983) provide a useful guide in the selection of the most appropriate strategies according to the level of public stance on the issue. The categorization can be found in Table 6.1.

Normative Strategies

If the public and policy makers involved in the advocacy issue are sympathetic and find proposed legislature or policy changes agreeable, then advocacy should be less complex. A good example of this normative advocacy is the initiation of Mothers Against Drunk Driving (MADD) in the United States, a support network for victims and families affected by drunk driving. Now a widely supported nongovernmental organization, MADD's origins can be traced back to Candace Lighter and Cindi Lamb, two mothers whose daughters were hit by drunk drivers.

In 1980, since the inception of the organization, the mothers participated in a national press conference on Capitol Hill on the issue and it received wide national support immediately (MADD, 2011). They organized press conferences and used newspaper articles and television talk shows to spread their message. This advocacy action awoke the nation's conscience against drunk driving. By 1983, 129 anti-drunk driving laws were passed. Although the catalyst for MADD's initiation was tragic, this case demonstrates how individuals can raise awareness, form alliances, and ultimately produce positive social impact and justice. By 1984, MADD had 330 chapters in 47 states. Their strategy is analyzed as normative, since their appeal was to the public's moral norms and they faced little resistance from legislative decision makers. Now, MADD is one of the most effective charities in the world.

Negotiation and Bargaining

Negotiation and bargaining may be appropriate if decision-makers are relatively neutral (or simply uninformed or indifferent) to the advocacy issue, as in the case of Action for Mental Illness (AMI) in India. AMI was founded in 2003 by Mrs. Laila Ollapally, a High Court advocate, and Dr. Nirmala Srinivasan, a disability activist (Offergeld, 2011). Their worthwhile efforts faced great obstacles due to the Indian general public's relatively negative perception of persons with mental illness (Lauber & Rossler, 2007). Unlike MADD, the lack of human resources and widespread stigmatization deterred prompt and supportive public responses to their advocacy efforts. Ollapally and Srinivasan responded by partaking in numerous lobbying efforts such as writing petitions and running public campaigns (Offergeld, 2011). They also battled pharmaceutical companies in their advocacy for access to affordable medication.

This negotiation and bargaining advocacy action resulted in a remarkable mental health plan for the Indian state of Karnataka. Their efforts became national as they partook in 7 years of lobbying and Supreme Court hearings, resulting in the amendment of the old Mental Health Act (1987). The AMI case highlights the reality and challenges that advocates face within a society that is not sympathetic to the needs of persons with mental illness. Only with persistent and long-term commitment can advocates achieve fundamental changes in underlying structures and legislation.

Confrontation

There is a general misconception that social workers should avoid confrontational strategies and that advocacy will inevitably lead to conflict. Such uncomfortable feelings about confrontation may deter social workers from participating in advocacy actions to bring about necessary changes in oppressive social policies and legislature. Confrontational actions may be required if there is strong opposition forces in society. For example, legalizing same-sex marriage is a heavily debated legal issue in the United States (Hatzenbuehler, McLaughlin, Keyes, & Hasin, 2010). Despite that, advocacy begun in the 1970s, and only six states have granted same-sex couples the right to marry. The majority of U.S. citizens voted to limit marriage to heterosexual couples (Hatzenbuehler et al., 2010), making advocacy extremely difficult as it is against the dominant social norm.

Here, confrontational actions may be a viable choice. For instance, Gay and Lesbian Advocates & Defenders (GLAD), has used litigation, judiciary hearings and public education to advocate for the legalization of same-sex marriage and alter public opinion since 1978 (GLAD, 2011). With GLAD's unceasing efforts, support for same-sex marriage has increased in recent years. According to Van Lohuizen and Beneson (2011), 50.6% of the public show support toward same-sex marriage. GLAD exemplifies that use of strategic confrontational action is a viable option in mainstreaming previously socially opposed issues.

Multimodal Strategies and Approaches

Social workers may adopt dynamic, multimodal and multilevel strategies for bringing about desired changes. Certain strategies may be more relevant under each circumstance. Hoefer (2012) suggests an "Advocacy Map" to facilitate planning and evaluating advocacy practices. Flexibility and creativity are crucial elements in the advocacy process. In order initiate advocacy efforts, the following steps as interconnected components alongside the CHEERS attributes are proposed:

Advocacy: Taking It One Step at a Time

Choosing the appropriate advocacy strategy will improve the probability of success. Showing the CHEERS attributes (see Figure 6.1) in the center, Figure 6.2 illustrates some of the key aspects of advocacy work.

Understand the Suffering

Advocacy can help provide a voice to the voiceless. One of the keys to effective advocacy is to develop an in-depth understanding of the clientele for whom social workers hope to advocate. This can be done through cultivating an empathic attitude and building trust. As in the case of children's rights advocacy, instead of perceiving children as vulnerable, weak, and

Figure 6.2

**Advocacy process
in the CHEERS model.**

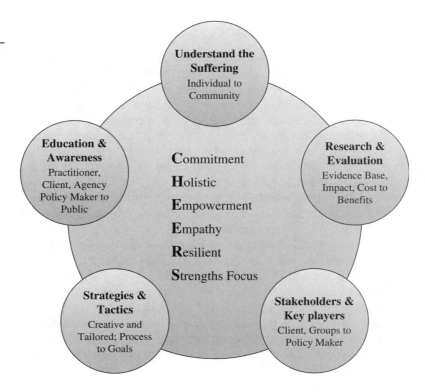

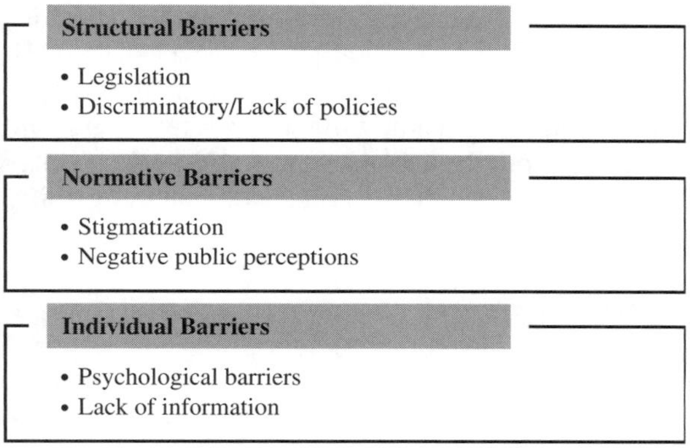

Figure 6.3

Barriers to equal access to rights of client groups in advocacy.

passive, regarding them as social actors who can offer valuable perspectives on their own issues may be more beneficial (Knight & Oliver, 2007).

Understanding the suffering also requires thorough examination of structural imbalances and policy inadequacies (determinants) that initiated these inequities. It has been demonstrated that inequalities in health, economics, and social outcomes are results of larger structural reasons and complex interplay between different policies (Carroll, Casswell, Huakau, Chapman, & Perry, 2011; Graham, 2000).

There are three main categories of barriers that advocates should help users articulate before they can formulate their advocacy goals. They are: (1) structural, (2) normative, and (3) individual barriers (see Figure 6.3).

1. *Structural barriers* may include discriminatory policies or the lack of certain necessary legislation to protect rights of certain sectors of the population. In the AMI case, mentally ill patients experience problems such as poor access to health care, absence of social assistance, and protective policies as results of structural barriers.

2. *Normative barriers* may include general misconceptions and stigmatization of this community. Public education by personal stories and research can help change public perceptions to rectify discrimination and misunderstanding.

3. *Individual barriers* may include individuals not knowing where to seek help. Equipping them with appropriate knowledge and facilitating empowerment would be important. Identifying these barriers accordingly will help formulate clearer advocacy strategies.

Research and Evaluation

Advocates must thoroughly research their respective advocacy subject as an initial step and tie it to "understanding the suffering" of the oppressed population. Participatory action research (PAR) can enable increased capacity to advocate. PAR can ensure accessible and meaningful knowledge production, as well as socially valid resource development and actions (Garcia-Iriarte, Kramer, Kramer, & Hammel, 2008; Townson et al., 2004). Conducting research will help to identify critical factors that may shape advocacy outcomes. Research may entail knowing the stakeholders and understanding key legislation around the issue. Systematic evaluation of efficacy of intervention can provide evidence for policy change and priority setting as well.

Stakeholders and Key Players

Knowing the stakeholders will enable development of appropriate advocacy strategy and facilitate advocacy efforts. Careful mapping of stakeholders and key players can provide insights of channels of advocacy. For instance, in advocating for mental health patients, liaising with the relevant departments like the Ministry of Health, as shown in Figure 6.4, and attaining a thorough understanding of the legal framework related to mental health may be fruitful.

Strategies and Tactics

There are many options in selection of strategies and tactics in advocacy. A combination of public education, advertising campaign, research, lobbying, mediation, persuasion, law drafting, legal proceedings, litigation, grassroots mobilization, and so forth can be used. The choice can be based on the assessment of public support so that normative, negotiation, or bargaining strategies can be developed. In most cases, a combination of tactics over a long period of time will be necessary to bring about change in policies and to sustain change efforts. Using a rights-based approach toward advocacy can have far-reaching impact on affected individuals by enabling knowledge sharing about legal entitlements and other structural oppression. Once the barriers to certain rights are realized, legislation change may be effectuated. In other instances, running campaigns or litigation may be needed. Strategies should be well thought out beforehand to inform advocacy goals and expected outcomes.

Figure 6.4

Stakeholders in mental health advocacy.

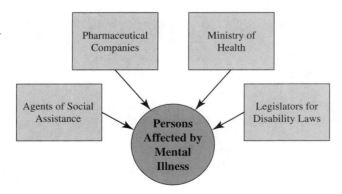

Education and Awareness

Public education is inherent in all advocacy work and public opinion motivates governments to implement changes. Education elements can be implemented for consensus building throughout the entire advocacy process. Clearly, when the public is receptive, as in the case of MADD, motions can be easily passed. But for cases that are more sensitive and have less public support, continuous investment into education campaigns for raising public awareness are essential.

A Differential Model of Advocacy

Different forms and types of advocacy will be needed under different circumstances. Freddolino et al. (2004) identify four primary approaches congruent with the social work tradition of working with the oppressed, marginalized and vulnerable.

1. Protecting the vulnerable
2. Creating supports to enhance functioning
3. Protecting and advancing claims or appeals
4. Fostering identity and control (adapted from Freddolino et al., 2004)

They further integrate the approaches with "professional" or "recipient" controlled advocacy process and outcomes. By combining these dimensions, a differential form of advocacy, independent of the traditional systems categorization, such as political versus clinical advocacy, is conceptualized (Freddolino et al., 2004).

User-Led Advocacy

User-led advocacy movements are gathering momentum in bringing about changes in society. Examples include persons with disability, survivors of mental illness, domestic violence, childhood sexual abuse, cancer, and women of divorce. Many small user groups are actively participating in advocacy and forming themselves into communal or district coalitions, national alliances, and ultimately international platforms for social and policy changes.

Chan and her colleagues contributed to the establishment of a patients' mutual help movement in Hong Kong. With groups of social work students from the University of Hong Kong, she mobilized patients to form themselves into self-help groups. The various patients' groups were then organized to form an Alliance of Patients' Mutual Help Organizations (Wong & Chan, 1994). She was also instrumental in organizing grassroots movements and mobilizing the support of environmental improvement projects (Chan & Hills, 1993).

Whistle-Blowing

Although better known in business and public administration arenas than in social work, whistle-blowing warrants discussion as a form of social work advocacy to protect clients' rights (Greene & Latting, 2004). Often social workers are mandated to speak about their agencies only in good terms; they may face dilemmas, feeling torn between protecting clients' needs and protecting themselves as employees. The protection of whistle-blowers and advocates in public organizations is usually not explicitly stated, and procedures for protection are far from elaborate. However, in the face of agency oppression, when internal resolution is not available, whistle-blowing could be used as an advocacy method. Greene and Latting (2004) discuss whistle-blowing in social work practice as well as practical knowledge and guidance in application.

Conflict Resolution: Negotiation and Spirituality of Advocacy

Conflict resolution is a natural part of being a social worker, as conflicts do occur in most settings and context of practice. Methods in resolving conflicts will be diverse and advocacy often plays a central role within the diversity of methods. Increasing the tools in a social worker's advocacy toolbox can be beneficial for the multilevel challenges and conflicts facing social workers today. Along these lines, Lens (2004) describes principled negotiation as a vital tool in advocacy and especially resonates with social work's value base. Principled negotiation strives for mutually beneficial conflict resolution and acknowledges the importance of ongoing relationships. It can be used across all levels of social work practice (Lens, 2004).

Canda and Furman (1999) propose a model of advocacy based on spirituality of reciprocity rather than alienation. It is very easy for us to fall into the trap of polarization and targeting the person whom we want to influence as our opponent or enemy.

> *In this enemy mentality, . . . we exploit, damage, or diminish others in our efforts for victory on behalf of the client, we become exactly what we opposed. This is a sin of omission—committing acts of violence or dehumanization. . . . And in returning indignity and harm to that opponent, we become just like the enemy. This approach does not afford any possibility of reconciliation or mutual benefit.*
>
> *(Canda and Furman, 1999, p. 203)*

In the reconciliatory style of advocacy, social workers treat clients, government officials, and opponents with respect and work toward win-win solutions in a persistent and collaborative manner and by seeking mutual growth and benefit through creative solutions. Chan et al. (2006) proposed a SMART model (**S**trengths-focused, **M**eaning-oriented, **A**pproach to **R**esilience and **T**ransformation) that advocates for a spiritual resilience toward trauma and adversity. The inner spiritual peace during the advocacy process is crucial in keeping the momentum for social change. "We respect all parties, even when we disagree or are in conflict. When conflict is unresolvable, we find ways to continue the conflict in a humane manner, or to forgive and move on. Mahatma Gandhi and Rev. Martin Luther King, Jr., were excellent examples of social activists who strove to put this ideal into action . . . the ideals of compassion, forgiveness, reconciliation, service and nonviolence" (Canda and Furman, 1999, pp. 203–204). Principles and steps include:

- Try to bring all parties into a dialogue based on mutual respect and willingness to understand each other. Assume the kind and altruistic nature of all parties involved.

- Do not reduce people to problems or enemies. Get to know each other as fellow people. Try to establish a genuine and warm relationship so that collaboration is possible.

- Identify shared visions, aspirations, and interests, common commitments, and passion as well as different positions of all parties concerned. Serve the most important principles and aspirations underlying their behavior and actions so that the deeper meaning can be established.

- Feelings touching feelings. Help each party to articulate their feelings, as the process will result in mutual appreciation from each other's point of view.

- Create a platform so that different parties can brainstorm to discover alternative solutions in which all parties would feel a sense of ownership to proposed solutions and feel that they have won.

- Accept a process of give and take. Stay in a continuous process of negotiation and communication. Select solutions that are ultimately acceptable to all parties.

- Develop an action plan and roles involving cooperative teamwork by representatives of all parties.

- Follow up with implementation of the plan, evaluating success in terms of common interests and different standards.

- Collaboratively examine the long-term impacts of the change, and revise activities as necessary. (Adapted from Canda and Furman, 1999, p. 205)

The proposed spirituality of advocacy can be seen as a checklist that adopts a flexible and collaborative style of negotiation and advocacy. Finding win-win situations for all would guarantee success in the long run.

Cyber-Activism: The Next Wave of Advocacy

Cyber-activism refers to advocacy for a specific cause using cyberspace as a platform for social change. The dissemination of information has never been as rapid, and its audience transcends social class, ethnicity, and national borders. Individuals can be both the informer and the informed, and can alert the public to any messages deemed important. Innovative social activists have capitalized on the Internet in order to advocate for positive social change using blogs, emails, podcasts, and popular social media such as Twitter, YouTube, and Facebook. A further unique phenomenon is the widespread use of handy multimedia communication devices, which have revolutionized recent advocacy efforts.

Not many would argue against the power of social media and its impact in forming public opinion and policy making (Cooper, 2005). Lim and Ting (2011) reported the power of cyber-activism in Malaysia: A policeman stopped a woman for speeding and invited her to partake in bribery and sexual misconduct. She recorded the incident on her phone and posted it to YouTube as an act of defiance. Within 1 week the video had 158,000 hits and more than 50,000 comments within the cyber community (Lim & Ting, 2011). The public rallied around the corruption problem and ultimately forced the government to launch the Whistle-Blower Protection Act and set up an Anti-Corruption Commission (MACC) in Malaysia.

Cyber-activism can be a key strategy and invaluable for organizing and launching campaigns, such as the widespread waves of demonstrations in the Arab world known as the "Arab Spring." Revolutions were initiated by the unemployed yet computer-literate youth in countries such as Tunisia, Egypt, Libya, and Syria. Online forums and social media were used to voice discontent with corrupt regimes and their oppressive political, economical, and social policies and human rights violations. Using Facebook and Twitter, protests were organized with hundreds of thousands of followers. These examples demonstrate how cyber-activism can contribute to positive policy change and social justice through effective mass mobilization within a short period of time of a large population who are strangers to each other.

The Role of Values

Advocacy efforts are often rooted in value choices and priorities. Values can be translated into programs that can affect individuals, agencies, communities, and the larger social system. People tend to support or oppose policies and programs because of the impact on their fundamental values (Jansson, 2011). A recent example is the controversy regarding the efforts of the Susan B. Komen Foundation to end funding for Planned Parenthood, a crucial provider for breast cancer and sexual and reproductive health information for low-income women.

The decision was allegedly influenced by prolife ideologies, values, and political leanings. The backlash of the decision resulted in an array of advocacy efforts from Planned Parenthood supporters, including letter-writing, online appeals, public rebuke by high-profile city leaders and increasing donations. Within weeks, the advocacy spurred the foundation to reverse its decision and restructure its grant-making policies. Also, a key decision maker resigned from her executive role. This serves as one of many global examples of existing oppressive structural power imbalances, where values on both sides were driving forces for oppression and for advocacy. Social workers can self-reflect and examine our own experiences of oppression, privilege and power, our values and passions, and our justification for advocacy efforts.

Acknowledging that strategies and tactics will be different in every situation, perhaps social work advocacy can be conceptualized beyond the systems classifications and framed in terms of what advocates seek to accomplish in their given situations (Freddolino et al., 2004). We encourage students and practitioners to implement and evaluate their own advocacy efforts and strategies and identify effective and innovative approaches to share with the profession.

National and International Advocacy Movements

Advocacy has had a vibrant history in many countries such as the United Kingdom. Hundreds of local advocacy agencies, both government and non-governmental organizations (NGOs), advocate for rights of the child and the persons with disabilities (Oliver, Knight, & Candappa, 2006). Through the combined efforts of politicians, advocates, legislators, policy makers, and social workers, the ratification of the 1989 United Nations Convention of Child Rights was a result of a long-fought battle over child rights. Despite cultural differences, an international consensus of children's fundamental rights was established and to date, as many as 194 countries have signed on to this Convention.

With changing socioeconomic, cultural, and political patterns come emerging dilemmas; advocacy is always needed for the betterment of humankind. It appears that advocacy topics and work are never exhaustive and take place in virtually all walks of life imaginable, from health, women's rights, disability rights, housing, environmental protection and so on. The International HIV/AIDS Alliance, World Institute on Disability, National Alliance for the Mentally Ill (NAMI), Reunite International Child Abduction Centre in the UK, From Grief to Action (FGTA) in Canada, Africa Advocacy Foundation (AAF) in the African region, and Kids' Dream in Hong Kong are some examples of social advocacy progressing into nationwide and international movements.

Grassroots Advocacy

Grassroots movements occur in affluent and resource-poor countries and communities. For instance, in the United States, immigrant and ethnic minority groups organize, advocate for social justice, and can change lives and laws. An organization, Adhikaar (meaning *rights*) for Human Rights and Social Justice, a New York City–based NGO serving Nepali-speaking people, uses a multimodal advocacy approach informed by the community it serves. Adhikaar is involved in assisting individuals whose labor rights were violated, facilitating literacy and education courses for women, conducting health fairs with partners for the community, and rallying at the state and federal levels for domestic workers' rights. Their advocacy has resulted in dramatic improvements for the Nepalese community as well as the passing of the first Domestic Workers Bill of Rights in the New York State government.

Grassroots advocacy can also be individually initiated, such as in the case of Indira Ranamagar of Prisoners Assistance Nepal (PA Nepal), who is the driving force for the empowerment of prisoners and their families. She also uses multilevel and multimodal advocacy. She works to improve dilapidated and overcrowded prisons, provides skills building and leadership training to prisoners, provides shelters for prisoners' children in several homes, and formed coalitions to support the movement. Social workers can choose to lead and support grassroots movements such as these. They can utilize their skills, training, knowledge, and backgrounds and be a great resource for various causes, while at the same time gaining valuable advocacy skills from the experience.

Global Social Work Advocacy

Recognizing barriers to advocacy, the profession has become active in its own advocacy. Social workers can form professional organizations, interest groups, and watchdog groups to ensure that continuous advocacy efforts can be sustained. National and international advocacy movements strive to advance and advocate for the profession and for just national and international policies. The National Association for Social Work (NASW) in the United States is the largest professional advocacy body in the profession and has established global precedents such as the Code of Ethics.

In 2010, a joint World Conference, organized by the International Association of Schools of Social Work (IASSW), International Council on Social Welfare (ICSW), and International Federation of Social Workers (IFSW), was held in Hong Kong to develop a "Global Agenda" for social work and social development action. The three established aims were:

1. To claim/reclaim the priority of "political" action and to develop a collective voice for social development and social work practitioners and social work educators.

2. To start a collective process of elaborating and setting a common Global Agenda for years to come that can unite those involved in social work and social development.

3. To strategize around mechanisms for the implementation of common actions and the development of modalities for monitoring our efforts. (Adapted from http://www.ifsw.org)

The 2012 conference in Stockholm reviewed the implementation strategies set forth in the 2010 Global Agenda in the hope of influencing global political, professional, and social change and development.

Conclusion

Within the multitude of diverse social work practice areas and educational settings, it is imperative that social workers act as advocates at the micro, mezzo, and macro levels and "celebrate the comprehensiveness of the profession" (Faust, 2008, p. 299). We emphasize that advocacy is a constant and dynamic force for all social workers to consider as a fundamental value and tool to advance individuals, groups, systems, and policies in the face of oppression. We suggest celebrating our successes, regardless of how small or big, as a method for promoting continuous momentum and inspiration. Emphasizing advocacy using a holistic perspective can enable the profession to realign its foundational core so that all social workers can and will want to participate in the global movement for human rights and social justice for all.

Key Terms

Advocacy	Collective action	Cyber-activism
Social justice	Whistle-blowing	Lobbying
Oppression	Stakeholder	Power and structural
Change agent	Resource mobilization	imbalance
Empowerment	Litigation	Policy change
Social activism	Negotiation	Public awareness

Review Questions for Critical Thinking

1. How is advocacy an important feature of the profession of social work?
2. What are concrete strategies and tactics for advocacy social work practice today?
3. How can advocacy be applied within the diversity of social work settings and roles?
4. What are the challenges of being an advocate for social workers today and what are ways to rectify these challenges?
5. How can clinicians become more active social justice advocates?

Online Resources

The International Council on Social Welfare (ICSW): http://www.icsw .org

Gathers and distributes information to civil society organizations, governments and intergovernmental organizations. It spreads information through journals, reports, electronic newsletters and its website. The bodies actively advocate to the United Nations and various governmental, policy and legislative bodies.

The International Association of Schools of Social Work (IASSW): http://www.iassw-aiets.org

The worldwide association of schools of social work, other tertiary level social work educational programs, and social work educators.

International Federation of Social Workers (IFSW): http://www.ifsw.org

A global organization striving for social justice, human rights and social development.

The National Association for Social Workers (NASW): http://www.naswdc.org

The national professional organization for social workers in the United States and largest professional social work advocacy body.

Association of Oncology Social Work (AOSW): http://www.aosw.org

Works to advance excellence in the psychosocial care of persons with cancer, their families, and caregivers through networking, education, advocacy, research, and resource development.

United Nations High Commissioner for Refugees (UNHCR): http://www.unhcr.org

This agency is mandated to lead and coordinate international action to protect refugees and resolve refugee problems worldwide. Its primary purpose is to safeguard the rights and well-being of refugees. It strives to ensure that everyone can exercise the right to seek asylum and find safe refuge in another state, with the option to return home voluntarily, integrate locally, or to resettle in a third country. It also has a mandate to help stateless people.

Adhikaar for Human Rights and Social Justice: http://www.adhikaar.org

A New York–based community organization serving Nepali-speaking people and focused on community development, advocacy, direct service, and health and education literacy.

The Advocacy Institute: http://www.advocacyinstitute.org

An organization dedicated to the development of products, projects, and services that work to improve the lives of people with disabilities.

References

Beresford, P., & Harding, T. (1993). *A call to change.* London, United Kingdom: National Institute for Social Work.

Brill, C. K. (2001). Looking at the social work profession through the eye of the NASW Code of Ethics. *Research on Social Work Practice, 11*, 223–234.

Canda, E., & Furman, L. (1999). *Spiritual diversity in social work practice: The heart of helping.* New York, NY: Free Press.

Carroll, P., Casswell, S., Huakau, J., Chapman, P., & Perry, P. (2011). The widening gap: Perceptions of poverty and income inequalities and implications for health and social outcomes. *Social Policy Journal of New Zealand*, *37*, 111–122.

Chan, C., & Hills, P. (Eds.). (1993). *Limited Gains: Grassroots Mobilization and Environmental Management in Hong Kong*. Hong Kong: Centre of Urban Planning and Environmental Management, University of Hong Kong.

Chan, C. L.-W., & Ng, S. M. (2004). The social work practitioner-researcher-educator: Encouraging innovations and empowerment in the 21st century. *International Social Work*, *47*, 312–320.

Chan, C. L.-W., Chan, T. H. Y., & Ng, S. M. (2006). The strength-focused and meaning-oriented approach to resilience and transformation (SMART): A body-mind-spirit approach to trauma management. *Social Work in Health Care. 43*(2/3), 9–36.

Cleaveland, C. (2010). "We are not criminals": Social work advocacy and unauthorized migrants. *Social Work*, *55*, 74–81.

Cooper, L. (2005). Implications of media scrutiny for a child protection agency. *Journal of Sociology & Social Welfare*, *32*, 107–121.

Davidson, W., & Rapp, C. (1976). Child advocacy in the justice system. *Social Work*, *21*, 225–232.

Dietz, C. A. (2000). Reshaping clinical practice for the New Millennium. *Journal of Social Work Education*, *36*(3).

Dominelli, L. (1996). Deprofessionalizing social work. *British Journal of Social Work. 26*, 153–175.

Donaldson, L. P., & Shields, J. (2008). Development of the Policy Advocacy Behavior Scale: Initial reliability and validity. *Research on Social Work Practice*, *19*, 83–92.

Ezell, M. (1994). Advocacy practice of social workers. *Families in Society*, *75*, 36–46.

Faust, J. R. (2008). Clinical social worker as patient advocate in a community mental health center. *Clinical Social Work Journal*, *36*, 293–300.

Freddolino, P. P., Moxley, D. P., & Hyduk, C. A. (2004). A differential model of advocacy in social work practice. *Families in Society*, *85*(1), 119–128.

Garcia-Iriarte, E., Kramer, J., Kramer, J., & Hammel, J. (2008). "Who did what?": A participatory action research project to increase group capacity for advocacy. *Journal of Applied Research in Intellectual Disabilities*, *22*, 10–22.

GLAD. (2011). Our work. Retrieved 009-02, 2012, from http://www.glad.org/work

Graham, H. (2000). *Understanding health inequalities*. Buckingham, U.K.: Oxford University Press.

Greene, A. D., & Latting, J. K. (2004). Whistle-blowing as a form of advocacy: Guidelines for the practitioner and organization. *Social Work*, *49*(2), 219–230.

Hatzenbuehler, M., McLaughlin, K., Keyes, K., & Hasin, D. (2010). The impact of institutional discrimination of psychiatric disorders in lesbians, gay, and bisexual populations: A prospective study. *American Journal of Public Health*, *100*, 452–459.

Haynes, K. S. & Mickelson, J. S. (1992). Social work and the Reagan era: Challenges to the profession. *Journal of Sociology and Social Welfare 19*(1), 169–183.

Herbert, M., & Levin, R. (1996). The advocacy role in hospital social work. *Social Work in Health Care*, *22*(3), 71–83.

Hoefer, R. (2012). *Advocacy practice for social justice* (2nd ed.). Chicago, IL: Lyceum Books.

Israel, B., Coombe, C., Cheezum, R., Schulz, A., McGranaghan, R., Lichtenstein, R., & Burris, A. (2010). Community-based participatory research: A capacity-building approach for policy advocacy aimed at eliminating health disparities. *American Journal of Public Health*, *100*, 2094–2102.

Jansson, B. S. (2011). *Becoming an effective policy advocate: From policy practice to social justice* (6th ed.). Belmont, CA: Brooks/Cole.

Knight, A., & Oliver, C. (2007). Advocacy for disabled children and young people: Benefits and dilemmas. *Child and Family Social Work*, *12*, 417–425.

Lauber, C., & Rossler, W. (2007). Stigma toward people with mental illness in Asia. *International Review of Psychiatry*, *19*, 157–178.

Lens, V. (2004). Principled negotiation: A new tool for case advocacy. *Social Work*, *49*, 506–513.

Lim, W., & Ting, D. (2011). Cyberactivism: Empowering advocacies for public policy. *World Journal of Management*, *3*(2), 201–217.

McLaughlin, A. M. (2009). Clinical social workers: Advocates for social justice. *Advances in Social Work 10*(1), 51–68.

McNutt, J. (2010). Is social work advocacy worth the cost? Issues and barriers to an economic analysis of social work political practice. *Research on Social Work Practice*, *21*, 397–403.

Mitchell, J., & Lynch, R. S. (2003). Beyond the rhetoric of social and economic justice. *Race, Gender & Class*, *10*(2), 8–26.

Mothers Against Drunk Driving (MADD). (2011). *Cari Lighter and Lauran Lamb Story*. Retrieved 09–02, 2012, from http://www.madd.org/about-us/history/cari-lightner-and-laura-lamb-story.pdf

O'Brien, G. (2011). Eugenics, genetics, and the minority group model of disabilities: Implications for social work advocacy. *Social Work*, *16*, 437–354.

Offergeld, J. (2011). *Action for Mental Illness India—A mental health advocacy initiative and its efforts to improve the living condition of persons living with mental illness and their families*. Retrieved from http://disabilityandhumanrights.com/2011/12/05/action-for-mental-illness-india-a-mental-health-advocacy-initiative-and-its-efforts-to-improve-the-living-condition-of-persons-living-with-mental-illness-and-their-families/

Oliver, C., Knight, A., & Candappa, M. (2006). *Advocacy for looked-after children and children in need*. Report for the Department for Education and Skills. London, U.K.: Thomas Coram Research Unit, Institute of Education.

Ritter, J. A. (2007). Evaluating the political participation of licensed social workers in the New Millennium. *Journal of Policy Practice*, *6*(4), 61–78.

Rome, S., & Hoechstetter, S. (2010). Social work and civic engagement: The political participation of professional social workers. *Journal of Sociology & Social Welfare*, *37*(3), 107–129.

Schneider, R. L. & Lester, L. (2001). *Social work advocacy: A new framework for action*. Belmont, CA: Brooks/Cole.

Sosin, M., & Caulum, S. (1983). Advocacy: A conceptualization for social work practice. *Social Work*, *28*(1), 12–17.

Spicuzza, F. J. (2003). Preparing students for social work advocacy. *Journal of Baccalaureate Social Work*, *8*(2), 49–68.

Swenson, C. R. (1998). Clinical social work's contribution to a social justice perspective. *Social Work*, *43*, 527.

Townson, L., Macauley, S., Harkness, E., Chapman, R., Docherty, A., Dias, J.,…McNulty, N. (2004). We are all in the same boat: Doing "people-led research." *British Journal of Learning Disabilities*, *32*, 72–76.

Van Lohuizen, J., & Beneson, J. (2011). 2011 public polling on marriage. Benenson Strategy Group & Voter Consumer Research. Downloaded from http://freemarry.3cdn.net/5ae85613318ade1b2e_8dm6bnq72.pdf

Vodde, R., & Gallant, J. (2002). Bridging the gap between micro and macro practice: Large-scale change and a unified model of narrative-deconstructive practice. *Journal of Social Work Education*, *38*, 439–458.

Warnecke, R., Oh, A., & Breen, N. (2008). Approaching health disparities from a population perspective: The National Institutes for Health Centers for Population Health and Health Disparities. *American Journal of Public Health*, *98*, 1608–1615.

White, M., & Epston, D. (1990). *Narrative means to therapeutic ends.* New York, NY: Norton.

Wong, D., & Chan, C. (1994). Advocacy on self-help for patients with chronic illness: The case of Hong Kong. *Prevention in Human Services* (Special Volume in Self-Help Groups), *11*(*1*), 117–139.

Kenneth R. Yeager, Albert R. Roberts, and Wendy Grainger

> When considering all aspects of social work practice within the framework of the stress–crisis–trauma continuum, to what degree do you believe crisis intervention is integrated into day-to-day social work practice?

Introduction

Crisis is a term that is used frequently. Pick up the daily newspaper and you will see headlines about the oil crisis, the AIDS crisis, or the citrus fruit crisis. While some usage of the word may be journalistic grandstanding, the fact remains that we live in a world in which sudden and unpredictable events are part of our existence. Every day, millions of people are negatively impacted by crisis-inducing events that they are not capable of resolving on their own. When such an event occurs, a crisis intervenor can provide assistance. Crisis intervenors come from a variety of backgrounds (e.g., mental health workers, police or fire responders, nurses, social workers, or physicians) and are skilled in addressing the various aspects of trauma. Crisis intervenors are called on to work in a variety of situations, including violent crime, natural disasters, traumatizing accidents, domestic violence, violence perpetrated upon children, the emergence of a severe mental illness, or the loss of a loved one to physical illness, accident, or suicide. The list of problems is long and varied.

Correspondingly, the crisis intervenor must tailor the approach to the problem to best meet the needs of the individual. What is the best way to achieve success? How does a professional provide a consistently effective approach to crisis intervention, regardless of the root event? One answer lies in Roberts's seven-stage model of crisis intervention. Using current best practices and an evidence-based framework, Roberts's model provides a consistent and comprehensive approach that providers can apply to a variety of crisis situations, and is the focus of this chapter.

Trends in Crisis Intervention

Since the publication of the first edition of *The Crisis Intervention Handbook: Assessment, Treatment, and Research* (Roberts, 1991), there has been a remarkable increase in interest in the appropriate methods to address crisis response, intervention, management, and stabilization. Expanding media coverage of large-scale crises such as school shootings, terrorist attacks, and natural disasters have raised the awareness of both professionals and the general public of the need for rapid, effective approaches to all kinds of critical events. As a result, crisis intervention practices and programs have become increasingly sophisticated and complex.

Crisis intervention programs have mushroomed in the past 20 years. There are now more than 1,400 grassroots crisis centers and units affiliated with the American Association of Suicidology or local community mental health centers. There are also more than 11,000 victim assistance programs, rape crisis programs, child sexual and physical abuse intervention programs, police-based crisis intervention programs, and programs for survivors and victims of domestic violence (Roberts, 2005). The method for treating acute mental health problems has also changed drastically. In 1990, the average length of stay (ALOS) for an inpatient mental health disorder was more than 30 days. By 2005, the ALOS had shortened to 8 days. At the same time, inpatient medical hospitalizations shifted from inpatient treatment models to outpatient forms of treatment (Yeager & Roberts, 2005).

The shift to outpatient care led to the development of crisis centers that are pivotal in providing persons in crisis with access to crisis information, assessment, and intervention. Crisis center personnel routinely assist callers with problems such as depression, substance dependence, health issues, and victimization by providing initial information and, when appropriate, triage. In addition, the staff and resources of crisis hotlines, hospital emergency departments, and first responders have been thoroughly tested because of their round-the-clock availability, rapid access, and ability to provide immediate, yet temporary, assistance (Roberts, 2005).

To complicate matters, trends show that an increasing number of persons have neither health care insurance nor the ability to pay for mental health services. Between 1998 and 2004, an annual percentage increase of 5.5% (95% confidence interval = 5.17% to 5.92%) of the population was unable to obtain medical care due to cost. When this kind of societal pattern emerges, crisis intervention centers become the access portals that link the caller to appropriate community resources.

Prevalence and Impact of Emotional Trauma

Emotional trauma occurs from many sources (physical, psychological, interpersonal, etc.) and can affect people in many diverse areas of functioning. This next section reviews the impact of trauma on mental health, followed by a discussion of how people can react to a crisis.

Mental Health and Trauma

When considering approaches to mental health, it is extremely important to understand and recognize the impact of trauma on mental health and wellness. Emotional trauma is often the central issue driving substance abuse, mental health, and co-occurring disorders. The facts are too great to ignore. According to The National Trauma Consortium ("A Few Facts about Trauma," n.d.) as many as 80% of men and women in psychiatric hospitals have experienced physical or sexual abuse, most of them as children. Murphy, Musser, and Maton (1998) report that 90% of public mental health clients have been exposed to and many have experienced multiple experiences of trauma. As many as 75% of men and women receiving substance abuse treatment report abuse and trauma histories (Jennings, 2004). LeBel and Stromberg (2004) reported that 82% of all adolescents and children in continuing care inpatient and intensive residential treatment programs in the state of Massachusetts were found to have histories of trauma as reflected by a point-in-time review of records.

A look at widely circulated information such as the *Surgeon General's Report*, the *U.S. Department of Health and Human Services Report* (1996), and updates from the *National Institute of Mental Health* (Drake et al., 2001) paints a broader picture of the impact of emotional trauma:

- 17% of the population has been victim to physical assault but not diagnosed with Posttraumatic Stress Disorder (PTSD).
- 40% of the population has *witnessed* serious violence.
- Among adolescents aged 12 to 17, an estimated 8% are victims of serious sexual abuse. Millions more suffer from a far less obvious condition, namely, the aftermath of trauma that stems from poor parental attachment in infancy.
- Mental disorders account for more than 15% of the overall burden of disease, slightly more than the burden associated with all forms of cancer and second only to cardiovascular disease. One in five Americans is affected by mental illness.
- Eleven million Americans become depressed every year. Twice as many women as men suffer depression.
- Twelve million Americans under age 18 suffer from some form of mental illness, with lifetime prevalence rates as high as 17%.
- More than 16 million adults in the United States aged 18 to 54 have anxiety disorders.
- The number of Americans encountering suicidal depression some time in their lives has increased from under 10% for baby boomers and their parents to as much as 25% for the post-baby boomer generations.
- The United States is the world's largest market for antidepressants, with annual sales estimated at $7.2 billion. However, these medications are not reducing mental health problems. There is a 50% chance

of recurrence after an individual's first episode of depression, 70% after the second, and 95% after the third.

Powerful evidence of the correlation between trauma and mental and physical heath has been provided through the results of the Adverse Childhood Experiences (ACE) Study (Felitti et al., 1998). In this collaborative study between the Centers for Disease Control and Prevention and Kaiser Permanente's Health Appraisal Clinic, more than 17,000 health maintenance organization (HMO) members undergoing a comprehensive physical examination elected to provide detailed information of childhood experiences of eight categories of abuse, neglect, and family dysfunction:

1. Recurrent physical abuse.
2. Recurrent severe emotional abuse.
3. Contact sexual abuse.
4. Growing up in a household where someone was in prison.
5. Where the mother was treated violently.
6. With an alcoholic or a drug abuser.
7. Where someone was chronically depressed, mentally ill, or suicidal.
8. Where at least one biological parent was lost to the patient during childhood regardless of cause.

Key findings of this study indicate that adverse childhood experiences are vastly more common than previously recognized or acknowledged. And these experiences have a powerful relationship to adult health. In fact, those who experienced adverse childhood experiences were more likely to experience strong correlations between adverse health impacts over the course of their lives that may be linked to adverse childhood experiences, depending on the extent of exposure to said adverse childhood experiences. Study outcomes reveal strong correlations between an individual's ACE score and the likelihood of that individual having a physical or emotional disorder. Examples include:

- *Smoking:* Individuals with a higher ACE Score were more likely to be a current smoker. In fact, 6% of those studied having an ACE score of 0 were found to be current smokers; however, 15% of those with a score of 6 or more were identified as current smokers.
- *Chronic obstructive pulmonary disease (COPD):* Individuals with an ACE Score of 4 are 260% more likely to have COPD than a person with an ACE Score of 0.
- *Hepatitis:* There is a 240% increase in the prevalence of hepatitis from patients with an ACE score of 0 to patients with a score of 4.
- *Depression:* Individuals with an ACE score of 4 are 260% more likely to be diagnosed with depression than individuals with a score of 0.

- *Attempted suicide:* Those with an ACE score of 4 are 1,200% more likely to attempt suicide than those with an ACE score of 0.

Crisis Response and Crisis Intervention

A crisis can be defined as a period of psychological disequilibrium experienced as a result of a hazardous event or situation and constitutes a significant problem that cannot be remedied by using familiar coping strategies. The main cause of a crisis is an intensely stressful, traumatic, or hazardous event that is accompanied by two other conditions: (1) the individual perceives the event as the cause of considerable upset and/or disruption, and (2) the individual is unable to resolve the disruption by previously used coping methods (Roberts, 2005).

These two factors combine with the event to create an upset in the steady state of the individual experiencing the crisis. While all crises are unique to the individual, each crisis episode has similar components. Episodes are usually comprised of five components: (1) a hazardous or traumatic event, (2) a vulnerable state, (3) a precipitating factor, (4) an active crisis state, and (5) the resolution of the crisis (Roberts, 2005).

A crisis reaction refers to the acute stage, which usually occurs shortly following the hazardous event. An individual may experience various forms of reactions during the acute phase, including, but not limited to, confusion, shock, disbelief, feelings of helplessness, hopelessness, hurt, loss, shame, shock, and anger. There is often an emergent state of depression or, in lesser severity, an impact on the level of self-confidence and self-esteem. A person who has recently experienced a crisis may appear confused and disorganized. They may experience an agitated, anxious, or volatile state. This stage is when the individual is most receptive to assistance and is generally aware that usual coping mechanisms are not going to be sufficient to resolve the crisis they have just experienced (Golan, 1978; Roberts, 2005).

Crisis intervention provides both challenges and opportunities for the clinician and the patient. The individual is challenged to apply new coping strategies. The clinician is challenged to help the patient maintain the level of motivation and risk-taking necessary to sustain the patient's acceptance of new and challenging tasks to aid in recovery. According to Roberts and Dziegielewski (1995), crisis clinicians are encouraged to examine psychological and situational crises in terms of "both danger and opportunity." The aftermath of a crisis often results in a significant change in the individual's ability to function. Immediate, effective crisis intervention can minimize the amount of psychological distress experienced by the individual and support optimal functioning during the time of crisis. The use of Roberts's seven-stage model facilitates crisis resolution, cognitive mastery, and personal growth at a critical time (Yeager & Roberts, 2005).

Helping a person in crisis requires an exceptional amount of emotional sensitivity, active listening skills, and the ability to effectively communicate genuine caring and understanding, while, at the same time, gathering information to facilitate effective decision making throughout intervention, assessment, and treatment. The clinician is challenged to rapidly establish rapport with an individual who may be emotionally guarded and, at best, marginally available psychologically for clinical interventions. The structure provided by Roberts provides the framework for establishing processes applied to the individual case in a systematic manner to support the individual's coping skills.

Historical Background

Physicians emphasized the significance of a hazardous life event as far back as 400 BC. Roberts (2005) notes that Hippocrates defined a crisis as a sudden state that gravely endangers life. However, the emergence of a comprehensive theory on the impact of crisis did not emerge until early in the 20th century. Among the first to provide crisis services was the National Save-a-Life Center in New York City, which focused on suicide prevention. The current approach to crisis intervention emerged in the 1940s and was influenced primarily by the work of Erich Lindemann and, later on, by Gerald Caplan.

Lindemann and his associates were employed by Massachusetts General Hospital in Boston, Massachusetts. On the night of November 28, 1942, approximately 1,000 persons, many of whom were preparing to go overseas on military duty, were at the Cocoanut Grove nightclub in Boston when a fire erupted that tragically took the lives of 492 persons. Many more were seriously injured. Evidence indicates that an employee used a lighted match to provide light while he changed a lightbulb, and the match ignited flammable decorations that rapidly spread the fire. In the aftermath, it was discovered that the two revolving doors at the main entrance had bodies stacked four and five deep (Lindemann, 1944).

Lindemann and colleagues based their emerging crisis theory on observations of the acute and delayed reactions of the survivors and grief-stricken relatives and friends of the victims. They noted that many individuals experiencing acute and delayed responses to grief and trauma demonstrated five related reactions:

1. Somatic distress.
2. Preoccupation with the image of the deceased.
3. Guilt.
4. Hostile reactions.
5. Loss of patterns of conduct.

Lindemann's observations led to an increased understanding of what became known as *grief work*. His major finding was that the duration of the grief reaction appeared to be dependent on the degree to which the bereaved person was able to conduct her or his mourning. In general, it was believed that grief work included actions toward emancipation from the deceased, adjustment to living within the environment from which the loved one is now absent, and developing new relationships. Lindemann's work taught us that people need to be encouraged to permit time for mourning in order to effectively respond to the loss and adjust to life without their loved one. Further, negative outcomes of crises develop if the normal grieving process is delayed. Lindemann's work was also applied in interventions with World War II veterans who were suffering from "combat neuroses" and bereaved family members.

Caplan (1964), who was also affiliated with Massachusetts General Hospital and Harvard School of Public Health, expanded on the ground-breaking work of Lindemann throughout the 1940s and 1950s. Caplan explored a variety of developmental crisis situations, for example, accidental and health-related crisis and death. He was the first to link the concept of homeostasis to crisis intervention. In 1961, he noted that crisis is an upset of a steady state in which the individual encounters an obstacle (usually to significant life goals) that cannot be overcome through traditional problem-solving activities. Caplan noted there was a homeostatic balance between affective and cognitive experience for each individual. Psychological functioning is threatened when opposing physiological, psychological, or social forces disrupt the balance. A crisis state will ensue if these forces overcome an individual's innate coping skill. Caplan further defined a crisis as an individual response to "stimuli which signals danger to a fundamental need satisfaction...and the circumstances are such that habitual problem-solving methods are unsuccessful within the time span of past expectation for success" (p. 39). Additionally, four stages of crisis reaction were described:

1. The initial rise of tension that comes from the precipitating event.

2. An increased level of disruption to daily living, as the individual is unable to resolve the crisis quickly.

3. The potential emergence of depressive or other primary mental health issues, that if unattended, result in stage 4.

4. A complete mental collapse or acute mental health episode *or* an alternative of partial resolution of the crisis, resulting in functioning for extended periods of time with diminished emotional skills and responses.

J. S. Tyhurst (1957) contributed to the crisis knowledge base through his study of transition states—for example, migration, retirement, civilian disaster, and the like. Based on his studies of individual patterns in response to community disaster, Tyhurst concluded that there are three overlapping phases, each with it own unique manifestation of stress:

1. A period of impact.

2. A period of recoil.

3. A posttraumatic period of recovery.

Tyhurst recommended state-specific intervention that focuses on reinforcing the relationship network and not removing a person who is experiencing transitional crisis from their life situation.

L. Rapoport (1962) expanded on the concept of disruption of the homeostasis by indicating that the "upset of a steady state" (p. 212) placed the individual in a hazardous condition. The crisis situation results in a problem frequently perceived as a threat, loss, or challenge and is linked to three interrelated factors that function to create or exacerbate the crisis:

1. A hazardous event.
2. A threat to life goals.
3. An inability to respond with adequate coping mechanisms.

Rapoport was the first to clinically conceptualize and apply a crisis intervention process. She asserted that persons experiencing crisis must have immediate access to the crisis worker stating, "A little help, rationally directed and purposefully focused at a strategic time, is more effective than more extensive help given at a period of less emotional accessibility" (Rapoport, 1967, p. 38). Additionally, Rapoport connected the process of establishing a primary diagnosis during the initial crisis assessment combined with conveying a sense of hope and optimism to the victim, in an effort to support the individual in the development of new problem-solving skills, along with clearly delineated goals and tasks. The result was the establishment of the initial working structure between the client and the therapist to resolve a crisis. Parad added the concept that the crisis is not the situation itself; rather, it is the person's perception of the event combined with the individual response to the situation that dictates the degree of reaction (Parad, 1971, p. 197).

N. Golan (1978) echoed the concepts set forth by Rapoport. Golan concluded that a person is frequently more amenable to suggestions and change during a state of active crisis. Golan noted that intensive, brief, appropriately focused treatment when the client is motivated produces more effective change than long-term therapy, when motivation and emotional accessibility may be lacking.

Roberts's Seven-Stage Practice Model for Crisis Intervention

Several practice models have emerged for crisis intervention work, which build on and synthesize the works of Caplan (1964), Rapoport (1962, 1967), Parad (1971), and Golan (1978). Each of the models focuses on therapeutic techniques designed to resolve immediate problems and emotional conflicts within a time-limited, goal-directed framework. Crisis-oriented treatment is designed to minimize the need for long-term treatment by capitalizing on the immediate emotional crisis and motivation that is present as a result of the crisis, thus providing optimal impact in a brief, time-limited approach. Roberts's (1991) seven-stage model of crisis intervention has been utilized for helping persons in acute psychological and situational crisis. Roberts's model has been tested and applied for 15 years with successes in numerous venues, including, but not limited to, addictions, psychiatric treatment, child welfare, domestic violence, battered women, school crisis health, and community crisis (Roberts, 2005, p. 20). The seven stages are:

1. Plan and conduct a thorough assessment (including lethality, dangerousness to self or others, and immediate psychosocial needs).

2. Make psychological contact, establish rapport, and rapidly establish the relationship (conveying genuine respect for the client, acceptance, reassurance, and a nonjudgmental attitude).

3. Examine the dimensions of the problem in order to define it (including the "last straw" or precipitating event).

4. Encourage an exploration of feelings and emotions.

5. Generate, explore, and assess past coping attempts.

6. Restore cognitive functioning through implementation of an action plan.

7. Follow up and leave the door open for booster sessions 3 and/or 6 months later.

Discussion

Practice with clients in crisis can be structured around a generally (but not always) sequential series of tasks, including conducting the initial assessment, establishing a relationship, explore any factors contributing to the crisis situation, help determine the client's feelings in regard to the situation, evaluate their past coping efforts, develop an action plan, and follow up on outcomes. Each of these tasks is described below.

Plan and Conduct a Thorough Assessment

Experienced clinicians frequently complete stages 1 and 2 concurrently. However, it is most important to assess the individual's risk for harm to self or others and the potential for rescue. The first and foremost task for the crisis intervenor is gathering basic information related to individual needs, experiences, perceptions, and plans to determine potential risk. Counselors, social workers, physicians, psychologists, and nurses are likely to encounter a full range of self-destructive individuals in crisis, including those who have taken potentially lethal actions to end their lives. Clinical staff dealing with crisis calls, or individuals in crisis centers or emergency rooms, often face cases where there is "some" potential danger for harm, but the individual is not forthcoming with enough information to determine the level of risk. In these situations, it is important to evaluate the patient in the following six areas:

1. Need for medical attention (e.g., drug overdose, suicide attempt, or victim of domestic violence).
2. Examination of general thoughts, specific plans, actions, or gathering of items that suggest a plan of self-harm. Ask about the patient's age, recent major life events, physical health, history of psychiatric diagnosis, family history, history of substance abuse, sexual orientation, previous attempts at self-harm, and personal beliefs related to self-harm. (Note: Risk factors for self-harm do not necessarily equal potential for self-harm, but must be carefully considered against environmental protective factors such as positive outlook on life, cultural beliefs that view suicide as negative, presence of positive coping skills, presence of positive social supports, and a positive relationship with family members. For a complete assessment of at-risk patients see the American Psychiatric Association Practice Guidelines for the Assessment and Treatment of Patients with Suicidal Behaviors.)
3. Determine whether any children are involved and are in danger.
4. Does the victim require emergency transportation to a hospital or shelter?
5. Is the crisis caller under the influence of alcohol or drugs?
6. Determine the potential for domestic violence and whether there are any violent persons living in the residence. (Roberts, 2005, pp. 21–22)

Make Psychological Contact, Establish Rapport, and Rapidly Establish the Relationship

Stage 2 involves the initial contact between the professional and the patient. The priority of the clinician is to rapidly establish rapport with the individual based on interactions that communicate respect for, and acceptance of, the person seeking assistance. In most cases, it is helpful to engage active listening skills. Taking time to hear and assess the individual's story, smiling, questioning, and coming from a position of interest are all important factors in establishing rapport with the individual experiencing crisis. Frequently, persons seeking assistance require assurance that they are going to be able to cope with the issues they are facing. Providing assurance and examples of approaches to help the person to stabilize assist the person in feeling he or she has "come to the right place" to address individual needs. It is important to remember that persons in crisis feel as if they are the first to have ever faced this issue or situation. It is essential that the care provider offer assurance of the potential for recovery (Roberts, 2005, p. 22).

Examine the Dimensions of the Problem in Order to Define It

It is useful to identify contributing factors to the crisis event. Questions that assist the clinician in understanding the patient's experience are paramount.

For example, ask a leading question, such as, "What is it that made today different from other difficult days you have experienced?" Examine the "last straw" or precipitating event. Ask the patient about previous coping methods, previous experiences with health care providers, previous experiences with treatments, and the success or failure of prior hospitalizations or therapeutic interactions. Use open-ended questions to examine the dimensions of the problem. Focus on the "now and how" of resolving the crisis rather than what has happened (Roberts, 2005, p. 23).

Encourage an Exploration of Feelings and Emotions

Stage 4 is closely related to stage 3, particularly when focusing on the precipitating event. It is presented here as a separate step because some therapists might be tempted to gloss over it in an effort to complete the assessment in a timely manner. Effective assessment takes time. Simply asking a few "key" questions cannot sum up the assessment of the situation. The intervener must permit the client to express feelings and emotions in an accepting and supportive, confidential, nonjudgmental manner. Frequently, important clues for stabilizing the patient begin to emerge (Roberts, 2005, p. 23).

Generate, Explore, and Assess Past Coping Attempts

Most youth and adults have established coping mechanisms. Some are more effective, some less effective, and some are completely inadequate or maladaptive. For example, substance abuse is frequently considered to be a common maladaptive coping mechanism. It is important to work with the patient to assess the presence of both positive and negative coping attempts and their relative application to the current crisis situation. The skilled clinician will be able to formulate an effective treatment plan building on the successful experiences of the client, working from a strengths perspective. Consider the use of solution-focused therapy at this stage of crisis intervention. Solution-focused therapy emphasizes working with existing client strengths to establish a pathway toward resolving the crisis through a series of agreed-on steps between the clinician and the patient. Both strengths perspective and solution-focused therapy view the patient as resilient. Both methods offer a two-pronged approach that is an effective tool for assessing past coping mechanisms that were effective and can again be applied to empower the patient to assume an active problem-solving role in the recovery process (Roberts, 2005, pp. 23–24).

Restore Cognitive Functioning Through Implementation of an Action Plan

Integral to the crisis intervention process is the restoration of cognitive stability, which involves three phases:

> *Phase I*: Establishment of a realistic understanding of what happened and what led to the crisis. Frequently, details surrounding the crisis are unclear. Establishing a clear understanding of what happened,

how and why it happened, the persons involved, and extenuating circumstances establishes the foundation on which cognitive mastery will be established.

Phase II: Evaluate the patient's understanding of the events' specific meanings. Crisis episodes tend to shatter an individual's future outlook. In an instant, everything the patient had understood as the pathway to the future can actually be or appear to be uncertain. Examining how the situation conflicts with his or her expectations, life goals, and belief systems will assist the individual in understanding and addressing current reality. Resist the temptation to identify the patient's irrational beliefs, but rather permit the client to discover cognitive distortions and/or irrational beliefs.

Phase III: Restructure or replace irrational beliefs. This phase frequently is completed in individual sessions, but can include homework assignments, journaling assignments, support groups, or other processes that assist the patient in formalizing thoughts and beliefs related to the crisis situation. (Roberts, 2005, pp. 24–25)

Follow Up

Closing sessions provide the client with opportunities to explore the progress they have made in therapy. Patients can examine the support systems available to them and discuss with group members how they can access ongoing support within the community. Offer follow-up sessions to support ongoing recovery processes. Make patients aware of potential trigger events, anniversaries of the crisis, and other high-risk times that may require additional support (Roberts, 2005, p. 25).

Summary of Current Evidence-Based and Informed Information on Crisis Intervention

Remarkable strides have been made within the past decade to clarify knowledge, practices, and processes supporting evidence-based approaches to crisis intervention since the last publication of this chapter. At that writing, we applied a simplistic but straightforward approach to understanding the increase in readily available knowledge related to evidence-based crisis intervention by searching on the Internet. A 2007 Google search for "evidence-based crisis intervention" retrieved 1,180,000 sites. When updating this chapter in 2011, the same search brought about 3,900,000 results. One can assume that this large increase in responses in a relatively short time period is reflective of the growing interest in this topic.

Compared to other disciplines, it is clear that social work has embraced evidence-based practice. In a similar methodology, a Google search for "evidence-based social work" pulled about 125,000,000 hits. "Evidence-based nursing" generated 9,920,000 hits. "Evidence-based psychology" demonstrated about 31,000,000 hits. "Evidence-based medicine" generated about 66,000,000 hits.

Examination of the data indicates there are great strides being made in increased awareness, knowledge base, application issues, integration of services, and needs management across time. It is clear to see by review of the data that evidence-based practice (EBP) is a worldwide undertaking, encompassing not only a great diversity of subjects but a wide diversity of persons, situations, and innovative approaches to care for persons experiencing physical health, mental health, social, and behavioral problems.

However, while evidence of interest in EBP is a necessary component facilitating establishment of such programs, it is not sufficient. This is referred to by some as the estrangement between knowing and doing. Research by Rosen (2003) and Walrath and colleagues (2006) suggest that if there is a weak link, it is the smaller agencies that experience greater difficulty in accurately implementing and sustaining evidence-based practices because there are fewer resources at their disposal. In order for EBP to be possible, agency staff must have access to Internet databases needed to conduct literature searches of the available evidence. Appropriate staff in-service training sessions are also key components in the implementation of EBP and are critical to success. Additionally, the impact of the EBP approach on staff work flow, administrative support, and management functionality must be figured into the adoption process.

Therefore, a successful EBP program is built from both the top down and the bottom up. The full implementation stage requires sustained management commitment, leadership rounding, program optimization, and daily feedback. It is important to note that evidence-based processes initially tend to magnify organization problems and weaknesses. It is important for administration to anticipate this process and support rather than blame staff for reductions in productivity or what may appear on the surface to be new problems.

In the final stages of implementation, the focus shifts to innovation and sustainability. Practice innovation evolves and the staff becomes comfortable with processes and are able to determine how best to apply the evidence to the population served. One caution is to be certain that staff members maintain fidelity to the model or theory. Tweaking the process can diminish effectiveness. A sustainable program cannot be taken for granted. Constant monitoring is needed to maintain new policies and practices. Maintenance involves frequent review and updating of evidence-based tools and monitoring processes within the context of ever-changing and shifting service delivery systems. Maynard (2010) recommends establishment of a learning organization as a guiding framework for bridging science and service in sustaining the implementation of evidence-based practices. Enthusiasm, guidance, and flexibility from management will serve to reduce barriers for staff. Additional resources of time, money, and training may be required to address unforeseen impacts of implementation and for staff support, recognition, and retention (Ganju, 2006; Goldman et al., 2001).

In addition to implementation in agency settings there are numerous efforts to establish EBP learning programs in both community practitioners and in educational settings. For example, Mullen, Bledsoe, and Bellamy (2009) have implemented pilot programs to study the effectiveness of training community practitioners in organizational settings. Rubin and Parrish (2009) are researching processes to validate and measure effectiveness of training and technical support related to evidence-based processes. Research with the focus of evaluation of implementation of evidence-based practice is critical as it addresses a serious challenge to the social work profession. The problem is the gap between theory and policy and practice. Soydan, Mullen, Alexandra, Rehnman, and Li (2010) indicate "Bridging the gap involves several complementary steps, from primary knowledge production, synthesis of accumulated knowledge, dissemination and translation to implementation in a timely manner" (p. 698).

Many new concepts for care have emerged from the EBP initiative. The most important is the use of EBP to improve care through application of the best available evidence. However, a close second is the concept of an integrative care approach. An integrative approach is one in which all disciplines interact to provide the best care to meet the individualized needs and preferences of the patient who presents in crisis. Current evidence has shown that rapid responses to trauma lead to more rapid recoveries and offer opportunities for practitioners to collaborate in ways not previously imagined.

One of the areas experiencing increasing integration is the crossroads of physical and mental health. Evidence-based practice guidelines for the treatment and management of common mental disorders were first introduced in the 1990s. These guidelines described effective treatments for mental illnesses commonly seen within the primary health-care setting (Roberts & Yeager, 2004; Schulberg, Katon, Simon, & Rush, 1998). However, mental illness is not neatly packaged as a single diagnosis. Frequently, depression is complicated by substance dependence. Additionally, many persons who present with co-occurring physical and mental illness also report additional somatic symptoms. Despite the guidelines and other diagnostic aids, as many as 75% of primary care providers indicate that they feel unprepared to address co-occurring diseases within the primary care setting (Wiest et al., 2002).

Evidence-based techniques can fill this knowledge gap and direct the implementation of collaborative care between medical and behavioral health providers. One group of studies has focused on "stepped care." Stepped care begins in the primary care office with low-intensity interventions and steps up the resistant patient to more intensive levels of care as necessary (Katon et al., 1995, 1996, 1997; Katon, Von Korff, Lin, & Simon, 2001; Von Korff & Tiemens, 2000).

The current literature includes several studies that demonstrate the potential for utilization of collaborative care models to improve patient compliance, outcome, and communication among care providers, patients, and families in crisis. Still unclear is the exact framework and/or nature of these collaborative efforts. Within the literature, there appears to be a range of what can best be referred to as "co-located services." Best practice models are recommending a "continuum of collaboration" between a variety of care providers, such as physicians, psychiatrists, and nurses, yet the degree to which collaboration actually occurs within current health care structures remains to be seen. However, as evidence increases and systems evolve over time, there will emerge a new model of service delivery that will encompass a variety of disciplines working to resolve the critical issues of the individual in carefully constructed, evidence-based interventions (Badamgarav et al., 2003; Schoenbaum et al., 2002; Schoenbaum, Miranda, Sherbourne, Duan, & Wells, 2004; Simon et al., 2001, 2002; Von Korff, Unutzer, Katon, & Wells, 2001; Wagner, Austin, & Von Korff, 1996).

Another key component of evidence-based crisis intervention is the utilization of technology. Since 1996, systematic reviews prepared and maintained by the Cochrane Collaboration have been published in the Cochrane Library, along with bibliographic and quality-assessed material on the effects of health care interventions submitted by others. Cochrane reviews have been published in the Cochrane Database of Systematic Reviews. These reviews are regularly updated as information becomes available and in response to comments and criticism. The reviews are now widely regarded as being of better quality, on average, than their counterparts in print journals (Roberts & Yeager, 2004). For evidence to be effective, technology must be available to deliver decision support. The emergence of decision support programs like the Cochrane Collaboration signifies remarkable progress in the application of evidence-based practices in all areas of crisis intervention.

As technology grows, so does the complexity of analysis. Decision-support and technical groups are growing rapidly. Evidence-based technology centers have been established in numerous areas of government, university, and private business sectors, such as:

- Blue Cross and Blue Shield Association, Technology Evaluation Center
- Duke University
- Agency for Healthcare Research and Quality
- Johns Hopkins University
- McMaster University
- Oregon Health & Science University
- RTI International, University of North Carolina
- Southern California
- Tufts University, New England Medical Center
- University of Alberta, Edmonton, Alberta, Canada
- University of Minnesota, Minneapolis
- University of Ottawa, Ottawa, Canada

The formation of decision-support systems and the means to access them is an important component to expanding evidence-based approaches to treatment. The process is one of a logical sequence of events:

1. As information on EBP becomes readily available, care providers are more likely to incorporate evidence-based approaches and protocols.

2. Inclusion of an interdisciplinary approach to crisis situations will move the knowledge base forward through the examination of outcomes, thus closing the loop.

3. New evidence will be examined and weighed against previously established best evidence.

Additional sources for the advancement of EBPs are the establishment of practice-based research groups who are applying evidence-based approaches following a crisis. It is important to note that evidence-based knowledge development is not a one-way street flowing from the scientific bench to the crisis situation. The practitioner has an equally important role in assessing and understanding the applicability of evidence in the management of crisis situations. Practitioners serve an important role of not only testing the protocols, but also improving the evidence as applied to crisis situations.

As you read and learn more about evidence-based approaches, you may find yourself wanting more information about your specific area of expertise, such as Police Crisis Intervention Teams (CIT), Crisis Intervention with HIV patients, or Children's Protective Services Crisis Intervention. Here is a six-step exercise to try:

1. Stop for just a moment and think about what you have just read. Then ask yourself, "Can I replicate the process described?" "Can I formulate a question in my area of interest that I want answered?"

2. Next, Google the area of interest. Look at the information available. Appraise the level of evidence you find.

3. Now refine your search in a more comprehensive manner by examining the Cochrane Collaboration, or InfoPOEMS, or any other evidence-based resource.

4. Now ask yourself the following questions:

   "Does the information apply to my patient or problem of interest?"
   "Does the information influence my approach to treatment?"
   "How does the information assist in diagnosis?"
   "Is there information about risk factors?"
   "Is there a comparison of treatment approaches?"
   "Can I use the information to develop a target for outcome measurement?"

5. Consider what information is still needed and search for those answers. Keep completing the process until you feel comfortable with your answers.

6. Review your findings with your team, colleagues, or supervisor.

While it is virtually impossible to cover all aspects of evidence-based crisis intervention within a single chapter, it is possible to provide resources that will assist you in developing the skills to conduct your own search for evidence. As we have said previously, crisis is a very broad term. The best approach is to provide a road map that gives each provider the means to answer his or her own questions.

The information on crisis intervention is growing and changing daily. Evidence-based crisis intervention is a field in transition. Best practices exist in some areas but are absent in others. The challenge to the clinician is to develop and evaluate the evidence in a systematic method, apply the information in his or her practice, and measure the outcomes to further inform yourself and others. As with any new methodology, barriers exist that impact establishment and acceptance. Commonly encountered challenges and possible remedies are discussed next.

Challenges in Implementing Evidence-Based Practice

The emergence of the evidence-based approach has presented challenges across the physical and behavioral health continuum. Some of the major challenges to implementing evidence-based practices for crisis intervention are discussed next.

Consumer Information Overload

We live in a scientific age in which new medical and social science advances are reported almost daily. The pace of change is breathtaking. Consumers are bombarded with information about medications, surgeries, alternative health care approaches, and psychological interventions that are "guaranteed" to ease their burden and enhance their lives each time they open their e-mail or postal box, turn on the TV, or surf the Internet. Individuals are faced with choices of herbal remedies, gadgets, intrusive physical interventions, and intriguingly named psychological treatments to manage everything from life-threatening illness to unappealing aspects of their appearance. People naturally apply information they hear to their problems and seek clarification from their care providers. This need for clarification usually comes in the form of a question such as "I saw this product on television; the ad said I should talk to you," or "I read about this in a magazine." It is the responsibility of the care provider to keep up with innovations, but what is the best method of evaluation? The answer: evidence-based approaches (Roberts & Yeager, 2004).

Professional Information Overload

Professionals are flooded with an overwhelming volume of information on a daily basis. Rosenthal (2004) estimates that the average professional must read an estimated 19 articles per day in his or her field just to keep up with the advances in clinical research (p. 20). The process required to do a thorough evidence-based search only adds to the burden. This process is generally defined as having five well-defined steps (Rosenthal, 2004; Sackett, Rosenberg, Gray, Haynes, & Richardson, 1996):

1. Format structured, clear, and answerable clinical questions about a patient's problem or information needed.
2. Search the literature for relevant clinical articles that might answer the question.
3. Conduct a critical appraisal on the selected research articles and rank the evidence for its validity and usefulness (clinical applicability).
4. Formulate and apply a clinical intervention based on the useful findings or "best evidence."
5. Conduct clinical audits to determine if the protocol was implemented properly (identify issues/problems).

Lack of Standardized Instruments

While the recurring emphasis in the literature is on assessment, there is a notable lack of standardized instruments with strong psychometric properties available to practitioners (Aguilera, 1998; Kanel, 1999; Roberts & Greene, 2002; Yeager & Roberts, 2005). Few studies have tested intervention models based on crisis theory (Aguilera, 1998; Kanel, 1999; Roberts, 1996; Slaikeu, 1984). Measurement instruments designed to objectively assess the degree of an individual's crisis state are not available (Corcoran & Roberts, 2000). The scales that have been developed are not capable of measuring the magnitude of a crisis state from the client's viewpoint (Roberts & Lewis, 2001). The science of EBP frequently does not transition well from "the bench to the bedside." Strategies are needed that will connect trusted psychometric measures to real-world referents and eliminate arbitrariness.

Effectiveness Training and Skill Set

Another challenge to implementation of EBPs in crisis intervention relates to workforce training. The objective of the National Survey of Psychotherapy Training in Psychiatry, Psychology, and Social Work was to determine the amount of evidence-based treatment taught in accredited training programs in these areas to identify whether the training was elective or required and presented as didactic (coursework) or clinical supervision. The major findings were as follows:

- Training programs offered a range of psychotherapies (mostly non-evidence-based practice [non-EBP]) as electives and often did not require the gold standard of didactic and clinical supervision for EBP. However, more recently, training programs have been seen offering a higher percentage of EBP courses that meet the training gold standard.
- The two disciplines with the largest number of students and the emphasis on training for clinical practice (PsyD and MSW) required

the lowest percentage of gold standard training in EBP. Although all of the disciplines offered elective courses in a range of psychotherapies, including EBP, the required clinical supervision training was largely in non-EBP, particularly in psychiatry. Among the EBPs, cognitive behavioral therapy (CBT) remained the best disseminated among all the disciplines. In psychiatry, this was likely due to the psychiatry accreditation board CBT requirement. Even though psychiatry reported the highest percentage of obstacles to EBP, more than 90% of the psychiatry residency programs were complying. Accreditation requirements, rather than voluntary changes, seemed to be effective in changing practice.

- The PhD clinical psychology programs were the most positive about EBP. This acceptance may be due to the success of CBT, which was developed in close collaboration with PhD psychologists who were often involved in the trials. Twenty percent of psychiatry training directors mentioned that EBP training was "too time consuming." Non-EBP may be less time consuming to teach because it may require less precision. (Weissman et al., 2006, p. 930)

Finally, the provider who performs an effective evidence-based crisis intervention assessment must possess a skill set that involves being able to find, rank, and analyze the best current evidence in a timely manner. Some providers will need continuing professional development education to become more comfortable with methods to incorporate these skills into daily practice.

Organizational Culture and Climate

The degree to which EBP is implemented in crisis intervention is complex and based on the reaction of those within the organization. Several recently proposed models target organizational factors that may support or hinder implementation of EBP and innovation in mental health settings (Aarons, 2004; Burns & Hoagwood, 2005). Additionally, a number of studies have identified certain constructs that are believed to be important in effective implementation of any innovation in organizations (Damanpour, 1991; Frambach & Schillewaert, 2002; Glisson, 2002).

Organizational culture and climate are two factors thought to influence attitudes toward adoption of new and innovative approaches in general, including EBP (Aarons, 2004). Although definitions vary, organizational culture can be defined as the organizational norms and expectations regarding how people behave and how things are done in an organization (Glisson & James, 2002). In contrast, organizational climate is more accurately a reflection of the staff's perceptions and emotional responses to not only the work environment, but also the potential impact that proposed changes may have on the workplace, workload, and overall functionality of the agency (Glisson & James, 2002). Thus, culture and climate are believed to be major contributing factors to attitudes in the workplace.

These characteristics are likely to impact dissemination and adoption of EBP (Gotham, 2004).

Studies across social work and mental-health delivery systems have shown organizational culture and climate are important contributors to the quality and outcomes of services provided. For example, organizational culture influences staff attitudes (e.g., job satisfaction, organizational commitment), service quality, turnover rate, and morale of the institution (Glisson & James, 2002). Constructive cultures are characterized by established organizational norms that are both reflective and rewarding of achievement, motivation, and individual accomplishment and satisfaction, combined with supportive and ethical approaches to all aspects of the workplace. Constructive cultures encourage supportive interactions and approaches to tasks that aid staff in meeting their goals for the task at hand and their individual satisfaction goals. In contrast, defensive cultures are characterized by seeking approval and consensus, requiring pre-established conventions, conforming, and a degree of subservient dependence. Defensive cultures encourage or implicitly require interaction with people in ways that will not threaten personal security (Cooke & Szumal, 2000). Carmazzi and Aarons (2003) found that staff working in child and adolescent mental health agencies with more positive cultures had more positive attitudes toward the adoption of EBP, whereas those with more negative cultures had more negative attitudes toward adoption of EBP.

Additionally, organizational culture has been shown to impact organizational change by facilitating or hindering the change process. When an organization's cultural values are in conflict with change, the result can be a lack of support, cooperation, and innovation (Feldman, 1993). Therefore, it is important to understand how organizational culture affects organizational change, including the implementation of EBP.

Studies in mental health service agencies and programs have examined a number of organizational-level factors that affect clinician attitudes. A positive organizational climate correlates positively with better organizational processes, work attitudes, and outcomes. A positive organizational climate is also associated with better long-term treatment outcomes (Schoenwald, Sheidow, Letourneau, & Liao, 2003). Work attitudes are also important contributing factors because they tend to mediate the effects of climate on employee performance and motivation (Parker et al., 2003). Positive organizational characteristics tend to positively correlate to employees' commitment to their organization and their job satisfaction (Glisson & Durick, 1988; Morris & Bloom, 2002). By developing a clearer understanding of the culture of an organization, it becomes possible to identify potential positive or negative attitudes that may affect the implementation of EBPs.

Provider Demographics

It is important to make an effort to consider and control for individual-level variables such as provider demographics when attempting to implement any innovation to a practice environment. Gotham (2004) suggests that provider demographics and attitudes can be influential in the willingness to adopt and implement an innovation such as EBPs. Levels of individual receptivity to change can be an important determinant of innovation success. Rogers (1995) suggested that higher levels of formal education among staff and favorable attitudes toward change and science are associated with increased adoption of innovation.

Remember to take the provider's level of professional development into consideration, as well as the time that has passed since completion of training, when attempting to introduce change into the practice environment. Findings suggest that psychiatric interns in specialty mental health clinics report more positive attitudes to using evidence-based assessment protocols (Garland, Kruse, & Aarons, 2003) and endorse more positive attitudes toward adopting EBPs than more experienced clinicians (Aarons, 2004; Ogborne, Wild, Braun, & Newton-Taylor, 1998). While senior leadership may decide to adopt an innovation, individual buy-in is the key element to acceptance, implementation, and development. Without the support of clinic staff, the implementation of any innovation is frequently long and less than effective (Moore, 2002; Rogers, 1995).

EBPs affect the structure and function of the agency and must be carefully considered in light of the patient population. Changes that may affect the patients need to be carefully thought out, planned, communicated, and tested. Current evidence demonstrates that positive consumer attitudes toward EBP can be achieved as a result (Roberts & Yeager, 2004).

Conclusion

Crisis intervention is a field that has expanded and evolved throughout the past 64 years. This expansion will continue as our understanding of the nature of crisis and the individual response to crisis evolves. There is an opportunity within each major crisis episode to improve professional practice and provide additional data to the applied form of crisis intervention. As with many forms of health and mental health interventions, the focus on evidence-based practice is still widely dispersed. Only moderate levels of evidence support the findings. However, the tide appears to be changing. Practitioners, educators, administrators, consumers, and researchers are becoming increasingly aware of the principals of evidence-based practice. Within each area, studies of varying sophistication are being developed to inform the evidence base.

The goals of this chapter are threefold. The first goal is to present an overview of the current issues and trends in evidence-based crisis intervention. The second goal is to provide the reader with a knowledge base of practical application. The third goal is to inform and inspire the practitioner to take up the challenges of evidence-based approaches, both in crisis intervention and in other practice areas. It is our belief that crisis intervention and evidence-based approaches have the potential to touch all areas of clinical practice. The body of evidence and knowledge will grow as practitioners apply systematic program evaluations, as researchers develop greater numbers of randomized control studies, and as consumer organizations provide data related to client satisfaction with services provided. We are confident that practitioners, when provided with the right tools, can produce compelling evidence that will direct the continued development of effective crisis intervention treatment.

Key Terms

Cognitive functioning	Crisis response	Social work
Crisis intervention	Evidence-based practice	
Crisis intervention teams	Emotional trauma	

Review Questions for Critical Thinking

1. What is meant by the term *crisis*?
2. Pick one stage of Roberts's practice model for crisis intervention and describe it.
3. How can one conduct an assessment of someone in crisis?
4. How has the adoption of evidence-based practice impacted the field of crisis counseling?

Online Resources

National Trauma Consortium: http://www.nationaltraumaconsortium.org

The consortium is dedicated to integrating research and practice in the field of trauma, engaging in advocacy and public education related to trauma issues, and promoting effective services in the field of trauma.

Social Work Policy Institute: http://www.socialworkpolicy.org/research/evidence-based-practice-2.html

This link provides useful information on the topic of evidence-based practice, supported by the Social Work Policy Institute of the National Association of Social Workers.

University of North Carolina: http://www.hsl.unc.edu/services/tutorials/ebm/welcome.htm

This is a web-based tutorial on evidence-based practice supported by the University of North Carolina.

Psychological First Aid Field Operations Guide: http://www.ptsd.va.gov/professional/manuals/psych-first-aid.asp

This guide was prepared by the United States Department of Veterans Affairs.

References

Aarons, G. A. (2004). Mental health provider attitudes toward adoption of evidence-based practice: The Evidence-Based Practice Attitude Scale (EBPAS). *Mental Health Services Research, 6*, 61–74.

Aguilera, D. (1998). *Crisis intervention: Theory and methodology.* St. Louis, MO: Mosby.

Badamgarav, E., Weingarten, S. R., Henning, J. M., Knight, K., Hasselblad, V., Gano, A. Jr., & Ofman, J. J. (2003). Effectiveness of disease management programs in depression: A systematic review. *American Journal of Psychiatry, 160*(12), 2080–2090.

Burns, B. J., & Hoagwood, K. E. (Eds.). (2005). Evidence-based practice: Pt. II. Effecting change [Special issue]. *Child and Adolescent Psychiatric Clinics of North America, 14*(2).

Caplan, G. (1964). *Principles of preventive psychiatry.* New York, NY: Basic Books.

Carmazzi, A., & Aarons, G. A. (2003, February). *Organizational culture and attitudes toward adoption of evidence-based practice*. Presented at the NASMHPD Research Institute's 2003 Conference on State Mental Health Agency Services Research, Program Evaluation, and Policy, Baltimore, Maryland.

Cooke, R. A., & Szumal, J. L. (2000). Using the organizational culture inventory to understand the operating cultures of organizations. In N. M. Ashkanasy, C. P. M. Wilderom, & M. F. Peterson (Eds.), *Handbook of organizational culture and climate* (pp. 147–162). Thousand Oaks, CA: Sage.

Corcoran, J., & Roberts, A. R. (2000). Research on crisis intervention and recommendations for future research. In A. R. Roberts (Ed.), *Crisis intervention handbook: Assessment treatment and research* (2nd ed., pp. 453–483). New York, NY: Oxford University Press.

Damanpour, F. (1991). Organizational innovation: A meta-analysis of effects of determinants and moderators. *Academy of Management Journal, 34*, 555–590.

Drake, R. E., Goldman, H. H., Leff, H. S., Lehman, A. F., Dixon, L., Mueser, K. T., & Torrey, W. C. (2001). Implementing evidence-based practices in routine mental health service settings. *Psychiatric Services, 52*, 179–182.

Feldman, S. P. (1993). How organizational culture can affect innovation. In L. Hirschhorn & C. K. E. Barnett (Eds.), *The psychodynamics of organizations: Labor and social change* (pp. 85–97). Philadelphia, PA: Temple University Press.

Felitti, V. J., Anda, R. F., Nordenbery, D., Williamson, D. F., Spitz, A. M., Edwards, V.,... Marks, J. S. (1998). Relationship of childhood abuse and household dysfunction to many of the leading causes of death in adults: The Adverse Childhood Experiences (ACE) Study. *American Journal of Preventive Medicine, 14*(4), 245–258.

Frambach, R. T., & Schillewaert, N. (2002). Organizational innovation adoption: A multi-level framework of determinants and opportunities for future research. [Special issue]: *Marketing Theory in the Next Millennium, Journal of Business Research, 55*, 163–176.

Ganju, V. (2006), Mental health quality and accountability: The role of evidence-based practices and performance measurement. *Administration and Policy in Mental Health & Mental Health Services Research, 33*(6), 659–665.

Garland, A. F., Kruse, M., & Aarons, G. A. (2003). Clinicians and outcome measurement: What's the use? *Journal of Behavioral Health Services and Research, 30*, 393–405.

Glisson, C. (2002). The organizational context of children's mental health services. *Clinical Child and Family Psychology Review, 5,* 233–253.

Glisson, C., & Durick, M. (1988). Predictors of job satisfaction and organizational commitment in human service organizations. *Administrative Science Quarterly, 33,* 61–81.

Glisson, C., & James, L. R. (2002). The cross-level effects of culture and climate in human service teams. *Journal of Organizational Behavior, 23,* 767–794.

Golan, N. (1978). *Treatment in crisis interventions.* New York, NY: Free Press.

Goldman, H. H., Ganju, V., Drake, R. E., Gorman, P., Hogan, M., Hyde, P. S., Morgan, O. (2001). Policy implications for implementing evidence-based practices. *Psychiatric Services 52*(12), 1591–1597.

Gotham, H. J. (2004). Diffusion of mental health and substance abuse treatments: Development, dissemination, and implementation. *Clinical Psychology: Science and Practice, 11,* 161–176.

Jennings, A. (2004). *The damaging consequences of violence and trauma: Facts, discussion points, and recommendations for the behavioral health system.* Alexandria, VA: National Association of State Mental Health Program Directors, National Technical Assistance Center for State Mental Health Planning.

Kanel, K. (1999). *A guide to crisis intervention.* Pacific Grove, CA: Brooks/Cole.

Katon, W., Robinson, P., Von Korff, M., Lin, E., Bush, T., Ludman, E., . . . Walker, E. (1996). A multifaceted intervention to improve treatment of depression in primary care. *Archives of General Psychiatry, 53*(10), 924–932.

Katon, W., Von Korff, M., Lin, E., & Simon, G. (2001). Rethinking practitioner roles in chronic illness: The specialist, primary care physician, and the practice nurse. *General Hospital Psychiatry, 23*(3), 138–144.

Katon, W., Von Korff, M., Lin, E., Unutzer, J., Simon, G., Walker, E., . . . Bush, T. (1997). Population-based care of depression: Effective disease management strategies to decrease prevalence. *General Hospital Psychiatry, 19*(3), 169–178.

Katon, W., Von Korff, M., Lin, E., Walker, E., Simon, G. E., Bush, T., . . . Russo, J. (1995). Collaborative management to achieve treatment guidelines: Impact on depression in primary care. *Journal of the American Medical Association, 273*(13), 1026–1031.

LeBel, J., & Stromberg, N. (2004). *State initiative to reduce the use of restraint and seclusion and promote strength-based care.* PowerPoint. Boston: Massachusetts Department of Mental Health.

Lindemann, E. (1944). Symptomology and management of acute grief. *American Journal of Psychiatry, 101,* 141–148.

Maynard, B.R., (2010). Social Service organizations in the era of evidence-based practice: The learning organization as a guiding framework for bridging science to service. *Journal of Social Work, 10*(3), 301–316.

Moore, G. A. (2002). *Crossing the chasm: Marketing and selling high-tech products to mainstream customers.* New York, NY: HarperCollins.

Morris, A., & Bloom, J. R. (2002). Contextual factors affecting job satisfaction and organizational commitment in community mental health centers undergoing system changes in the financing of care. *Mental Health Services Research, 4,* 71–83.

Mueser, K., Rosenberg, S., Goodman, L., & Trumbetta, S. (2002). Trauma, PTSD, and the course of schizophrenia: An interactive model. *Schizophrenia Research, 53,* 123–143.

Mullen, E. J., Bledsoe, S. E., & Bellamy, J. L. (2009). Implementing evidence-based social work practice. *Research on Social Work Practice. 18,* 325–338.

Murphy, C. M., Musser, P. H., & Maton, K. I. (1998). Coordinated community intervention for domestic abusers: Intervention system involvement and criminal recidivism. *Journal of Family Violence, 13*, 263–284.

Ogborne, A. C., Wild, T. C., Braun, K., & Newton-Taylor, B. (1998). Measuring treatment process beliefs among staff of specialized addiction treatment services. *Journal of Substance Abuse Treatment, 15*, 301–312.

Parad, H. J. (1971). Crisis intervention. In R. Morris (Ed.), *Encyclopedia of social work* (16th ed., Vol. 1, p. 197). New York, NY: National Association of Social Workers Press.

Parker, C. P., Baltes, B. B., Young, S. A., Huff, J. W., Altmann, R. A., Lacost, H. A., . . . Roberts, J. (2003). Relationships between psychological climate perceptions and work outcomes: A meta-analytic review. *Journal of Organizational Behavior, 24*, 389–416.

Rapoport, L. (1962). The state of crisis: Some theoretical considerations. *Social Service Review, 36*, 211–217.

Rapoport, L. (1967). Crisis-oriented short-term casework. *Social Service Review, 41*, 31–43.

Roberts, A. R. (1991). Conceptualizing crisis theory and the crisis intervention model. In A. R. Roberts (Ed.), *Contemporary perspectives on crisis intervention and prevention* (pp. 3–17). Englewood Cliffs, NJ: Prentice-Hall.

Roberts, A. R. (1996). Epidemiology and definitions of acute crisis in American society. In A. R. Roberts (Ed.), *Crisis management and brief treatment: Theory, technique, and applications* (pp. 16–33). Chicago, IL: Nelson-Hall.

Roberts, A. R. (2005). Bridging the past and present to the future of crisis intervention and crisis management. In A. R. Roberts (Ed.), *Crisis intervention handbook: Assessment, treatment, and research* (3rd ed., pp. 3–34). New York, NY: Oxford University Press.

Roberts, A. R., & Dziegielewski, S. F. (1995). Foundation skills and applications of crisis intervention and cognitive therapy. In A. R. Roberts (Ed.), *Crisis intervention and time limited cognitive treatment* (pp. 3–27). Thousand Oaks, CA: Sage.

Roberts, A. R., & Greene, G. J. (2002). *Social workers' desk reference.* New York, NY: Oxford University Press.

Roberts, A. R., & Lewis, S. (2001). Crisis assessment tools: The good, the bad, and the available. *Brief Treatment and Crisis Intervention, 1*, 17–28.

Roberts, A. R., & Yeager, K. R. (2004). Systematic reviews of evidence-based studies and practice-based research: How to search for, develop and use them. In A. R. Roberts & K. R. Yeager (Eds.), *Handbook of evidence-based practice: Research and outcome measures in health and human services* (pp. 3–14). New York, NY: Oxford University Press.

Rogers, E. M. (1995). *Diffusion of innovations* (4th ed.). New York, NY: Free Press.

Rosen, A., (2003). Evidence-based social work practice: Challenges and promises. *Social Work Research 27*(4), 197–208.

Rosenthal, R. N. (2004). Overview of evidence-based practice. In A. R. Roberts & K. R. Yeager (Eds.), *Handbook of evidence-based practice: Research and outcome measures in health and human services* (pp. 20–29). New York, NY: Oxford University Press.

Rubin, A., & Parrish, D., (2009) Development and validation of the Evidence-Based Practice Process Assessment Scale. *Research on Social Work Practice, 21*(1), 106–118.

Sackett, D. L., Rosenberg, W. M. C., Gray, J. A. M., Haynes, R. B., & Richardson, W. S. (1996). Evidence-based medicine: What it is and what it isn't. *British Medical Journal, 312*, 71–72.

Schoenbaum, M., Miranda, J., Sherbourne, C., Duan, N., & Wells, K. (2004). Cost-effectiveness of interventions for depressed Latinos. *Journal of Mental Health Policy and Economics, 7*(2), 69–76.

Schoenbaum, M., Unutzer, J., McCaffrey, D., Duan, N., Sherbourne, C., & Wells, K. B. (2002). The effects of primary care depression treatment on patients' clinical status and employment. *Health Services Research, 37*(5), 1145–1158.

Schoenwald, S. K., Sheidow, A. J., Letourneau, E. J., Liao, J. G. (2003). Transportability of multisystemic therapy: Evidence for multilevel influences. *Mental Health Services Research, 5*, 223–239.

Schulberg, H. C., Katon, W., Simon, G. E., & Rush, A. J. (1998). Treating major depression in primary care practice: An update of the Agency for Health Care Policy and Research Practice Guidelines. *Archives of General Psychiatry, 55*(12), 1121–1127.

Simon, G. E., Katon, W. J., Von Korff, M., Unutzer, J., Lin, E. H., Walker, E. A., ... Ludman, E. (2001). Cost-effectiveness of a collaborative care program for primary care patients with persistent depression. *American Journal of Psychiatry, 158*(10), 1638–1644.

Simon, G. E., Von Korff, M., Ludman, E. J., Katon, W. J., Rutter, C., Unutzer, J., ... Walker, E. (2002). Cost-effectiveness of a program to prevent depression relapse in primary care. *Medical Care, 40*(10), 941–950.

Slaikeu, K. (1984). *Crisis intervention: A handbook for practice and research.* Boston, MA: Allyn & Bacon.

Soydan, H., Mullen, E. J., Alexandra, L., Rehnman, J., & Li, Y. P. (2010). Evidence-based clearinghouses in social work. *Research on Social Work Practice, 20*(6), 690–700.

Tyhurst, J. S. (1957). The role of transition states—including disasters—in mental illness. In *Symposium on preventive and social psychiatry* (pp. 1–23). Washington, DC: Walter Reed Army Institute of Research.

U.S. Department of Health and Human Services. (1996). *Physical activity and health: A report of the surgeon general.* Atlanta, GA: National Center for Chronic Disease Prevention and Health.

Von Korff, M., & Tiemens, B. (2000). Individualized stepped care of chronic illness. *Western Journal of Medicine, 172*(2), 133–137.

Von Korff, M., Unutzer, J., Katon, W., & Wells, K. (2001). Improving care for depression in organized health care systems. *Journal of Family Practice, 50*(6), 530–531.

Wagner, E. H., Austin, B. T., & Von Korff, M. (1996). Improving outcomes in chronic illness. *Managed Care Quarterly, 4*(2), 12–25.

Walrath, C. M., Sheehan, A. K., Holden, E. W., Hernandez, M., & Blau, G. M., (2006). Evidence-based treatments in the field: A brief report on provider knowledge implementation and practice. *The Journal of Behavioral Health Services and Research 33*(2), 244–253.

Weissman, M. M., Verdeli, H., Gameroff, M. J., Bledsoe, S. E., Betts, K., Mufson, L., ... Wickramaratne, P. (2006). National survey of psychotherapy training in psychiatry, psychology, and social work. *Archives of General Psychiatry, 63*(8), 925–934.

Wiest, F. C., Ferris, T. G., Gokhale, M., Campbell, E. G., Weissman, J. S., & Blumenthal, D. (2002). Preparedness of internal medicine and family practice residents for treating common conditions. *Journal of the American Medical Association*, *288*(20), 2609–2614.

Yeager, K. R., & Roberts, A. R. (2005). Differentiating among stress, acute stress disorder, acute crisis episodes, trauma and PTSD: Paradigm and treatment goals. In A. R. Roberts (Ed.), *Crisis intervention handbook: Assessment, treatment, and research* (3rd ed., pp. 90–119). New York, NY: Oxford University Press.

Chapter 8
Practice Evaluation

Bruce A. Thyer

> What practical methods can social work practitioners use to evaluate the outcomes of their interventions with clients?

Practice evaluation refers to the efforts made by individual social workers to appraise the results of their interventions with clients. This chapter is limited to a review of evaluation efforts that are practicable when undertaken by clinicians operating within the domain of direct practice — efforts at interpersonal helping focused on the problems and situations of individuals, couples, marriages, families, and small groups. Even more narrowly, this chapter focuses on efforts made to empirically ascertain the actual outcomes of practice: how people's lives have been changed following their experience of services by a professional social worker and in some circumstances, how it may be possible to determine not only the possible changes in peoples' lives, but to empirically determine if these observed changes can be plausibly attributed to have been *caused* by the client's receipt of social work services. These efforts, when successful, constitute the highest form of scientifically credible evidence relating to empirically demonstrating a cause-and-effect relationship between intervention and outcome at the level of the individual case.

The term *clients*, as used in this chapter, refers not simply to individuals but also to couples, families, and so on. The term *intervention* is used synonymously with *treatment*. The evaluation practices described in this chapter can be employed with all types of clients, with the very young and the very old, with people of all races and ethnicities, and, equally importantly, by practitioners using virtually any type of social work intervention. It does not matter if you are a psychodynamically oriented clinician, a cognitive-behaviorist, a client-centered practitioner, or a solution-focused therapist; the evaluation methods described herein are genuinely *atheoretical* — they are not derived from any particular formal theory of behavior or of mind. They are *methods of evaluation* capable of being adopted by any practitioner who hopes that his or her interventions will produce pragmatic changes in the way clients think, feel, act, or cope with their environment.

This chapter, by focusing on evaluating your interpersonal practice with clients, omits several other areas of evaluating social work intervention. It does not present various methods to conduct client needs assessments, to undertake formative or summative evaluations of a service program, or to conduct sweeping appraisals of the overall results of program outcomes. Nor is attention given to evaluating social work interventions at a more macro level, for example, by the analysis of the effects of social welfare policies (e.g., changes in the well-being of welfare clients as the nation transitioned from AFDC to TANF). Also omitted are efforts using nomothetic (e.g., group) research designs such as pre-experimental studies, quasi-experiments, or randomized controlled trials to evaluate practice outcomes. While these are all admittedly important and engaging topics, they are beyond the more limited scope of the present chapter. See Royse, Thyer, and Padgett (2010) and Thyer and Myers (2007) for more encompassing reviews of evaluation research methods).

This chapter focuses on the use of single-system research designs, also known as single-subject designs (SSDs), defined as:

> A research procedure often used in clinical situations to evaluate the effectiveness of an intervention. Behavior of a single subject, such as an individual client, is used as a comparison and as a control. Typically the results of progress or change are plotted graphically. Single-subject design is also known as N = 1 design or single system design.

> (Barker, 2003, p. 398)

Keep in mind that the term *client* is used not only for an individual person, but also for larger systems such as couples, families, and small groups. It is also important to keep in mind the inclusive definition of *behavior*:

> Any action or response by an individual, including observable activity, measurable physiological changes, cognitive images, fantasies, and emotions.

> (Barker, 2003, p. 40)

Behavior does not only refer to the observable actions of clients. It refers to everything they publicly or privately experience.

Brief Background

From the very beginnings of professional social work in North America, individual practitioners have been concerned with obtaining credible evidence as to whether social work clients actually benefit from the services they received. Mary Richmond's (1917) classic text *Social Diagnosis* was one early attempt to teach social workers how to gather systematic and reliable information on client circumstances and functioning, so as to better serve clients and to evaluate outcomes more credibly. A few decades later, social workers began experimenting with an outcome measure called the Hunt-Kogan Movement Scale, a way of assessing client functioning and measuring changes occurring during and after social work intervention with individual clients. Although some formal studies were undertaken on this instrument's reliability and validity (see Gershenson, 1952; Hunt, Blenkner, & Kogan, 1950; Kogan, Kogan, & Hunt, 1952; Wessel, 1953), it never really became widely used. This scale was cited by Wolins in an early social work book chapter devoted to the topic of practice evaluation. Wolins also noted that one very legitimate focus of social work evaluation is "the effect of the caseworker in a minute operation with a single client" (1960, p. 248). The word "minute" in this quote does not refer to time; it means something small, pronounced "my-newt," as in an individual session(s).

The earliest known published study authored by a social worker who used an SSD to evaluate practice appeared in 1965, written by Arthur Staats (a psychologist) and William Butterfield, a social worker, and involved evaluating the results of providing academic tutoring to an Hispanic juvenile delinquent. Since that time, many SSDs have appeared in the social work literature (see Thyer & Thyer, 1992).

Evidence-Based Information on Practice Evaluation

There are actually only two essential features needed to undertake single-system research designs useful to evaluate your own practice, and to some extent these are consistent with the dictates of sound practice in general. The first is to be able to locate and apply one or more reliable and valid outcome measures pertinent to the client's problem and/or situation. And the second prerequisite is to then actually apply this outcome measure repeatedly over time. All SSDs are simply variants on these two principles, which are discussed in sequence.

All social worker therapists make use of outcome measures in their practice. Most commonly, we rely on what clients tell us during clinical interviews. The client lives his or her life, encountering other people, circumstances, and events, and then comes to see us for 50 minutes or so each week. During these therapy sessions, we invite the client to relate the week's events, what they did, how they felt, and what they thought. From such primary source material, we make inferences about client functioning, their possible progress or deterioration, and then we adjust our interventions accordingly. Occasionally we also seek information from others involved in the client's life—a parent, a spouse, a partner, more rarely coworkers, employers, or friends. Even more rarely, we may obtain more objective information from agency records, health care facilities, schools, and so forth. As noted previously, Mary Richmond's (1917) *Social Diagnosis* laid the empirical foundations for clinical interviewing by professional social workers, and its most contemporary parallel is *Clinical Assessment for Social Workers* (Jordan & Franklin, 2011).

Rather striking advances have been made in assessment methodology in the past few decades, advances that have the potential to markedly improve the reliability, validity, and pragmatic usefulness of the information we can obtain from our interactions with and on behalf of clients.

For example, rapid assessment instruments (RAIs) have been developed that consist of short standardized questionnaires or inventories focused on particular problem areas or strengths. Sometimes these are related to specific disorders, such as depressive conditions, anxiety disorders, trauma, alcohol abuse, or psychosis, and an overall score is calculated that provides a systematic if approximate quantitative measure of the problem. Others deal with more complex issues, such as domestic violence, child abuse or neglect, social support, life satisfaction, or quality of life. These RAIs can be completed by clients periodically—weekly, biweekly, or monthly—and the results used to augment our judgments heretofore solely informed from our clinical interviews. Fischer and Corcoran (2007) have assembled a comprehensive listing of such RAIs, including copies of the actual scales, how to score them, and where to obtain more primary information about them. The *Association for Behavioral and Cognitive Therapies* (http://abct.org/Home/) sponsors a series of reference books that also provide compilations of actual assessment measures for use in clinical practice. Among the titles available are the *Practitioner's Guide to Empirically-Based Measures of School Behavior, Practitioner's Guide to Empirically-Based Measures of Anxiety, Practitioner's Guide to Empirically-Based Measures for Depression*, and the *Practitioner's Guide to Empirically-Based Measures of Social Skills*. Social worker Walter Hudson developed a couple of dozen assessment instruments for use in evaluating social work practice, and these are available at http://www.walmyr.com. Useful RAIs can be found for virtually any clinical problem encountered, and new ones are constantly being developed and published. The journal *Research on Social Work Practice* usually has several reports of new or expanded RAIs appearing in each of its bimonthly issues. Recent issues (http://rsw.sagepub.com/) featured presentations on assessment measures related to a school-support scale for low-income mothers, an elementary school success profile for teachers to use with children, client satisfaction, child and youth resilience, an empathy scale, and a measure for use with antisocial students.

Another development in clinical assessment related to practice evaluation has been the considerable advances made in the systematic measurement of client behavior via direct observation. Virtually all conditions for which clients seek help from social workers present with important behavioral manifestations. These may be behavioral excesses such as drinking too much (alcoholism), weeping too much (depression), or talking too long or rapidly (manic behavior). Others are behavioral deficits, such as a lack of social skills on the part of the schizophrenic, a failure to get out of bed on the part of the catatonic, or an inability to find a job on the part of the unemployed. A client may suffer from a lack of appropriate stimulus control in behaviors that are displayed at the wrong time, place, or circumstance, but are otherwise appropriate (e.g., randomly giggling). Social workers of all theoretical persuasions are keenly interested in helping clients change their behavior along more functional lines. Even those practitioners who theorize that overt behavior is primarily a symptom of intrapsychic processes that are the true focus of treatment endorse the principle that at some point therapeutic gains should be manifested as positive behavioral change. Within the social literature, Rosen and Polansky (1975) and Polster and Collins (1993) provide very good, if a bit dated, overviews of behavioral assessment, whereas Baer, Harrison, Fradenburg, Petersen, and Milla (2005) have published a more contemporary presentation.

The third domain that may be the focus of clinical assessment for the purposes of practice evaluation consists of selected physiological indicators. Urine screens, blood tests, and hair analyses are sometimes used to assess a client's use of illegal (or abused but legal) drugs. Medical social workers sometimes examine clients' charts for records of blood pressure or blood sugar to assess compliance with health care regimens. Some social workers make use of biofeedback instrumentation that assesses various indicators of anxiety (e.g., muscle tension, skin temperature, perspiration, brain waves) to help clients acquire skills in becoming less stressed.

These three domains pretty much cover all the various approaches to assessing client functioning. Environmental appraisal and relationship variables are other important elements of social work assessment, but these are not usually the focus of evaluation studies making use of SSDs (although there is no inherent reason they could not be).

Case Studies

The case study or history is the oldest method of appraising the outcomes of social work practice. It is a primarily a qualitative evaluation methodology that uses verbal narratives, diagrams, and pictures to assess and evaluate client changes. Gilbert and Franklin (2003), Brandell and Varkas (2010), and Gilgun (1994) provide reviews of this approach specific to social work, while Yin (1989) provides a more general description. Almost all social work journals regularly publish case histories or studies of clients that have been used for a variety purposes—to illustrate practice technique, to enrich clinical theory, and to try and document client changes. Historically and currently, many prominent social workers and psychotherapists have achieved great acclaim and recognition through their publication of clinical case studies. Case studies may be grounded in the epistemologies of mainstream or conventional science (e.g., positivism) or based on alternative philosophical perspectives (e.g., postmodernism and constructivism). The approach is not intrinsically linked to either orientation, although it is more closely associated with the methodologies collectively known as qualitative research. Narrative case studies can be as brief as a few pages or as long as an entire book. I have published a number of them myself, illustrating the usefulness that I personally place on this form of practice evaluation (Cameron & Thyer, 1985; Koepke & Thyer, 1985; Pergeron, Curtis, & Thyer, 1986; Thyer, 1980, 1981; Thyer & Stocks, 1986). Many new schools of psychotherapy begin to establish their research foundations with the publication of case studies, and some approaches such as classical psychoanalysis remain strongly linked to this approach as the primary method of evaluating practice outcomes (e.g., Colby, 1960).

The strengths of the case study are in its apparent ability to place clinical events in their situational contexts, which greatly facilitates making inferences about etiology and response to treatment. Many case studies can be considered classics—think of the influence of some of Sigmund Freud's case histories, the conditioning studies of John Watson the behavioral psychologist, or the sexual dysfunction cures achieved by Masters and Johnson. Very rarely can the results of individual case studies be aggregated in an attempt to produce more generalizable findings; usually, case histories are narratively presented as isolated instances of some phenomenon.

In a paper titled "Drawing Valid Inferences from Case Studies," psychologist Alan Kazdin (1981) is appropriately cautious regarding the internal validity of the single narrative case study, noting:

> Despite its recognized heuristic value, the case study is usually considered to be inadequate as a basis for drawing valid scientific inferences. Relationships between independent and dependent variables are difficult to discern in a typical case study because of the ambiguity of the factor(s) responsible for the performance. For example, treatment for a particular clinical case may be associated with therapeutic change. However the basis for the change cannot be determined from an uncontrolled case study. Even if treatment were responsible for change, several alternative interpretations of the case might be proposed. These alternative interpretations have been catalogued under the rubric of "threats to internal validity." (p. 184)

Kazdin goes on to discuss some special design features by which the case study can be strengthened so that valid causal inferences regarding the effects of treatment may become more legitimate, consisting of practices such as gathering more objective data, repeatedly assessing client functioning using these more objective indicators, taking baseline measures of client functioning prior to treatment, observing immediate and marked changes in the clients immediately after treatment is initiated, repeating this methodology across a number of similar cases, and hopefully obtaining similar results. This discussion of Kazdin leads us to the topic of single-system research designs, which form the balance of this chapter's presentation on clinician-friendly approaches to practice evaluation.

The B Design

To begin with, imagine the typical narrative case study of social work intervention with a client, but with the addition of some more objective indicator of functioning obtained prior to the beginning of treatment and again after treatment has been terminated. For some clinical issues, the choice of such outcome measures is obvious and noncontroversial. If a client is seeking assistance in losing weight, weighing him or her once at the beginning of therapy and again at its conclusion provides a rather obvious way to look at clinical success (or its lack). Or if a client is seeking assistance in abstaining from cocaine, a urine test can be administered upon initial assessment (a positive result would indicate recent cocaine ingestion) and again after termination (a negative result, hopefully). But outcome measures need not be so blunt. For example, a depressed client could complete the well-known Beck Depression Inventory (BDI) pre- and posttreatment. Measures such as these would add to the narratively provided clinical evidence of treatment success.

The limitations of such singularly administered outcome assessments are obvious, however. Prior to treatment, the client's problem may be very labile and an isolated measure may not accurately reflect long-term functioning. The same caveat applies to posttreatment assessments. Also, many clients tend to seek treatment when problems reach a crisis and in the natural ebb and flow of life's circumstances the passage of time alone, or the tendency for extreme variations to regress to average or more normative functioning, means that any single pretreatment assessment will, if repeated after some time has passed, likely indicate lessened severity of the presenting problem. One possible solution to these barriers to making causal inferences about the true effects of social work intervention is to obtain *repeated* assessments of the client's state over time. In this way, trends can be determined in a more reliable fashion than relying on a single benchmark pre- and posttreatment. This approach is also congruent with the advice of Richmond (1917) who asserted:

> Special efforts should be made to ascertain whether abnormal manifestations are increasing *or* decreasing *in number and intensity, as this often has a practical bearing on the management of the case.* (p. 435, emphasis in original)

What could be a clearer historical precedent for what has become known as single-system research designs?

The simplest form of an SSD can be called the B design, and refers to the social worker beginning treatment and formal assessment with one or more structured outcome measures at the same time. As an example, during an initial assessment session the social worker has a depressed client tell his or her story; conducts a psychosocial assessment; offers empathy, support, and encouragement; and concludes with arriving at a formal treatment contract (verbal or written) with the client, and the client is asked to complete a Beck Depression Inventory (BDI). Research-informed psychosocial treatment begins the following week and continues with weekly sessions. At the beginning of each session, the client is asked to once again complete the BDI. These BDIs are scored by the social worker and depicted on a graph, with the vertical axis indicating the BDI score and the horizontal axis the time intervals, say weeks or treatment sessions. Over time it will be evident if the client's BDI scores are remaining stable (depressed), improving, or growing worse. This information, combined with the usual rich clinical narrative material disclosed in therapy, augments the social worker's ability to judge whether the client is getting any better. After a reasonable period of time, lack of progress may call for a reevaluation of the treatment being provided. Please note that the more objective measure is never intended to supplant the social worker's clinical judgment. If BDI scores and the client's narrative do not jibe, this can serve to direct attention in treatment to the apparent disparity.

Simply taking a single assessment pre- and posttreatment would not constitute an SSD since such limited evaluations provide no evidence as to change, trends, or (in)stability in client functioning, so that leaves us with the question of how many data points are needed. This is a murky area. The general rule is that more is better. Two is better than one, but you need at least three data points to infer any trend. Four is better than three, five is better than four, and so on. Any inferences made using this approach to practice evaluation are very much qualitative in nature. There are no widely applied quantitative tests to add in this process. If you do observe a trend, the best check on the reliability of your judgment is to show the graph to one or more colleagues and ask what they think, after you fill them in on the clinical background material. If your colleagues concur with your views, then you have a rough form of interrater agreement. But if they disagree with you, or among each other, then the clarity of inference you had hoped for is absent, and you'd best defer drawing any conclusions or, more conservatively, infer that no changes are obvious. If the clinical situation permits, then simply continuing treatment and gathering more data is the best option. This rough guide to making inferences from data presented on line graphs can be called the "intra-ocular trauma test," that is, the conclusion must jump out at you and hit you between the eyes. Lacking such striking changes, it is best to infer nothing, which is itself informative—knowing that the outcome measure does not clearly indicate any client improvement.

Outcome measures in SSDs need not be quantitative. For example, weekly urine screens of illicit drug use can be depicted on a line graph using "Yes" or "No" as a pair of labels on the vertical axis and the dates of the tests labeled on the horizontal axis. Over time, you would hope that with successful treatment for substance abuse, the frequency of the Yes test results (indicating that the client had used drugs) would diminish and be replaced with an eventual succession of No results. A child might be asked to indicate his or her mood by placing adhesive smiley or frowny faces on a graph each week. Such an approach to an SSD would render this a purely qualitative method of outcomes assessment.

The absence of a formal baseline period wherein assessments are systematically made prior to beginning actual treatment makes the B design rather ineffectual for trying to determine if the client improved *because* of social work intervention, but it can be an excellent way to more objectively document the client's status throughout the course of treatment. Wong and his colleagues used a B design to see how an institutionalized psychotic individual's problematic behavior diminished over a 35-week period (Wong, Woolsey, & Gallegos, 1987). Vonk used a B design to see how a client's previously intractable sexual phobia changed over several months of treatment (Vonk & Thyer, 1995). These SSDs are obviously more than a simple case history. The use of more systematic assessments of client functioning adds to the richness of the narrative and background material and augments your ability to infer meaningful change. But the B design does not usually allow the worker to make *causal* inferences about the effects of treatment. To do that, more stringent design requirements are needed, like the one discussed next.

The AB Design

The AB design builds on the features of the B design by adding one further element, and that is the repeated assessment of client functioning *before* social work intervention formally begins. This is an operationalization of the social work dictum, "Beginning where the client is at." This baseline phase—an A phase of a single system design—attempts to exclude the possibility that the client's functioning is so labile that it would be hard to determine if any meaningful change occurred following treatment. In the best of all circumstances (in an inferential sense), several baseline measures of some reliable and valid outcome measure indicate that a serious problem is present and that the values of the outcome measure are neither fluctuating wildly nor trending in the direction of improvement. Then treatment is initiated and measurement of the client's problem/situation continues as before, using the same reliable and valid outcome indicator(s). If, in the best of all possible worlds (in an inferential sense), the client's situation immediately and markedly improves and stays better during this treatment or B phase of the AB design, you are in a marginally better position to tentatively claim that intervention caused this change. This ability to make such as inference is enhanced by having a larger rather than a small number of baseline measurements, by having a very stable baseline, and by the presence of an abrupt and clinically important improvement at the beginning of the B phase, an improvement that is maintained or even enhanced throughout the entirety of the B phase. Such inferences are also affected by the nature of the problem. Serious issues known to be generally intractable, or whose natural history does not indicate that improvements are likely, or problems not known to be responsive to placebo or nonspecific treatment factors all augment the strength of the inferences that can potentially be drawn.

Over 25 years ago, Stanley Witkin, the distinguished social worker and past editor of the NASW journal *Social Work*, illustrated the use of AB designs in his evaluations of social work practice in the field of marital counseling. He provided a very favorable appraisal of this approach, saying:

> This chapter recounts how in a marital intervention training program for social workers in a public agency...intervention and evaluation was highly compatible with the exigencies and needs of the workers and couples served. Assessment was clear and provided clients and workers with ongoing feedback. Intervention was directive and action-oriented; evaluation was straightforward and relevant....Measurement of intervention efficacy provided accountability data.

(Witkin, 1981, p. 286)

The ABA Design

The next incrementally complex SSD can be called the ABA design. An ABA design consists of conducting a regular AB design and then discontinuing treatment while continuing to assess your outcome measure(s). ABA designs begin to approximate what have been called *experiments*. Here are some definitions of this term:

> *A study in which an intervention is deliberately introduced to observe its effects.*
>
> (Shadish, Cook, & Campbell, 2002, p. 12)

> *One or more independent variables are manipulated to observe their effects on one or more dependent variables.*
>
> (Shadish et al., 2002, p. 12)

> **Experiment**. *The manipulation of one or more independent variables conducted under controlled conditions to test one or more hypotheses, especially for making inferences of a cause-effect character. Involves the measurement of one or more dependent variables.*
>
> (Corsini, 2002, p. 351, bold in original)

Digging deeper into our indigenous social work literature we find a similar definition:

> *Manipulation of subject and/or intervention is the essence of experimental method ... The demands of science and of practice have lead to a whole array of experiments. They include experiments designed ... with the subjects serving as controls for themselves.*
>
> (Wolins, 1960, p. 255)

Although you may associate the term *experiment* with the use of research designs involving large numbers of participants, perhaps randomly selected from some population on interest and perhaps randomly assigned to active treatment and to control groups, such group research designs are only one type of experiment. Certain forms of SSDs also qualify.

The landmark book *Evidence-Based Medicine* (Straus, Glasziou, Richardson, & Haynes, 2011) discusses the use of $N = 1$ studies as an important component of evidence-based practice. In fact, selected forms of SSDs are asserted in the *Users' Guide to the Medical Literature: Essentials of Evidence-Based Clinical Practice* (Guyatt & Rennie, 2002, p. 12) to be the *strongest* form of evidence to make treatment decisions with individual clients, rated superior to systematic reviews or randomized controlled trials. If this flies in the face of everything you have been taught about any presumptive hierarchy of research evidence, I encourage you to read primary sources on this methodology to help you in understanding the inferential logic behind such assertions (e.g., Guyatt & Rennie, 2002; Hersen & Barlow, 1985; Sidman, 1960; Straus et al., 2011; Thyer & Myers, 2007).

The issue relates to the direction of inference. If you are attempting to make an inference about the effects of social work treatment for *this particular client*, then an SSD is indeed a superior form of evidence. If you wish to make inferences from a sample of clients who responded favorably to a specific social work treatment to a larger population of interest (e.g., everyone with problem X), then larger scale group studies will usually provide a stronger evidentiary foundation for such inferences. Curiously, a single randomized controlled trial or even a comprehensive systematic review of the effects of some intervention for problem X may actually provide *little* guidance on how to care for an individual with that problem who sits in your consulting room. Friston, Homles, and Worsley (1999, p. 1) addressed this issue in their paper titled "How Many Subjects Constitute a Study?" "A critical distinction that determines the number of subjects included in a . . . study is between inferences about *the particular subjects studied* and inferences that pertain to *the population* from which these subjects came" [italics added]. To see if treatment X really helped *Mr. Smith*, an SSD is needed. To see if treatment X is reliably effective for many clients with the same problem that Mr. Smith experiences requires a group outcome study with a sample of clients representative of folks with that problem. Given that social workers in direct practice are primarily concerned with evaluating the outcomes of the interventions they provided to *their* clients, you can grasp the potential superiority of using SSD methodology in micropractice evaluation relative to group research designs.

Going back as far as Aristotle, we find references to the idea that gaining evidence by deliberately introducing or removing a purported cause and systematically observing its apparent effects, provides the most credible evidence for making cause-and-effect determinations. The experimental SSDs make use of this principle. Take a baseline (the A phase). Introduce social work treatment (B phase). Remove social work treatment (restore the conditions of the A phase). If (happily) the problem gets better when B is introduced and then relapses (unhappily) when B is removed and A reinstated, we have considerably stronger evidence of the causal role of B in bringing about these changes than with the more simple AB design alone. This design, the ABA, was used in landmark investigations by Truax and Carkhuff (1965) to evaluate the processes of Rogerian psychotherapy.

The ABA design is primarily useful when the effects of intervention are predicted to be short-lived, not durable. Yet, many social work treatments can be anticipated to produce durable changes. For example, the insights achieved via psychotherapy do not evaporate if therapy is halted. If the client is taught a social or academic skill, these will not vanish. If a client has been cured of a phobia via exposure therapy, the phobic condition is unlikely to return. In instances of treatments producing well-maintained effects, the experimental logic of the ABA design and other SSDs using withdrawal phases will collapse. If during the second A phase, client gains seen during the B phase are maintained, then you have, logically, only the results of an AB design in terms of making causal inferences about treatment.

This is good clinically, but not for experimental demonstration purposes. This is okay for the direct practitioner who would undoubtedly prefer, as would the client, that gains made via intervention be maintained after treatment is terminated. Such designs do, after all, provide a good test of how genuinely successful treatment was. But if the client does relapse during the second A phase, then the opportunity for a more rigorous experimental demonstration of the effects of social work treatment becomes possible, as discussed next.

The ABAB Design

The ABAB design is simply a continuation of the principles outlined previously. If the client regresses during the second baseline (A phase), reinstate treatment B. If the problem resolves again, you have three consecutive demonstrations of an apparent cause-effect relationship between treatment and outcome. The first is the improvement seen during the first B phase when the client gets better after treatment begins. The second is the deterioration when treatment is removed, during the second A phase. The third is the second demonstration of improvement when the treatment is reapplied during the second B phase. Such shifts in the data pattern, clearly linked to the introduction or the removal of treatment, provides a very high level of confidence in inferring that treatment was responsible for these changes. The ABAB design was used by Thyer, Irvine, and Santa (1984) to examine the effects of a reinforcement program on promoting aerobic exercise among individuals with chronic mental illness and by Martinez and Wong (2009) to evaluate a method of improving participation in a self-help group for survivors of domestic violence.

Multiple Baseline Designs

Multiple baseline (MBL) designs make use of the same experimental logic as withdrawal designs such as the ABA and ABAB SSDs, namely attempting to see if a problem improves when, and only when, a given social work intervention is provided to clients. In addition, MBL designs attempt to demonstrate such an apparent relationship several times, with each successful replication enhancing confidence that treatment caused improvements. There are three major variations of the MBL designs, as outlined below.

Multiple Baseline Design Across Clients

This novel design requires that the social worker have access at the same point in time to two or more clients with the same problem who will receive the same intervention. Although this may sound unlikely, in many practice contexts (e.g., large mental health agencies) it is not an uncommon situation. How many social workers have two clients with major depression seek treatment during the same week, or month? If you do, then using this type of design might be one way to evaluate your practice outcomes. As with all SSDs, you must choose a reliable and valid outcome measure and begin a baseline for your clients (two, three, or even more clients) around the same time. Prepare an AB graph at the top of the page, and label this *Client 1*. The values of the outcome measure appear on the left or vertical axis, and the dimension of time (date, week, session, etc.) is depicted on the bottom, horizontal axis. Obtain a baseline (the A phase) consisting of a certain number of data points (e.g., three, four, five, whatever), then begin the intervention (the B phase). Continue monitoring the outcome measure(s). When you begin baselining Client 1, also begin baselining Client 2 on a second AB graph positioned or drawn on the page directly under Client 1's graph, with the bottom axes aligned so that the labels for both graphs refer to the same time periods (date, week, session, etc.). Now, for Client 2, have his or her baseline extend beyond that of Client 1, so that, say if Client 1's baseline was four data points, Client 2's is six or eight data points. After the extended baseline without treatment, provide Client 2 with the same treatment that you delivered to Client 1. In ideal circumstances, you are looking for a situation wherein Client 1 has a baseline indicating a stable, serious problem; and when treatment is provided, his or her outcome measure indicates a rapid, meaningful improvement. However, for the purposes of experimental inferences, you would like to see that Client 2's baseline remains stable, indicating continuing problems. If, when you subsequently provide the same intervention to Client 2 and problem resolution/improvement is also immediately observed, you have two demonstrations of the treatment application apparently resulting in problem improvement. This replicated effect is more convincing evidence than a single AB study, and the lengthier baseline of Client 2, which remains unchanged when Client 1's treatment data reflects improvement, serves as a partial control for some sort of historical event (spring break, Christmas, etc.) as being responsible for these improvements. If you conduct this MBL across clients with three rather than two clients, the evidence can be even more persuasive. Besa (1994) used this type of design with several families to evaluate the effects of narrative therapy, a study he used as his doctoral dissertation. Pinkston, Howe, and Blackman (1987) also used a MBL design across clients to assess the effectiveness of social work intervention designed to help nursing home residents achieve a greater degree of urinary continence.

Multiple Baseline Design Across Problems

In the MBL across problems approach to practice evaluation, the social worker must have one client with two or more problems or difficulties that will be treated using the same intervention. Appropriate outcome measures will be selected for each problem and graphed on separate AB designs, aligned one over the other. Like before, the horizontal axis reflects the dimension of time and the vertical axes measure the different problems. As an example, let's say that our client, Allen, suffers from three different phobias, to dogs, snakes, and bugs, each of which will be treated *sequentially*, not concurrently. The top graph is an AB design measuring Allen's fear of dogs. The social worker locates reliable and valid measures of phobic anxiety (they do indeed exist). A baseline is taken and then a specific treatment, say graduated real-life exposure therapy, is undertaken involving dogs. No therapy is applied to snakes or bugs, but concurrent baseline measures are taken of these fears while treatment for the dog phobia is applied. After a longer baseline than that of the dog phobia, treatment begins for Allen's snake phobia. But his bug phobia is not yet treated, and the bug phobia baseline is continued. Then following a longer baseline than that used for snake fears, the social worker begins treatment for the bug phobia. In the ideal situation, all baselines display stable, profound levels of fear for their specific phobic stimulus. When treatment, exposure therapy, is applied to the dog phobia, this problem quickly improves but the snake and bug fear baselines remain unchanged. Then, a bit later when the snake fear is treated, also with exposure therapy, snake fears quickly improve but bug fears remain. Last, treatment begins for the bug phobia, and it too rapidly resolves. In this example, three distinct problems remain intact until they are individually treated, and then and only then are they resolved. This provides three demonstrations of an apparent treatment effect. You can do a MBL across problems with only two problems, and this is stronger in terms of internal validity than a single AB study.

Multiple Baseline Design Across Situations

This variation of SSDs requires a client with a particular problem that manifests itself across several different circumstances, and sequentially applies the same intervention to this problem in these differing settings, so as to provide a convincing demonstration that it was indeed treatment that caused these (hopefully) observed improvements. Allen (1973) provides a nice illustration of this design to evaluate a psychosocial intervention targeting bizarre speech in a youth with brain damage residing at a summer camp. Baselines were made of the child's frequency of odd speech in four different settings while he was at a summer camp:

1. While walking on a trail during evening activities.
2. In the dining hall.
3. In the cabin where the boy lived.
4. During education classes.

A 6-day baseline was taken of bizarre talk while on the trail, then intervention began on day 7. Bizarre talk quickly reduced in frequency. But the baselined bizarre talk in the other three settings continued unabated. After 12 days of baseline, intervention was also applied in the dining hall. Bizarre talk again declined. Bizarre talk was baselined for 16 days in the cabin, then intervention was applied, and the bizarre talk declined, and last, following 20 days of baseline, intervention was introduced during education classes, and again, for the fourth demonstration, peculiar talk subsided to near zero levels. Such a data pattern is rather convincing evidence that for this child, with this problem, this intervention was causally responsible for the improved behavior.

Alternating Treatments Design

The alternating treatment design is an innovative approach to examine the relative effectiveness of two of more interventions with the same client. Following a baseline period, assessing some problem or situation, a coin is tossed and the client is provided with one of, say two, possible treatments (call them Treatment X or Treatment Y), based on the random fall of the coin. The next session, the coin is tossed again to determine if the client receives Treatment X or Y. This process is repeated. The experimental logic is that if X and Y are differentially effective, a line connecting the data points for the session when Treatment X was provided and another line connecting the data points for the sessions when Treatment Y was provided, will not overlap and indeed show marked divergence. This ATD is only appropriate for treatments with effects that are expected to be immediate and pronounced.

Social worker Stephen Wong and his colleagues used such an approach with a 37-year-old man called Tom who was diagnosed with schizophrenia and who resided at a state mental hospital. One of Tom's problems was that he rather constantly engaged in mumbling or solitary laughter, behaviors that hindered his ability to be placed in a less restrictive community setting. Tom's occurrence of mumbling and solitary laughter was measured in the hospital dayroom setting for five sessions. Following the baseline, the client was randomly presented, at the beginning of free-time periods in the dayroom, with the opportunity to select from a variety of magazines. In other words, given something interesting to do (his history indicated he enjoyed reading) or not given anything to do and just left to his own devices in the dayroom with other patients (similar to the baseline period). During the baseline period and during the similar sessions when baseline and reading opportunities were randomly alternated, Tom displayed stereotypic vocalizations about 77% of the time when he had nothing to do. However, when he was provided with magazines to read, mumbling and solitary laughter declined to about 24% of the time, a rather marked and clinically significant decline. This was striking evidence that providing Tom (and perhaps others suffering from chronic mental illnesses) the opportunity to engage in something interesting to do, rather than being bored, can produce dramatic reductions in bizarre symptoms See Wong, Terranova et al. (1987) for a fuller description of this SSD, and Wong, Seroka, and Ogisi (2000) for another example of this type of design, involving a diabetic client with memory impairments who was helped to achieve greater accuracy in assessing her blood glucose levels.

The ATD is similar to what is labeled an $N = 1$ randomized controlled trial within the field of evidence-based practice, although they have been in use with psychology and education for years prior to their discovery by medicine (Guyatt et al., 1986; Janosky, 2005). Kent, Camfield, and Camfield (1999) demonstrate their usefulness with 50 families of children diagnosed with Attention-Deficit/Hyperactivity Disorder (ADHD). The families were provided with bottles of identical capsules containing either standard medication (Ritalin) or placebo. The child, family, teacher, and physician were unaware of the true content of the capsules, administered in random order each day to the child. Careful assessment was made of ADHD symptoms during the baseline and during 3 weeks of treatment. Sometimes (randomly) the children got placebo and sometimes Ritalin. After 3 weeks of daily treatment, data were analyzed to see if medication was really having an effect on the children's behavior. This approach was extremely useful in determining the real effects of Ritalin versus placebo on ADHD. A similar $N = 1$ randomized trial (an ATD) was conducted by McBride (1988) and the medical literature is rapidly embracing this method of practice evaluation to compare the effects of two of more treatments.

I plan to illustrate the use of this design in my own teaching of evaluation research. Using student volunteers in my research course, I will ask them to rate their sleepiness at the beginning of class, and again at the end, and baseline their "sleepiness" for a few classes. I will then offer them, randomly, one of two identical pills. One pill will be a real homeopathic sleeping pill, and the other will be a real homeopathic energy booster pill. In reality, homeopathic medicines contain NO active ingredients and are merely credible placebos, so offering these to students will be very safe. After baselines are completed, at the next class students will rate their sleepiness at the beginning and end of class, but half will take the sleeping pill and half the energy pill, after the initial rating. A couple of hours later, near the end of class, they will rate their sleepiness again. This will continue for a number of classes with the type of pill they swallow being determined by a coin toss each class. Toward the end of the school term we will halt the study, break the code, and identify for each class whether the individual student took the sleeping pill or the energy pill, and compare their sleepiness ratings under the two conditions. Students will graph their own data in the form of an alternating treatments design. I predict that the two pills will have indistinguishable effects and this exercise will provide a striking example of how the ATD can be used to evaluate something at the level of an individual client. I could also embed testing homeopathic medicines this way using either ABAB or multiple baseline designs. Stay tuned.

This brief overview just touched on the general principles of conducting single system designs. Before attempting these designs, consult various book-length treatments of the topic to be found in the social work literature, such as Thyer and Myers (2007); Bloom, Fischer, and Orme (2009); Kazi (1998); and Tripodi (1994).

Is There a Hierarchy of Research Evidence?

There have been several attempts to conceptualize research evidence in terms of its credibility and usefulness in informing clinical practice. In the mid-1950s, a group of psychiatrists were invited to participate in one of the first-ever randomized controlled trials of the effects of psychotropic medication. Their reaction? "The psychiatrists immediately betrayed their skepticism by declaring the supremacy of knowledge acquired by doctors at the bedside and clinical intuition to be above any other methodology" (Tansella, 2002, p. 4). Another similar statement made with respect to the treatment of clinical depression is representative of the evidentiary hierarchy prevalent at the time:

> There is no psychiatric illness in which bedside knowledge and long clinical experience pays better dividends and we are never going to learn how to treat depression properly from double blind sampling. (Sargant, as cited in Tansella, 2002, p. 4, from a 1965 letter in the British Medical Journal)

Thus, 50 years ago clinical observations, practitioner intuition, and experience were widely viewed as the most credible sources of information to guide the care of individual clients. Suffice it say, although such views continue to be maintained by a minority of social workers, most contemporary professionals acknowledge the limitations of clinical experience alone as a guide to evaluating practice and accept the general idea that scientific investigations of the effects of interventions have something to contribute as well and in many instances can provide more valid and useful information.

One of the more influential efforts to develop an explicit hierarchy of research evidence was undertaken by members of Division 12 (Clinical Psychology) of the American Psychological Association, who comprised a *Task Force on Treatments That Work*, formed in the early 1990s. This group was charged with three ambitious projects — to determine what amount of evidence would suffice to claim that a given psychosocial treatment was empirically supported, to create lists of such empirically supported treatments, and to help disseminate these empirically supported treatments to the practice community. The first task was completed (not without considerable contention), and they determined that there were two paths through which a given intervention could be described as "empirically supported" (Chambless et al., 1998). The first path is by a given treatment that has been demonstrated as effective through at least two well-designed randomized controlled experimental studies, with "effective" meaning better than a credible placebo therapy and/or equivalent to an already established treatment. The other path was the publication of a relatively large ($\geq$ 9 participants) series of well-designed SSDs demonstrating that the experimental treatment was also superior to placebo or to an established intervention. Both approaches could be used to designate an intervention as empirically supported and this dual pathway to accruing evidence remains the research benchmark used by this APA group (see http://www.div12 .org/PsychologicalTreatments/faq.html). These criteria strikingly illustrate the value of SSDs to arrive at causal knowledge regarding the effects of social work treatments at the levels of individual practice, being seen by one influential group as logically and experimentally equivalent to randomized controlled group studies.

Another hierarchy of research evidence developed by the proponents of evidence-based practice appears in the *Users' Guides to the Medical Literature: Essentials of Evidence-Based Clinical Practice* (Guyatt & Rennie, 2002). Contained in this volume is a small section called "A Hierarchy of Evidence" in which the authors lay out the following position:

> What is the nature of the "evidence" in EBM? We suggest a broad definition: any empirical observation about the apparent relation between events constitutes potential evidence. Thus the unsystematic observations of the individual clinician constitute one source of evidence...Unsystematic observations can lead to profound insight, and experienced clinicians develop a healthy respect for the insights of their senior colleagues...At the same time, unsystematic clinical observations are limited by small sample size and more importantly, by deficiencies in human processes of making inferences. Given the limitations of unsystematic clinical observations...EBM suggests a hierarchy of evidence. (p. 11)

These authors' suggested hierarchy is as follows, beginning with the type of evidence possessing the greatest potential internal validity, through forms of evidence usually seen as offering less solid evidence relating to what treatments to offer individual clients: (1) $N = 1$ randomized controlled trials, (2) systematic reviews of randomized trials, (3) single randomized controlled trial, (4) systematic review of quasi-experimental studies addressing client-important outcomes, (4) single quasi-experimental study addressing client outcomes, and (5) unsystematic clinical observations. However, they do include cautionary language regarding the interpretation of this framework:

> This hierarchy is not absolute. If treatment effects are sufficiently large and consistent, for instance, observational studies may provide more compelling evidence than most RCTs...The hierarchy implies a clear course of action for (clinicians) addressing patient problems: They should look for the highest available evidence from the hierarchy. The hierarchy makes clear that any statement to the effect that there is no evidence addressing the effect of a particular treatment is a non sequitur. The evidence may be extremely weak—it may be the unsystematic observation of a single clinician or a generalization from physiological studies that are related only indirectly—but there is always evidence. (pp. 13–14)

It is very important to stress this point: EBP prefers stronger evidence over weaker evidence and suggests that clinicians should not only seek out the highest levels of evidence, but clearly indicates that additional forms of evidence of lesser internal validity should also be appraised. It is important to stress the inclusive nature of all of the evidence being consulted because the misperception is widespread that EBP relies only on studies of the highest quality, as in the following definition for EBP found in *The Social Work Dictionary*: "The use of the best available scientific knowledge derived from randomized controlled outcome studies and meta-analyses of existing outcome studies" (Barker, 2003, p. 149). Given that substantial domains of social work field of practice have yet to have their interventions investigated by well-designed RCTs, the hapless social worker reading such misleading descriptions may shrug his or her shoulders and conclude (incorrectly) that the process of EBP has little to offer clinicians in their area of practice. Evidence-based practice says if there are no experimental SSDs, look for systematic reviews. If there are none of these, look for randomized controlled trials of interventions applied to persons similar to your client with similar problems. If none can be located, drill down the evidentiary strata to the quasi-experiments, then consensus-based practice guidelines perhaps, then case studies. The most comprehensive systematic reviews of this nature may be located on the websites of the Cochrane (related to health and mental health) and Campbell (related to social welfare, education, and criminal justice) Collaborations, available at http://www.cochrane.org and http://www.campbellcollaboration.org, respectively. Although some forms of evidence may be deemed of greater credibility that others, EBP suggests that all forms of relevant evidence be judiciously considered and critically reviewed. Anyone who implies that EBP exclusively focuses only on randomized controlled trials, meta-analyses, or systematic reviews is simply ignorant.

Limitations of This Approach

Twenty-five years ago, the Council on Social Work Education (CSWE) accreditation standards stated that training in practice skills needed to include "data gathering . . . and evaluation relevant to social work practice" (p. 10) and that the content on research should incorporate " . . . designs for the systematic evaluation of the student's own practice" (CSWE, 1982). Soon some social work programs did indeed begin including such content. Early in the last decade, the CSWE's *Educational Policy and Accreditation Standards* (CSWE, 2002, p. 8) continued to include as a foundation program objective the requirement that students demonstrate the ability to "Evaluate research studies, apply research findings to practice, and evaluate their own practice interventions." In the concentration year, the research objectives stated that "The content prepares students to develop, use, and effectively communicate empirically based knowledge, including evidence-based interventions. Research knowledge is used by students . . . to evaluate their own practice" (CSWE, 2002, p. 10).

The more recent revision of the EPAS (CSWE, 2008) has weakened the above standards and now reads, under Educational Standards 2.1.10(d), that "Social workers critically analyze, monitor and evaluate interventions." Nevertheless, it would appear that training-in-practice methods of program and clinical evaluation remain an essential component of professional social work education. On paper these are fine aspirations. But there is relatively little evidence to suggest that we are doing a good job at this. In the 1980s there was a flurry of articles that followed up on the post-MSW graduation use of SSDs in real-life practice, generally finding that they were relatively rarely used (e.g., Cheatham, 1987). A recent survey on a related topic, the extent to which social work programs actually provide didactic instruction and clinical supervision in empirically supported treatments, found them to be very rarely taught indeed (Bledsoe et al., 2007; Weissman et al., 2006). One is tempted to conclude that if the CSWE accreditation standard mandating teaching empirically supported interventions as well as research designs to evaluate one's own practice found that the former is infrequently taught, then it seems likely that the latter is not well covered either. About 25 years ago, I reported on a survey of the extent to which training in SSDs was covered in MSW programs (Thyer & Maddox, 1988). At that time, a large majority appeared to ignore this content, but these old results cannot be extrapolated to the present. However, I venture to speculate that training in SSDs remains rarely taught and when it is covered, it is perhaps not well addressed nor required during internships. A recent more positive exception is the report by Wong & Vakharia (2012) describing the student outcomes they obtained when having students design and conduct SSDs during their MSW evaluation research class. Most are able to do so successfully.

An unfortunate hindrance to the adoption of SSDs within social work is the perceived link between this method and the approach to practice called behavioral social work. This is important because behavioral social work has a long history of being misrepresented, to its detriment, within the social work literature to such an extent that the model is often viewed with disfavor. By inaccurately linking the use of SSDs with behavioral methods, the former topic is tainted by the latter (see Thyer, 1991, 2005). The reality is that the atheoretical methodology of SSDs originated in early nonbehaviorist psychological research and within medicine, physiology, and related disciplines during the late 1800s. In the middle of the last century, researchers began advocating for using SSDs to examine the outcomes and processes of nonbehavioral psychotherapy (e.g., Chassan, 1967; Shapiro, 1961; Shapiro & Ravenette, 1959) and the person-centered therapy developed by Carl Rogers was also subjected to analysis using ABA SSDs (e.g., Truax & Carkhuff, 1965). Within social work, SSDs have been used to evaluate the outcomes of psychodynamic therapy (e.g., Broxmeyer, 1978), task-centered practice (e.g., Tolson, 1977), and treatment informed by communication theory (Nelsen, 1978). The fact that behaviorally oriented practitioners have admittedly made greater use of SSDs should not overshadow the fact that these research techniques can and should be used to evaluate the outcomes of all forms of practice.

It also cannot be denied, in discussing limitations of using SSDs, that some of the designs possess fairly restrictive methodological requirements (e.g., staggered baselines, withdrawal phases) that are difficult to meet, which limits their applicability. Also most agencies seem to provide little in the way of organizational support to reinforce practitioner efforts to undertake these designs, and, as we well know, that which has not been reinforced in the past is much less likely to be engaged in.

Implications for Social Work on Micro,
Mezzo, and Macro Levels

At the micro level, it will be obvious that I advocate the wider use of SSDs by social workers to evaluate the outcomes of their own practice. This is not only congruent with what is required by the CSWE; such evaluations are also compatible with the practice standards and the Code of Ethics promulgated by the National Association of Social Workers, which call for social workers to engage in such systematic practice evaluations (these standards are reviewed in Royse et al., 2010, p. 16). I encourage practitioners to start with relatively simple designs, such as the B or AB, prior to undertaking more complex SSDs, so that your skills in applying these research methods can be honed. Try it with one client, then perhaps another. No one, certainly not me, is suggesting social workers should be required to use these designs with all clients. Advocates of SSDs are simply urging their gradual incorporation into some cases. Quite apart from the desirability of enhancing this aspect of professional practice, if greater numbers of social workers undertook such SSDs, they would be in a better position to submit such cases to the various professional journals that welcome examples of such evaluations. It would certainly be a good thing for our professional journals to have greater representation from the practice community among its published authors.

Supervisors also can encourage their supervisees to undertake SSDs and incorporate a review of graphed data into their supervisory sessions with social workers (see Artelt & Thyer, 1998). As Gambrill has aptly noted: "The quality of services you offer should be enhanced by the supervision you receive and supervisors should be evaluated by reviewing the outcomes achieved by those whom they supervise" (1983, pp. 400–401). This is a very radical idea! There are a few examples of social workers receiving supervision that incorporated the use of SSDs (e.g., Isaacs, Embry, & Baer, 1982; Jones, Morris, & Barnard, 1986), so this approach is not without precedent, nor is it impractical.

Artelt and Thyer (1998, pp. 419–420) provided three even more directive recommendations:

1. Supervisors should encourage social workers to use, as first-choice assessment options, empirically supported methods of assessment, where such knowledge is available.

2. Supervisors should encourage social workers to repeatedly gather quantitative and qualitative data on the client's situation throughout the course of treatment. This information should be presented in records as an up-to-date graph.

3. Supervisors should encourage social workers to use as first-choice treatment options empirically supported methods of intervention, where such knowledge is available.

Again, such recommendations can be seen as compatible with contemporary practice standards and ethical admonitions. See Myers and Thyer

(1997) for an expanded argument for the client's right to receive empirically supported treatments.

Earlier, Thyer (1995, p. 95) provided the following statement as a proposed addition to the NASW's Code of Ethics:

> *Clinicians should routinely gather empirical data on client's relevant behavior, affect, and reports of thoughts, using reliable and valid measures, where such measures have been developed. These measures should be repeated throughout the course of treatment, and used in clinical decision making to supplement professional judgments pertaining to the alteration or termination of treatment.*

This recommendation, of course, is identical with using SSDs in your own practice.

At the macro level, several larger-scale practices suggest themselves. The CSWE could strengthen its required content related to research so that each student specializing in direct practice would be expected to actually undertake an SSD during his or her clinical internship. This is not a requirement at present. So we have the very odd accreditation standard situation wherein students are supposed to be taught something (how to evaluate their own practice), but they are not ever required to actually do so. An even stiffer standard for individual programs to adopt, if not the CSWE, would be for each direct practice student to be required, during his or her internship, to provide convincing evidence that he or she has helped at least one client! When, over the years, I have voiced this suggested requirement among groups of students or faculty, it usually has been met with grins or nervous laughter. I wonder why?

Going up the mezzo/macro scale of implications, third-party vendors (e.g., insurance companies) who pay for clinical social work services could adopt some of these suggestions—such as requiring clinical social workers to provide objective data of client functioning presented via graphs. Many already ask for some information from clinicians such as client diagnoses, time and duration of therapy sessions, and the nature of treatment being provided. Asking for additional data related to client functioning before, during, and perhaps after the social work services they are paying for could exert a significant leavening effect on the field.

Conclusion

Social work practice can be evaluated using a variety of methodological tools. Single-system designs are one very good tool for evaluating practice outcomes. They have been advocated within social work for the past 40 years, and a rather substantial literature describing the methodology of SSDs, as well as hundreds of real-life examples of using them in direct social work practice, is available (Thyer & Thyer, 1992). SSDs can range in internal validity from the very weak to the very strong. Some practitioners within the empirically supported treatments and evidence-based practice communities consider well-conducted SSDs to be among the strongest forms of evidence available for practitioners to make causal inferences about the effects of treatment with their individual clients.

SSDs can be used by practitioners operating from any conceivable theoretical framework, and they can be usefully employed to evaluate outcomes across all the client systems encountered in direct practice—individuals, couples, families, and small groups. There is much that our major professional organizations could do to promote the greater use of SSDs in social work practice, but individual clinicians need not wait for external contingencies to be established to begin experimenting with applying these approaches to practice evaluation. So using SSDs has the potential to help clients more effectively, to contribute to the knowledge base of the field, and to more tightly knit together the art of social work practice with the science of human behavior.

Key Terms

AB design

ABAB design

Alternating treatments design

Case studies

Causal inference

Evidence-based practice

Multiple baseline designs

Rapid assessment instruments

Single-system designs

Visual inference

Review Questions for Critical Thinking

1. What are the two prerequisites for conducting a single-system research design?

2. Why do you suppose these designs are not more commonly used within social work practice?

3. What practical steps could be taken to encourage social work students and practitioners to make greater use of these designs in their work?

4. Think of a practice situation you have encountered and describe how you could have used an SSD to evaluate clinical outcomes.

5. Describe the experimental logic behind causal inferences that may be drawn from the more rigorous SSDs such as the ABAB or multiple-baseline designs.

Online Resources

Association for Behavior Analysis International http://www.abainternational.org/in

A membership organization for individuals concerned with the applied and experimental analysis of behavior.

Association of Professional Behavior Analysts (APBA) http://www.apbahome.net/

An organization for practitioners holding credentials as Board Certified Behavior Analysts. The APBA holds an annual convention, publishes a journal, and promotes the ethical and scientific use of single-system designs in everyday practice.

This is a nice 10-minute video overview of the use of SSDs in clinical practice.

http://www.youtube.com/watch?v = exnuZS4Av08

Here is a link to a short instruction video on how to make a single-system graph using Google Docs.

http://www.youtube.com/watch?v = G6Biv0IWZ9s

References

Allen, G. J. (1973). Case study: Implementation of behavior modification in summer camp settings. *Behavior Therapy, 4,* 570–575.

Artelt, T., & Thyer, B. A. (1998). Empirical approaches to social work supervision. In J. S. Wodarski & B. A. Thyer (Eds.), *Handbook of empirical social work practice, Vol. 2: Social problems and practice issues* (pp. 413–431). New York, NY: Wiley.

Baer, D. M., Harrison, R., Fradenburg, L., Petersen, D., & Milla, S. (2005). Some pragmatics in the valid and reliable recording of directly observed behavior. *Research on Social Work Practice, 15,* 440–451.

Barker, R. (Ed.). (2003). *The social work dictionary* (5th ed.). Washington, DC: National Association of Social Workers Press.

Besa, D. (1994). Evaluating narrative family therapy using single-system designs. *Research on Social Work Practice, 4,* 309–325.

Bledsoe, S. E., Weissman, M. M., Mullen, E. J., Betts, K., Gameroff, M. J., Verdeli, H., et al. (2007). Empirically supported psychotherapy in social work training: Does the definition of evidence matter? *Research on Social Work Practice, 17,* 449–455.

Bloom, M., Fischer, J., & Orme, J. (2009). *Evaluating practice: Guidelines for the accountable professional* (6th ed.). Boston, MA: Allyn & Bacon.

Brandell, J. R., & Varkas, T. (2010). Narrative case studies. In B. A. Thyer (Ed.), *Handbook of social work research methods* (2nd ed., pp. 376–398). Thousand Oaks, CA: Sage.

Broxmeyer, N. (1978). Practitioner-research in treating a borderline child. *Social Work Research and Abstracts, 14*(4), 5–10.

Cameron, O. G., & Thyer, B. A. (1985). Treatment of pavor nocturnus with alprazolam [Letter]. *Journal of Clinical Psychiatry, 46,* 504.

Chambless, D. L., Baker, M. J., Baucom, D. H., Beutler, L. E., Calhoun, K. S., Crits-Critsoph, P., . . . Woody, S. R. (1998). Update on empirically validated therapies (Pt. II). *Clinical Psychologist, 51*(1), 3–16.

Chassan, J. B. (1967). *Research design in clinical psychology and psychiatry.* New York, NY: Appleton-Century-Crofts.

Cheatham, J. M. (1987). The empirical evaluation of clinical practice: A survey of four groups of practitioners. *Journal of Social Service Research*, *10*(2/3/4), 163–177.

Colby, K. M. (1960). *An introduction to psychoanalytic research*. New York, NY: Basic Books.

Corsini, R. J. (2002). *The dictionary of psychology*. New York, NY: Brunner-Routledge.

Council on Social Work Education. (1982). Curriculum policy for the master's degree and the baccalaureate degree programs in social work education. *Social Work Education Reporter*, *30*(3), 5–12.

Council on Social Work Education. (2002). *Educational policy and accreditation standards*. Alexandria, VA: Author.

Council on Social Work Education. (2008). *Educational policy and accreditation standards*. Alexandria, VA: Author.

Fischer, J., & Corcoran, K. (Eds.). (2007). *Measures for clinical practice* (4th ed.). New York, NY: Free Press.

Friston, K. J., Homles, A. P., & Worsley, K. J. (1999). How many subjects constitute a study? *NeuroImage*, *10*, 1–5.

Gambrill, E. (1983). *Casework: A competency approach*. Englewood Cliffs, NJ: Prentice Hall.

Gershenson, C. P. (1952). The reliability of the movement scale. *Social Casework*, *33*, 294–300.

Gilbert, D. J., & Franklin, C. (2003). Qualitative assessment methods. In C. Jordan & C. Franklin (Eds.), *Clinical assessment for social workers* (2nd ed., pp. 139–178). Chicago, IL: Lyceum Books.

Gilgun, J. (1994). A case for case studies in social work research. *Social Work*, *39*, 371–380.

Guyatt, G., Haynes, B., Jaeschke, R., Cook, D., Greenhalgh, T., Meade, M.,... Richardson, W. S. (2002). Introduction: The philosophy of evidence-based medicine. In G. Guyatt & D. Rennie (Eds.), *Users' guides to the medical literature: Essentials of evidence-based clinical practice* (pp. 5–20). Chicago, IL: American Medical Association.

Guyatt, G., & Rennie, D. (Eds.). (2002). *Users' guides to the medical literature: Essentials of evidence-based clinical practice*. Chicago, IL: American Medical Association.

Guyatt, G., Sackett, D., Taylor, D. W., Chong, J., Roberts, R., & Pugsley, S. (1986). Determining optimal therapy: Randomized trials in individual patients. *New England Journal of Medicine*, *314*, 889–892.

Hersen, M., & Barlow, D. H. (1985). *Single case experimental designs*. New York, NY: Pergamon Press.

Hunt, J., Blenkner, M., & Kogan, L. S. (1950). A field test of the movement scale. *Social Casework*, *31*, 267–277.

Isaacs, C. D., Embry, L. H., & Baer, D. M. (1982). Training family therapists: An experimental analysis. *Journal of Applied Behavior Analysis*, *15*, 505–520.

Janosky, J. E. (2005). Use of the single subject design for practice-based primary care research. *Postgraduate Medicine Journal*, *81*, 549–551.

Jones, H. H., Morris, E. K., & Barnard, J. D. (1986). Increasing staff completion of civil commitment forms through instructions and graphed group performance feedback. *Journal of Organizational Behavior Management*, *7*(3/4), 29–43.

Jordan, C., & Franklin, C. (Eds.). (2011). *Clinical assessment for social workers* (2nd ed.). Chicago, IL: Lyceum Books.

Kazdin, A. E. (1981). Drawing valid inferences from case studies. *Journal of Consulting and Clinical Psychology, 49,* 183–192.

Kazi, M. A. F. (1998). *Single-case evaluation by social workers.* Aldershot, U.K.: Ashgate.

Kent, M. A., Camfield, C. S., & Camfield, P. R. (1999). Double-blind methylphenidate trials: Practical and highly endorsed by families. *Archives of Pediatric and Adolescent Medicine, 153,* 1292–1296.

Koepke, J., & Thyer, B. A. (1985). Behavioral treatment of failure to thrive in a two-year-old infant. *Child Welfare, 64,* 511–516.

Kogan, N., Kogan, L. S., & Hunt, J. (1952). Expansion and extension of use of the movement scale. *Social Casework, 33,* 10–12.

Martinez, K. K. & Wong, S. E. (2009). Using prompts to increase attendance at groups for survivors of domestic violence. *Research on Social Work Practice, 19,* 460–463.

McBride, M. (1988). An individual double-blind cross-over trial for assessing methylphenidate response in children with attention deficit disorder. *Journal of Pediatrics, 113,* 137–145.

Myers, L. L., & Thyer, B. A. (1997). Should clients have the right to effective treatment? *Social Work, 42,* 288–298.

Nelsen, J. (1978). Use of communication theory in single-subject research. *Social Work Research and Abstracts, 14*(4), 12–19.

Pergeron, J. P., Curtis, G. C., & Thyer, B. A. (1986). Simple phobia leading to suicide: A case study [Letter]. *The Behavior Therapist, 9,* 134–135.

Pinkston, E. M., Howe, M. W., & Blackman, D. K. (1987). Medical social work management of urinary incontinence in the elderly. *Journal of Social Service Research, 10*(2/3/4), 179–194.

Polster, R. A., & Collins, D. (1993). Structured observation. In R. M. Grinnell (Ed.), *Social work research and evaluation* (4th ed., pp. 244–261). Itasca, IL: Peacock.

Richmond, M. (1917). *Social diagnosis.* New York, NY: Sage.

Rosen, S., & Polansky, N. A. (1975). Observation of social interaction. In N. A. Polansky (Ed.), *Social work research* (2nd ed., pp. 154–181). Chicago, IL: University of Chicago Press.

Royse, D., Thyer, B. A., & Padgett, D. K. (2010). *Program evaluation: An introduction* (5th ed.). Belmont, CA: Thomson-Brooks/Cole.

Shadish, W. R., Cook, T. D., & Campbell, D. T. (2002). *Experimental and quasi-experimental designs for generalized causal inference.* New York, NY: Houghton Mifflin.

Shapiro, M. B. (1961). The single-case in clinical-psychological research. *British Journal of Medical Psychology, 34,* 255–263.

Shapiro, M. B., & Ravenette, A. T. (1959). A preliminary experiment of paranoid delusions. *Journal of Mental Science, 105,* 295–312.

Sidman, M. (1960). *Tactics of scientific research: Evaluating experimental data in psychology.* New York, NY: Basic Books.

Staats, A. W., & Butterfield, W. (1965). Treatment of nonreading in a culturally deprived juvenile delinquent. *Child Development, 36,* 925–942.

Straus, S. E., Glasziou, Richardson, W. S., & Haynes, R. B. (2011). *Evidence-based medicine: How to practice and teach EBM* (4th ed.). New York, NY: Elsevier.

Tansella, M. (2002). The scientific evaluation of mental health treatments: An historical perspective. *Evidence-Based Mental Health, 5,* 4–5.

Thyer, B. A. (1980). Phobia sufferers take a journey into fear. *Practice Digest, 3*(3), 8–10.

Thyer, B. A. (1981). Prolonged in-vivo exposure therapy with a 70-year-old woman. *Journal of Behavior Therapy and Experimental Psychiatry, 12,* 47–51.

Thyer, B. A. (1991). Behavioral social work: It is not what you think. *Arete, 16*(2), 1–9.

Thyer, B. A. (1995). Promoting an empiricist agenda in the human services: An ethical and humanistic imperative. *Journal of Behavior Therapy and Experimental Psychiatry, 26,* 93–98.

Thyer, B. A. (2005). The misfortunes of behavioral social work: Misprized, misread, and misconstrued. In S. A. Kirk (Ed.), *Mental disorders in the social environment: Critical perspectives* (pp. 230–243). New York, NY: Columbia University Press.

Thyer, B. A., Irvine, S., & Santa, C. (1984). Contingency management of exercise among chronic schizophrenics. *Perceptual and Motor Skills, 58,* 419–425.

Thyer, B. A., & Maddox, K. (1988). Behavioral social work: Results of a national survey of graduate curricula. *Psychological Reports, 63,* 239–242.

Thyer, B. A., & Myers, L. L. (2007). *A social worker's guide to evaluating practice outcomes.* Alexandria, VA: Council on Social Work Education.

Thyer, B. A., & Stocks, J. T. (1986). Exposure therapy in the treatment of a phobic blind person. *Journal of Visual Impairment and Blindness, 80,* 1001–1003.

Thyer, B. A., & Thyer, K. B. (1992). Single system research designs in social work practice: A bibliography from 1965–1990. *Research on Social Work Practice, 2,* 99–116.

Tolson, E. (1977). Alleviating marital communication problems. In W. Reid & L. Epstein (Eds.), *Task-centered practice* (pp. 100–112). Chicago, IL: University of Chicago Press.

Tripodi, T. (1994). *A primer on single-subject design for clinical social workers.* Washington, DC: National Association of Social Workers Press.

Truax, C. B., & Carkhuff, R. R. (1965). Experimental manipulation of therapeutic conditions. *Journal of Consulting Psychology, 29,* 119–124.

Vonk, E. M., & Thyer, B. A. (1995). Exposure therapy in the treatment of vaginal penetration phobia. *Journal of Behavior Therapy and Experimental Psychiatry, 29,* 359–363.

Weissman, M. M., Verdeli, H., Gameroff, M., Bledsoe, S. E., Betts, K., Mufson L., . . . Wickramaratne, P. (2006). National survey of psychotherapy training programs in psychiatry, psychology, and social work. *Archives of General Psychiatry, 63,* 925–934.

Wessel, S. L. (1953). A study of the Hunt Movement Scale at family service of Philadelphia. *Smith College Studies in Social Work, 24,* 7–40.

Witkin, S. (1981). Preparing for marital counseling in nontraditional settings. In S. P. Schinke (Ed.), *Behavioral methods in social welfare* (pp. 269–286). New York, NY: Aldine de Gruyter.

Wolins, M. (1960). Measuring the effect of social work intervention. In N. A. Polansky (Ed.), *Social work research* (pp. 247–272). Chicago, IL: University of Chicago Press.

Wong, S. E., Seroka, P. L., & Ogisi, J. (2000). Effects of a checklist on self-assessment of blood glucose levels by a memory-impaired woman with diabetes mellitus. *Journal of Applied Behavior Analysis, 33,* 251–254.

Wong, S. E., Terranova, M. D., Bowen, L., Zarate, R., Massel, H. K., & Liberman, R. P. (1987). Providing independent recreational activities to reduce stereotypic vocalizations in chronic schizophrenics. *Journal of Applied Behavior Analysis, 20,* 77–81.

Wong, S. E. & Vakharia, S. P. (2011). Teaching research and practice evaluation skills to graduate social work students. *Research on Social Work Practice, 22,* 714–718.

Wong, S. E., Woolsey, J. E., & Gallegos, E. (1987). Behavioral treatment of chronic psychiatric patients. *Journal of Social Service Research, 10*(2/3/4), 7–35.

Yin, R. K. (1989). *Case study research: Design and methods.* Newbury Park, CA: Sage.

Chapter 9

Termination, Stabilization, and Continuity of Care

Samuel A. MacMaster and Sara Sanders

> How can social workers proactively prepare clients and themselves for the completion of a treatment relationship?

Termination and stabilization are quite possibly the most important phases in the entire clinical process. It is in these phases that changes initiated during the course of services are solidified, the individual or client system envisions a future in this new state, and the groundwork is laid for any future service use with the current or any other service provider. Yet, despite the overall importance of these critical phases of treatment, there is a paucity of literature dedicated to the ending of clinical services and the maintenance of any changes that have been realized.

Both termination and stabilization have been broadly defined within the social work literature and are often conceptualized as two closely and interrelated processes. This chapter treats them as two phases of what is essentially the same process. In an ideal world, once the client stabilizes, and has met all goals, services naturally come to an end. Therefore, stabilization is the process that indicates an ending point or termination of services.

Ideally, stabilization and termination are linear processes in which a stabilized client who has met the treatment goals and experienced a resolution to the presenting problem initiates an ending to services with interpersonal growth. However, stabilization and termination are rarely carried out in this fashion. Depending on the mode of service delivery and, unfortunately, more often than not, external environmental factors, service termination and stabilization may not always occur as a smooth transition or may not even be related to each other.

This chapter provides a brief overview of the historical trends of termination and stabilization and an overview from a transtheoretical perspective. We discuss the importance of these phases for the overall clinical process, provide a discussion of stabilization beyond the settling of a crisis, introduce ideal termination process, discuss perspectives on planned and unplanned terminations, and finally provide perspectives of termination and stabilization in areas of social work practice that do not follow the idealized clinical process.

Historical Trends

As argued by many clinicians and clinical researchers, preparation for stabilizing the client and terminating the clinical relationship starts from the first day of treatment (Woods & Hollis, 1990). The need for this type of practice approach has become more pronounced as the requirements for documenting clinical outcomes, justifying ongoing treatment and reimbursement have taken a prominent role in clinical practice. With reductions in mental health care in an attempt to control climbing fees for service (Anderson, 2000; Ligon, 1997; Strom, 1992), it is becoming more critical to develop intervention plans that are geared toward timely termination and long-term client stabilization.

Third-party reimbursement has received criticism for its impact on the clinical relationship between the social worker and client in all phases of the treatment process, as well as at termination. The result is that clients often have a reduced length of treatment (i.e., termination too soon) because of the inability to justify the continued need for treatment (Strom, 1992). This was further echoed by Petryshen and Petryshen (1992) as they discussed the drive toward fiscally responsible lengths of treatment. Third-party reimbursement has also created concern about premature termination because of the lack of insurance funding. This has ramifications for the client who loses insurance before treatment has been completed. Does the social worker continue the treatment process knowing that the client is unable to pay; thus, the social worker loses financially? Or does the social worker terminate the therapeutic relationship with the client prior to client stabilization (Strom, 1992)? These questions create an ethical dilemma for social workers as they continue to strive to provide cost-effective treatment and positive clinical outcomes.

A Broader Perspective on Service Delivery

A discussion of stabilization and termination requires not only a broader view of the clinical process, but also incorporation of what we know about the process of behavior change. Any change stabilized and ultimately maintained throughout and after termination must first be initiated in the early stages of the clinical process. Through research and practice experiences, it has become clear that individuals rarely make behavior changes rapidly in response to professional interventions, but rather changes occur through a slow and steady ongoing process with the *assistance of* professional interventions. This conceptualization of the change process has become known as the stages of change or transtheoretical model (Table 9.1). Developed by Prochaska and DiClemente (1983), the transtheoretical model helps explain how both self-initiated and professionally assisted changes occur for individuals with problematic behavior. Prochaska and DiClemente put forth a five-stage theory based on a review of all empirical research on professionally assisted behavior change. The basic premise of

Table 9.1 Transtheoretical Model

1. Precontemplation Stage

No intention to change in the foreseeable future.
Unaware or underaware that there is even a problem.
Present to treatment because of outside influences.
May even demonstrate change while pressure is on.
Resistance to recognizing or modifying a problem is the hallmark; for example, "I don't have any problems."

2. Contemplation Stage

Aware problem exists—seriously thinking about overcoming it, but have not yet made a commitment to take action.
May be stuck here for a long time.
"Knowing where you want to go, but not quite ready yet."
Weigh pros and cons of problem and solution—struggle with positive evaluations of their addiction and the amount of energy, effort, and loss it will cost to overcome the problem.

3. Preparation Stage

Combines intention and behavioral criteria, for example, individuals in this stage are intending to take action in the next month and have unsuccessfully taken action in the past year.
Typically will report some action such as a decrease in the behavior—but have not yet reached a criterion for effective action.
They are, however, intending to take such action in the future.

4. Action Stage

Individuals modify their behavior, experiences, or environment to overcome their problems.
Involves the most overt behavioral changes and requires considerable commitment of time and energy.
Modifications here tend to be the most visible and receive greatest external recognition.
Do not confuse this stage with change, which often happens, as you will overlook the requisite work that prepares changers for action and important efforts necessary to maintain the changes following action.
They have successfully altered the behavior for a period of 1 day to 6 months, for example, reaching a certain criterion.
Modification of the target behavior to an acceptable criterion and significant overt efforts to change are the hallmarks of action.

5. Maintenance

People work to prevent relapse into the changed behavior and consolidate the gains attained during action.
Maintenance is not static and is viewed as a continuation of change. It extends from about 6 months to an indeterminate period past the initial action—for some, it's a lifetime of change.
Being able to remain free of the behavior and being able to consistently engage in new, incompatible behavior for more than 6 months are the criteria for this stage.
Stabilizing behavior change and avoiding relapse into old behavior patterns are the hallmarks of maintenance.
Since relapse into old behaviors is the rule rather than the exception, cannot conceptualize this model as a linear model with people neatly going from one stage to another; rather, the authors present it as a spiral pattern.
In relapse to old behavior patterns, some return to the stage before relapse. Others begin again somewhere in the middle. The majority recycle back to later stages, that is, they potentially learn from their mistakes.
In a cohort of individuals, the number of successes continues to increase gradually over time, but a large number stay in the precontemplation and contemplation stages.

their work is that stages of change are temporal dimensions that determine when particular shifts in attitudes, intentions, and behaviors occur within a much larger dynamic process.

In general, each stage represents a period of time, as well as a set of tasks needed for movement to the next stage. Although the time an individual spends in each stage may vary, tasks to be accomplished are assumed to be uniform. With regard to implications for stabilization and termination, it is important to note that the vast majority of people are neither highly motivated nor are they in the action stage. However most social work interventions are oriented toward individuals seeking services in an action stage of change or minimally assume an action orientation toward the presenting problem. Studies indicate that of the individuals seeking professional services, only 10% to 15% are prepared for action; 30% to 40% are in the contemplation stages; and the majority, 50% to 60%, are in the precontemplation stages (Prochaska, DiClemente, & Norcross, 1992). Therefore, most social workers and social work programs will underserve, misserve, or not serve the majority of their target populations in the beginning stages of services and set up problems that will continue until the ending stages. The amount of measurable progress clients make following an intervention tends to be a function of their pretreatment stage of change.

Research has also shown that if clients progress from one stage to the next in the first month of treatment, they can double their chances of taking actions during the initial 6 months of services. It is important for social workers to remember that action-oriented treatment with definitive beginnings and endings may be ideal and may work with people who initially present in the preparation or action stages. However, this assumption will lead to a mismatch between the intervention and the stage change and will likely be totally ineffective with individuals in the precontemplation or contemplation stages. Just as individuals will be poorly conceptualized to be in preparation or action stages at the beginning of services, it is often quite common for misconceptions to continue with the assumption that individuals are in the maintenance stage. Therefore, it is quite likely that services will end with little hope of stabilization, and termination will not be the smooth end to an idyllic process, but services are likely to end abruptly and/or prematurely (Prochaska & Velicer, 1997; Prochaska, Velicer, DiClemente, & Fava, 1988; Prochaska, Velicer, DiClemente, Guadagnoli, & Rossi, 1991).

There are clear markers for determining where an individual may be relative to their stage of change. In the precontemplative stage, people processed less information about their problems, devoted less time and energy to reevaluating themselves and experienced fewer emotional reactions to the negative aspects of their problems. These clients tended to be less open with others about their problems and did little to shift their attention or their environment in the direction of overcoming problems—they were the most resistant and least active patients. In the contemplation stage, they were most open to consciousness-raising techniques, such as confrontations or educational processes. They reevaluated themselves more and struggled with questions such as "How do I think and feel about living in a deteriorating environment that places my families or friends at increasing risk for disease, poverty, or imprisonment?" In the preparation stage, people began to take small steps toward action—this is where is it appropriate to use counterconditioning and stimulus-control techniques to begin reducing the targeted behavior. During the action stage, individuals endorsed higher levels of self-liberation, believed they had the autonomy to change their lives, and relied increasingly on support and understanding from helping relationships. In the maintenance stage, clients relied on all the processes that came before it. This stage entails an assessment of the conditions under which a person was likely to relapse into the old behaviors and development of alternative responses for coping with such conditions.

This broader perspective on social work practice clearly suggests the need to assess the stage of a client's readiness for change and to tailor interventions accordingly throughout the clinical process. Ultimately, effective and efficient professionally assisted change depends on doing the right things (processes) at the right time (stages). While not assuming a linear process through these stages, the stabilization of client gains and the termination of services do rely on the accomplishment of certain markers in the previous stages. The lack of awareness or lack of recognition of these markers by clinicians will determine the ability to effectively stabilize targeted behaviors and, ultimately, the experience of both the service recipient and the service provider in the termination of services.

Importance of Termination and Stabilization

While a great deal of literature, training, research, and resources are dedicated to the beginning stages of treatment in which a social worker engages with the client, it is quite clear that the ending stages of the same services are just as, if not more, important for the long-term health of the client. The manner in which the clinician handles these interrelated processes has significant implications for the client long after formal professional services are complete. Woods and Hollis (1990) describe five features that highlight the importance of this stage and the need for heightened skill, care, and sensitivity to the client or client system.

The most important feature is the crisis focus that many clients seeking services present with at the beginning of treatment. When entering the stabilization and termination phases, this crisis may have abated and the motivation to continue to seek growth may decrease. The first struggle for a social worker working with a client in this phase is that as the momentum decreases, it becomes necessary to assist the client in maintaining focus and continuing to seek and foster growth.

Heightened sensitivity to client's emotional reactions to services is also necessary at this time. As services are initiated, discussions of the relationship between the client and the social worker naturally occur; however, as stabilization begins to occur and termination may be seen as imminent, clients may have heightened emotions regarding the therapeutic relationship and transference and countertransference issues may arise. Unlike the beginning stages of services, clients at this point may experience less awareness of these issues and are much less likely to acknowledge these feelings.

Increased vigilance at this point in the relationship is also necessary because it is a very vulnerable time for clients. This vulnerability is related to both the new growth experienced in services and the nature of the transitional period, which may heighten a desire to return to ineffective coping mechanisms. If handled poorly, this transition may negate any growth developed during the therapeutic process, and more importantly it may be so damaging that the client may be reluctant to reconnect with services in the future. Mistakes made at this time are also further exacerbated because there may be little time to become aware of and/or correct any issues that arise.

Another factor that is often overlooked when planning and beginning services is that very few clients actually follow an ideal pattern of stabilization and termination. There are a host of issues that may be completely unplanned that often cause an individual to prematurely end services. As a result, there may be little or no time for stabilization and/or a formal termination process. Likewise, the nature of the event or factor that leads to the ending or reduction of the length of services is also important. The way that this is viewed within the therapeutic relationship has a definitive impact on the opportunities for stabilization and termination. Who initiates the ending of services, whether this is planned or unplanned, and the reasoning behind it may influence how this is viewed within the relationship, particularly if these events are not conceptualized by both parties in the same way.

While these previous factors are discussed in the literature on stabilization and termination, Woods and Hollis (1990) make particular mention of the difficulties in the process from the vantage point of the social worker. They suggest that unresolved ambivalence around both the client and the nature of therapeutic process with the system will impact stabilization and termination. The social worker will likely have increased emotions around both issues that he or she may not recognize. More important, they suggest that the relationship the social worker has with separation will directly impact this stage. Again, similar to the other previously mentioned issues, the social worker is likely to have less self-awareness at the ending of services versus the beginning; and at the same time the potential impact that these issues have for the overall health of the client is much greater. Because of the nature of delivering social work services over time, social workers, unless extremely self-aware, are likely to somewhat deny the impact of termination on emotions simply because these emotions may be experienced on a regular basis, and they may not connect these experiences to their own potential issues around separation or attachment.

Stabilization and termination are potentially the most important stages of the therapeutic process because it is here that the potential for real-world growth of the client is developed. Despite this importance, stabilization and termination are frequently overlooked and rarely focused on. Intensifying the potential for problems at this stage of the process is the need for the clinician to be aware of and plan for the complex set of factors that serve as barriers to a smooth transition to stabilization and from stabilization to termination. Dorfman (1996) refers to this as a time for mourning or a time for celebration; however, it is important for social workers to be aware of all of these factors so that they can adequately address the grief or the celebration.

Stabilization

Typically, writings on social work practice assume a linear process conceptualizing the interactions between a social worker and a client system, which has a beginning, middle and an end. There are many of these models in the social work and other related literatures (Corey, 1991; Northen, 1995; Woods & Hollis, 1990), which tend to be closely related on a conceptual basis to the one posited by Hepworth, Rooney, and Larsen (2002) that suggests a three-phase process of a beginning, described as exploration, assessment, and planning; followed by a middle stage, described as implementation and goal attainment; and a final or ending stage or termination. While there are many such conceptualizations for these processes, they often overlook the all-too-important stage of stabilization. It is within this stage that a client is able to incorporate changes to overcome the presenting problem, return to a new state of homeostasis, and develop new mechanisms for coping with the environment that include any gains and/or new skills developed as a direct result of the received services. Stabilization is not an event—signaling the need for termination—but is rather a process unto itself.

Contrasting with the previously described conceptualization of stabilization is another broader perspective that takes in both the individuals and environmental factors over a longer period of time. From this perspective, services are not complete when a presenting crisis is over and/or has been successfully dealt with through an intervention. For many individuals seeking social work services, the presenting issue rarely exists in a vacuum, but is often symptomatic of an extended, often lifelong, pattern of poor coping with environmental stressors. However, most service recipients seek services during a crisis and through this myopia are only able to be aware of the presenting problem. When the crisis is resolved, individuals often seek to terminate services. However, for true stabilization to occur, a skilled social worker must assist the individual in identifying these underlying patterns and working toward their abatement.

A four-stage model for conceptualizing this broader perspective has been posited by Smets (1988). This model includes an incubation phase, the crisis, the development of an intervention plan, and finally stabilization. The inclusion of an early, pretreatment seeking phase of incubation provides a conceptualization that is more in line with what we know about behavior change from the transtheoretical model's stages of change. This conceptualization from a broader perspective also assists clinicians in providing services that will be more efficient because they are tailored to the underlying issue and not the immediate crisis; thus interventions are specifically directed at the root cause and not symptoms of the issue and are tailored to the appropriate stage of change. Clinicians will also therefore be more effective at achieving the treatment goal both in the short term, but more importantly over the long term.

Usually services are initiated at the high point of the crisis phase, which naturally passes with time. It is the clinicians' responsibility to not assume stabilization once this crisis has passed, but to direct services to the underlying issues that incubated the presenting problem (Smets, 1988). Within this model, stabilization and termination occur in stage 4—only after the client and the social worker have mutually achieved stabilization of the underlying issue. This model assumes that true stabilization of the client or client system rarely occurs because the focus is on stabilizing the crisis and not on the stabilization of the underlying issue.

In order to effectively stabilize a client, the clinician must first have the long-term perspective of the nature of presenting problems. Similarly, the clinician must be willing and able to take services to a deeper level beyond the superficial crisis. From an environmental perspective, an opportunity must exist for the client to engage with a service provider over a long enough time period for the underlying issue or issues to emerge. The social worker's time is often the most frequently discussed resource in service delivery; however, the client too must have the available time and energy to devote to this endeavor. Similarly, the client must maintain motivation toward change. However, regardless of how high the motivational state may be, it is the opportunity that is most lacking and that creates the most barriers for vulnerable client populations. Once the clinician and client both possess the opportunity, willingness, and perspective, stabilization can occur, but only if the clinician maintains vigilance against the issues previously raised that so often interfere with ideal stabilization.

Case Management, Brief Therapy, and Crisis Intervention

Much of the literature on stabilization and termination in social work practice assumes a highly clinical or therapeutic style of service delivery, which is most often typified by weekly outpatient office visits where time is not a constraining resource. While this type of service delivery is in no way typical of the work that all, or even most, social workers perform, it is the type of service that is described when ideal therapeutic processes are presented in the literature. To fully describe stabilization and termination as it relates to social work practice, there are some areas that need special attention because of time constraints or the nature of the service delivery mechanism.

Case Management

Case management is a primary social work service for frail elders, children and youth, individuals with cognitive or physical disabilities, individuals with physical or mental health problems, and those who are experiencing poverty or other disabling life circumstances (Fiene & Taylor, 1991; Levine et al., 2006). Through the roles of brokering, counseling, educating, and advocating, case managers strive to enhance the functioning of the client through locating and securing necessary support services from the community (Fiene & Taylor, 1991; Moxley, 1989). The coordination of services looks different based on the client and his or her needs. For some, the case management may be simply assessing the clients' needs and then connecting them to other providers of services, but for others it may be more intensive, including counseling, interdisciplinary assessment and care planning, scheduling and transporting to appointments, monitoring medications and follow-up with medical care, serving as a liaison between the client and other providers, and ensuring that daily needs, including activities of daily living, are being met. The length of time that clients receive case management services will also vary based on the clients' needs, the structure of the case management program, and agency resources.

Stabilization and termination also look different based on the case management program. For instance, in health care-related case management programs, termination of client services is based on client progress and reimbursement issues. In home health care, for example, if the patients' condition stabilizes, many insurance programs cease paying for services. As found in the work of Levine and colleagues (2006), the decision to terminate services may occur within 24 to 48 hours, giving the patient and family little time to make alternative care arrangements. The ramification of this type of termination is that family support systems often do not have time to prepare for losing assistance; thus, termination occurs before stabilization happens in the home.

In the area of child welfare, termination may also occur prior to stabilization. For instance, case managers within the child welfare system work with families to obtain resources to strengthen their family unit and address individual needs, such as substance abuse, domestic violence, and parenting skills. If the family system is strengthened, termination will occur with the child returning to or remaining in the home. However, if these goals are not accomplished, it is determined that stabilization within the family unit has not occurred. Thus, termination of parent rights or continued work will occur.

With other client populations, social service agencies work on stabilization and termination simultaneously. This has been seen predominantly in the areas of substance abuse and criminal justice, where clients are terminated from one type of treatment program when they reach a certain level of stabilization only to then be enrolled in a case management program to ensure long-term stabilization. Rich and colleagues (2001) presented a program such as this for ex-offenders who have HIV. As ex-offenders left prison, they enrolled in a community-based case management program to assist them in maintaining their involvement with medical care. These researchers concluded that through this case management program, ex-offenders were able to remain connected to the medical services they needed and maintain stabilization postprison.

A variant of this form of termination and stabilization process has also been found to be effective in work with older adults. Naleppa and Reid (1998) used a task-focused case management program with older adults. They found that within a few weeks, the needs of most older adults were met. At this point, they could be transferred into a longer-term case management program or discharged completely from case management services. Morrow-Howell, Becker-Kemppainen, and Judy (1998) also found that older adults, following an intensive telephone-based case management program, had fewer unmet needs and improved life situations at termination. The relationships that had been formed through the case management referrals created stabilization over time.

Finally, some case management programs place a greater emphasis on client stabilization with the hopes of keeping the clients from leaving the program. This model has been seen in the areas of mental health and substance abuse. Noel (2006) found that in adolescent substance abusers, premature termination from the case management program was more associated with programmatic elements than frequency of case management service. Thus, for some populations, stabilization through case management has to be related to client motivation; otherwise, they may opt for prematurely terminating the program. This could also apply to the area of child welfare.

As case management services continue to grow, particularly state-funded case management programs, stabilization and termination needs to be given greater attention. Although stabilization and termination may look different based on the case management program and the population that is being served, considering these two elements of practice early in the case management process is essential for long-term client outcomes.

Brief Therapy

Brief therapy has become a common form of treatment for clients of all ages because of issues relating to reimbursement, insurance, and managed care (Anderson-Klontz, Dayton, & Anderson-Klontz, 1999). Instead of having a relationship with a therapist that lasts years, brief therapy on average lasts 5.5 sessions over a period of less than 4 months (Lee, 1997). Other estimates suggest that brief therapy lasts no more than eight sessions. While there are different schools of brief therapy, including solution-focused, behavioral, or Adlerian, the stabilization and termination process of brief therapy models is similar. These concepts will be discussed in general, instead of focusing specifically on one form of brief therapy.

Brief therapy is based on a treatment model to enable clients to work on "achievable goals within a limited time period" (Anderson-Klontz et al.,

1999, p. 115). As a result of this approach, brief therapy models have received criticism for not providing sufficient time for a thorough exploration of client problems; instead, problems are examined at a "surface level" (Walter & Peller, 1992). It has been suggested that brief therapy approaches restrict clients from working through the emotions related to their problems as well as discovering unresolved issues that may inhibit stabilization in the future.

Professionals who provide brief therapy are often hesitant to use the word "termination" when working with a client. Some brief therapy models, specifically Adlerian brief therapists, use the word "interrupted" instead of "terminated" at the end of a client period (Bitter & Nicoll, 2000). From this perspective, interruption leaves the door open for the client and therapist to reconnect in the future to continue to work on problematic issues. Others have focused less on the "finished product" or the long-term sustainable outcomes and instead on the incremental changes that were seen during the therapeutic process (Watts & Pietrzak, 2000, p. 445). Thus, sustainable change is not necessarily the goal; instead, the focus is on the change process and client growth.

The effectiveness of brief therapy approaches for creating long-term client stabilization is starting to be documented (Gingerich & Eisengart, 2000), with some researchers suggesting that short-term approaches are as effective as long-term approaches in creating client stabilization (Smyrnios & Kirby, 1993; Weisz, Thurber, Sweeney, Proffitt, & LeGagnoux, 1997). However, the sophistication of the intervention models has made this a slow process (Gingerich & Eisengart, 2000).

Research has also suggested that long-term stabilization of clients following brief therapy may be hard to obtain without adequate follow-up plans. Allison, Roeger, Dadds, and Martin (2000) found that 27% of children who received brief therapy for mental health problems were still experiencing difficulty posttermination. It was suggested that maintaining contact with the parents of the child via telephone posttermination may have led to greater stabilization of the children because treatment could have been reinitiated before the problem escalated to pretreatment levels. One way to address issues of stabilization posttermination from brief therapy may be what Shakeshaft, Bowman, Burrows, Doran, and Sanson-Fisher (1997) proposed. They proposed that following brief therapy for alcohol abuse, individuals who need more intensive intervention or follow-up could start a longer-term cognitive behavioral program.

The rates of stabilization post–brief therapy have varied. Lee (1997) found that brief therapy had a 65% success rate in achieving treatment outcomes in children with mental health problems. While this rate was lower than what was found in other studies (de Shazer, 1991), it does provide some evidence of the effectiveness of brief therapy approaches for client stabilization, at least in the short term. Franklin, Biever, Moore, Clemons, and Scamardo (2001) found that brief therapy, specifically solution-focused, was effective with children in school-based settings who were experiencing learning and behavioral problems. In this study, only one student at follow-up had returned to preintervention clinical levels.

Brief intervention models have also been found to be effective in creating stabilization in adolescents admitted to psychiatric hospitals. Balkin and Roland (2007) found that adolescent stabilization was connected to the attainment of therapeutic goals. Stabilization occurred as the adolescents became better at articulating their problems and committing to follow-up posthospitalization as determined by a reduction in psychiatric symptoms. This obviously played an important role as the patient was preparing for discharge or termination from the hospital program.

Finally, brief therapy has also been found to be effective in stabilization in adult populations. Barkham, Shapiro, Hardy, and Rees (1999) presented a two-plus-one brief therapy model for adults with depression, as measured by the Beck's Depression Inventory (Beck, Ward, & Mendelson, 1961). They found that gains made by the clients were still evident up to 1 year posttreatment, thereby suggesting client stabilization.

While brief therapy has been found to have short-term effectiveness in resolving client issues, long-term client stabilization rates are not known. As brief therapy receives more empirical attention, focus should be given to documenting client stabilization over time.

Crisis Intervention Therapy

Stressful life events lead to crises when individuals feel as though they have lost control over their particular circumstances. Depending on the person's coping ability and resolution of previous crises, life crises can lead to dysfunctional and at times self-destructive behavior. Crisis intervention therapy is frequently provided to individuals who experience distress following "normal" life stressors. Crisis intervention therapy can also be provided to individuals who experience significant trauma; however, crisis intervention in this context may appear different and include additional forms of intervention.

When considering termination and stabilization in a crisis intervention format, it is critical to consider the person's history of crisis, functional ability following a crisis, use and effectiveness of coping strategies, available formal and informal support systems, and ability to access additional assistance should a crisis stage reoccur. Anthony (1992) found that individuals who had been admitted to a crisis inpatient psychiatric unit were more successful at discharge if they had greater support from families and greater compliance with treatment protocols.

For stabilization postcrisis, part of crisis intervention is working with the client to determine how to prevent the next crisis, as well as how to respond when the next crisis occurs (Smets, 1988). Equally important to long-term stabilization postcrisis is considering ways to prepare clients for resolving future crises that may or may not be related to the same stressful event. Following crises, clients are reluctant to hear that the problems that led to the crisis may reappear, but part of termination and ensuring a stabilized client is being cognizant of how prepared the client is for the reoccurrence of events that precipitated the crisis in his or her life (Smets, 1988).

Research on crisis intervention has been found within multiple areas of social work, including health care, child welfare, suicide and mental health, and substance abuse. This literature, while rich and informative, has yet to provide sufficient detail into how termination and stabilization are assessed and evaluated within a crisis situation. However, the literature emphasizes the importance of the person in crisis having the opportunity to work on time-limited tasks and developing some form of follow-up plan to get future intervention if necessary (Poindexter, 1997).

Research on the effectiveness of crisis intervention therapy has found mixed results for creating stabilization in client. Rossi (1992) suggested that family preservation programs that provided crisis intervention were not successful with families who were experiencing extreme amounts of stress. However, Ruffin and colleagues (Ruffin, Spencer, Abel, Gage, & Miles, 1993) determined that a crisis stabilization program that consisted of daytime crisis work, after-hours assistance, and the ability to broker additional services that were beyond outpatient and inpatient care was effective in reducing the number of youth who were admitted to psychiatric facilities. Evans and colleagues (2003) found that in-home intensive crisis services for children and their families were successful in creating family cohesion by termination, as well as increased social support at termination and follow-up. Thus, as seen in this research, stabilization over time did occur following crisis-based services.

Conclusion

Greater attention needs to be directed to discussing termination and stabilization within the therapeutic process. Termination and stabilization are critical phases in the therapeutic relationship between the social worker and the client; however, they frequently receive scant empirical and clinical attention. While these two processes may appear different based on the clinical model and the client's circumstances, termination and stabilization should be incorporated into all phases of treatment and not introduced only at the end of therapy.

Key Terms

Continuity of care

Maintenance

Precipitating crisis

Service interruption

Stabilization

Termination

Transtheoretical model

Review Questions for Critical Thinking

1. Termination has been described as a key to the success of the clinical process. Why do you think this is true?

2. Why is it important to begin the termination process as early as possible?

3. What is the difference between stabilization and the end of a precipitating crisis?

4. From a historical perspective, termination and stabilization occur much earlier than they have in the past. What do you think are positive and negative aspects of accelerating the process?

5. There are situations when termination occurs before stabilization. What are some things social workers can do to ensure the process ends appropriately?

Online Resources

National Association of Social Workers www.socialworkers.org/practice/default.asp

This is a link to a series of practice standards promoted by the National Association of Social Workers, which address an array of important fields of practice.

This is a blog prepared by an individual MSW-level social worker, who has posted a very insightful personal essay on the termination process:

www.dorleem.com/2011/04/reflections-about-termination-in.html

This link connects to a doctoral dissertation describing research on the termination process among clinical social workers:

http://repository.upenn.edu/edissertations_sp2/12

This is a link to a brief article taken from a NASW state chapter newsletter, which focuses on our ethical responsibilities pertaining to the termination process:

www.socwel.ku.edu/jimk/711handouts/11.1.htm

This is another essay on the ethical aspects of termination, written by one of social work's leading experts on the topic of termination:

www.socialworktoday.com/news/eoe_0506.shtml

References

Allison, S., Roeger, L., Dadds, V., & Martin, G. (2000). Brief therapy for children's mental health problems: Outcomes in a rural setting. *Australian Journal of Rural Health, 8*, 161–166.

Anderson, C. E. (2000). Dealing constructively with managed care: Suggestions from an insider. *Journal of Mental Health Counseling, 22*, 343–354.

Anderson-Klontz, B. T., Dayton, T., & Anderson-Klontz, L. S. (1999). The use of psychodramatic techniques within solution-focused brief therapy: A theoretical and technical integration. *International Journal of Action Methods: Psychodrama, Skill Training, and Role Playing*, 53(3), 113–120.

Anthony, D. J. (1992). A retrospective evaluation of factors influencing successful outcomes on an inpatient psychiatric crisis unit. *Research on Social Work Practice*, 2, 56–64.

Balkin, R. S., & Roland, C. B. (2007). Reconceptualizing stabilization for counseling adolescents in brief psychiatric hospitalization: A new model. *Journal of Counseling and Development*, 85, 64–72.

Barkham, M., Shapiro, D. A., Hardy, G. E., & Rees, A. (1999). Psychotherapy in two-plus-one sessions: Outcomes of a randomized control trail of cognitive-behavioral and psychodynamic-interpersonal therapy for subsyndromal depression. *Journal of Consulting and Clinical Psychology*, 67, 201–211.

Beck, A. T., Ward C., & Mendelson, M. (1961). Beck Depression Inventory (BDI). *Archives of General Psychiatry*, 4, 561–571.

Bitter, J. R., & Nicoll, W. G. (2000). Alderian brief therapy with individuals: Process and practice. *Journal of Individual Psychology*, 56, 31–44.

Corey, G. (1991). *Theory and practice of counseling and psychotherapy*. Pacific Grove, CA: Brooks/Cole.

de Shazer, S. (1991). *Putting difference to work*. New York, NY: Norton.

Dorfman, R. (1996). *Clinical social work: Definition, practice, and wisdom*. New York, NY: Brunner/Mazel.

Evans, M. E., Boothroyd, R. A., Armstrong, M. I., Greenbaum, P. E., Crown, E. C., & Kuppinger, A. D. (2003). An experimental study of the effectiveness of intensive in-home crisis services for children and their families: Program outcomes. *Journal of Emotional and Behavioral Disorders*, 11, 92–104.

Fiene, J. I., & Taylor, P. A. (1991). Serving rural families of developmentally disabled children: A case management model. *Social Work*, 36, 323–327.

Franklin, C., Biever, J., Moore, K., Clemons, D., & Scamardo, M. (2001). The effectiveness of solution-focused therapy with children in a school setting. *Research on Social Work Practice*, 11, 411–434.

Gingerich, W. J., & Eisengart, S. (2000). Solution-focused brief therapy: A review of the outcome research. *Family Processes*, 477–498.

Hepworth, D., Rooney, R., & Larsen, J. (2002). *Direct social work practice: Theory and skills*. Pacific Grove, CA: Brooks/Cole.

Lee, M. (1997). A study of solution-focused brief family therapy: Outcomes and issues. *American Journal of Family Therapy*, 25, 3–17.

Levine, C., Albert, S. M., Hokenstad, A., Halper, D. E., Hart, A. Y., & Gould, D. A. (2006). "This case is closed": Family caregivers and the termination of home health care services for stroke patients. *Milbank Quarterly*, 84, 305–331.

Ligon, J. (1997). Brief crisis stabilization of an African American woman: Integrating cultural and ecological approaches. *Journal of Multicultural Social Work*, 6, 111–122.

Morrow-Howell, N., Becker-Kemppainen, S., & Judy, L. (1998). Evaluating an intervention for the elderly at increased risk for suicide. *Research on Social Work Practice*, 8, 28–46.

Moxley, D. P. (1989). *The practice of case management*. Newbury Park, CA: Sage.

Naleppa, M. J., & Reid, W. J. (1998). Task-centered case management for the elderly: Developing a practice model. *Research on Social Work Practice*, 8, 63–85.

Noel, P. E. (2006). The impact of therapeutic case management on participation in adolescent substance abuse treatment. *American Journal of Drug and Alcohol Abuse, 32,* 322–327.

Northen, H. (1995). *Clinical social work: Knowledge and skills.* New York, NY: Columbia University Press.

Petryshen, P. R., & Petryshen, P. M. (1992). The case management model: An innovative approach to the delivery of patient care. *Journal of Advanced Nursing, 17,* 1188–1194.

Poindexter, C. (1997). In the aftermath: Serial crisis intervention for people with HIV. *Health and Social Work, 22,* 23–35.

Prochaska, J. O., & DiClemente, C. C. (1983). Stages and processes of self-change of smoking: Toward an integrative model of change. *Journal of Consulting and Clinical Psychology, 51,* 390–395.

Prochaska, J. O., DiClemente, C. C., & Norcross, J. C. (1992). In search of how people change: Applications to addictive behaviors. *American Psychologist, 47*(9), 1102–1114.

Prochaska, J. O., & Velicer, W. F. (1997). The transtheoretical model of health behavior change. *American Journal of Health Promotion, 12,* 38–48.

Prochaska, J. O., Velicer, W. F., DiClemente, C. C., & Fava, J. L. (1988). Measuring the processes of change: Applications to the cessation of smoking. *Journal of Consulting and Clinical Psychology, 56,* 520–528.

Prochaska, J. O., Velicer, W. F., DiClemente, C. C., Guadagnoli, E., & Rossi, J. (1991). Patterns of change: A dynamic typology applied to smoking cessation. *Multivariate Behavioral Research, 26,* 83–107.

Rich, J. D., Holmes, L., Salas, C., Macalino, G., Davis, D., Ryczek, J., & Flanigan, T. (2001). Successful linkage of medical care and community services for HIV-positive offenders being released from prison. *Journal of Urban Health, 78,* 279–289.

Rossi, P.H. (1992). *Using theory to improve program and policy evaluations.* Westport, CT: Greenwood.

Ruffin, J. E., Spencer, H. R., Abel, A., Gage, G., & Miles, L. (1993). Crisis stabilization services for children and adolescents: A brokerage model to reduce admissions to state psychiatric facilities. *Community Mental Health Journal, 29,* 433–441.

Shakeshaft, A. P., Bowman, J. A., Burrows, S., Doran, C. M., & Sanson-Fisher, R. W. (1997). Community-based alcohol counseling: A randomized clinical trial. *Addictions, 97,* 1449–1463.

Smets, A. C. (1988). What to do when the crisis is over? *Journal of Strategic and Systemic Therapies, 4,* 20–29.

Smyrnios, K. X., & Kirby, R. J. (1993). Long-term comparison of brief versus unlimited psychodynamic treatments with children and their parents. *Journal of Consulting and Clinical Psychology, 61,* 1020–1027.

Strom, K. (1992). Reimbursement demands and treatment decisions: A growing dilemma for social workers. *Social Work, 37,* 398–404.

Walter, J. L., & Peller, J. E. (1992). *Becoming solution-focused in brief therapy.* New York, NY: Brunner/Mazel.

Watts, R. E., & Pietrzak, D. (2000). Adlerian encouragement and the therapeutic process of solution-focused brief therapy. *Journal of Counseling and Development, 78,* 442–227.

Weisz, J. R., Thurber, C. A., Sweeney, L., Proffitt, V. D., & Le Gagnoux, G. L. (1997). Brief treatment of mild-to-moderate children depression using primary and secondary control enhancement training. *Journal of Consulting and Clinical Psychology, 65*, 703–707.

Woods, M., & Hollis, F. (Eds.). (1990). *Casework: A psychosocial therapy.* New York, NY: McGraw-Hill.

Author Index

Subject Index